The Intellectual Origins
of the
European Reformation

B

The Intellectual Origins
of the
European Reformation

Alister McGrath

BLACKWELL
Oxford UK & Cambridge USA

First published 1987
First published in paperback 1993

Blackwell Publishers
108 Cowley Road, Oxford OX4 1JF, UK

238 Main Street, Suite 501
Cambridge, Massachusetts 02142, USA

British Library Cataloguing in Publication Data
A CIP catalogue record for this book is available from the British Library.

Library of Congress Cataloging in Publication Data
McGrath, Alister E., 1953–
    The intellectual origins of the European Reformation.
    Bibliography: p.
    Includes index.
    1. Reformation.   2. Theology, Doctrinal—History—
Middle Ages, 600–1500.   3. Theology, Doctrinal—History
—16th century.   4. Philosophy, Medieval.   5. Philosophy,
Renaissance.   I. Title.
BR307.M44   1987   274'.06   86–24473
ISBN 0–631–15144–3   ISBN 0–631–18688–3 (pbk.)

Typeset in 11/12½ pt Baskerville by System 4 Associates, Gerrards Cross
Printed in Great Britain by
T.J. Press Ltd, Padstow, Cornwall

This book is printed on acid-free paper

Contents

Preface

The quest for the intellectual origins of the European Reformation of the sixteenth century is increasingly gaining recognition as one of the most important recent undertakings in the study of intellectual history. Despite the tendency within certain schools of historical interpretation to disinvest the Reformation of any religious or intellectual character, in order to facilitate its analysis as a purely social phenomenon, there is a growing realization that there is an irreducible intellectual element to the Reformation which demands and deserves careful analysis. This book is concerned with one crucial question: how may the religious ideas of the Reformers be accounted for? The quest for the intellectual origins of the Reformation involves the detailed analysis of the continuities and discontinuities between two eras in the history of thought, raising questions of fundamental importance for the historian of ideas and the theologian. It is hoped that this book will go some way towards identifying those questions, and providing provisional answers to them.

My thanks are due to many for their kindnesses during the preparation of this work. The stimulus for writing it was provided by my students at Wycliffe Hall, Oxford, who demanded better answers to their questions than they had hitherto found. Much of the research underlying this work was carried out at the Zentralbibliothek and Institut für schweizerische Reformationsgeschichte of the University of Zurich. I owe these institutions thanks for their hospitality and the use of their enviable facilities and resources. The British Academy made funds available for this work, and I gratefully acknowledge this invaluable assistance. Finally, my thanks are again due to the staff and students of Wycliffe Hall, Oxford, for providing such an outstanding environment in which to teach, study and think.

Abbreviations

ARG	*Archiv für Reformationsgeschichte*
BHR	*Bibliothèque d'Humanisme et Renaissance*
CR	Corpus Reformatorum
EThL	*Ephemerides Theologicae Lovanienses*
FS	*Franziskanische Studien*
FcS	*Franciscan Studies*
HThR	*Harvard Theological Review*
RThAM	*Recherches de théologie ancienne et médiévale*
WA	Luthers Werke: Kritische Gesamtausgabe
WABr	Luthers Werke: Kritische Gesamtausgabe, Briefwechsel
WATr	Luthers Werke: Kritische Gesamtausgabe, Tischreden
ZKG	*Zeitschrift für Kirchengeschichte*
ZKTh	*Zeitschrift für katholische Theologie*
ZThK	*Zeitschrift für Theologie und Kirche*

Introduction

The European Reformation of the sixteenth century continues to retain its inherent fascination for the historian, whether he is concerned with its social, political or intellectual dimensions. Of the many questions to be thrown up by the present intense scholarly activity in the field, perhaps the most intriguing is the question of the intellectual origins of the Reformation. How may the origins of the distinctive religious ideas of the Reformation be accounted for in terms of the overall development of thought in the period 1300–1600? To what extent does the Reformation mark a break with the thought of an earlier period, and to what extent is it continuous with it? Four questions are of particular importance in this connection.

First, were there 'Forerunners of the Reformation'? In other words, were there anticipations of aspects of the thought of the Reformation in the medieval period which immediately preceded it? Second, what is the relationship between the Reformation and the Renaissance? Was the Reformation merely an aspect of the Renaissance, or does it possess special significance on account of its subject matter, presuppositions, sources or methods? Third, what is the relationship between the Reformation and late medieval theological schools of thought, particularly the *via moderna* and the *schola Augustiniana moderna*? This question has been the subject of intense debate in relation to Luther's early theological development, but it is also important in relation to Karlstadt, Zwingli, Peter Martyr and Calvin, to name but the more prominent among the Reformers. Fourth, how was it that a movement which was initially so hostile towards scholasticism came to develop a scholasticism of its own within so short a period? The full importance of this question has only recently been appreciated, as it appears to point to an important link between late Renaissance Aristotelian humanism and Protestant (especially Reformed) theology. It is this question of the intellectual – as opposed to the political, social or institutional – origins of the Reformation which urgently requires detailed critical examination.

It is all too easy to overlook the fact that the European Reformation of the sixteenth century was concerned with religious ideas. The deep and wide currents which the Reformation created in the flow of European history are an adequate testimony to the political and social dimensions of the movement. Nevertheless, those at the forefront of the Swiss and German Reformations appear to have been primarily concerned with religious ideas, and to have based their political and social programmes upon them. The historical significance of the Reformation is not merely inseparable from, but is largely a consequence of, the religious views of the major Reformers. Any attempt to understand the complexity of the sixteenth century Reformation must involve a serious engagement with the ideas that lay behind it.[1] But what are the distinctive ideas of the Reformation? And in what way do these ideas differ from those of the centuries prior to the Reformation? Is the religious thought of the Reformation a natural outcome of late medieval thought, or does it represent a break with a hitherto homogeneous intellectual tradition?

To answer these questions with any degree of precision and conviction, it is necessary to examine the way in which theological ideas were developed and analysed in the late medieval period, as well as the extent to which they could be – and were! – controlled and regulated by both society and the church. Late medieval church and society exercised an ambiguous attitude towards religious ideas, which was both creative and repressive. By establishing a political and intellectual climate throughout much of western Europe in which theological scholarship and speculation could proceed, the church may be said to have adopted a creative attitude towards the development of new religious ideas; by establishing means by which unacceptable new ideas might be eliminated or suppressed, by force if necessary, the church may be said to have adopted a repressive attitude in the same area. Perhaps one of the more significant features of the fifteenth century is the evident growth in theological speculation – and hence doctrinal pluralism – in the religious houses and universities of

---

1 Recent protests concerning the tendency of some Reformation historians to indulge in a 'flight from history' by concentrating upon matters of theology do, of course, make an important point. See Max Steinmetz, 'Probleme der frühbürgerlichen Revolution in Deutschland in der ersten Hälfte des 16. Jahrhundert', in *Die frühbürgerlichen Revolution in Deutschland*, ed. Gerhard Brendler (Berlin, 1961), pp. 17–52, especially p. 32; Berndt Moeller, 'Probleme der Reformations-geschichtsforschung', *ZKG* 76 (1965), pp. 246–57. But this hardly excuses an equally illegitimate 'flight from theology', by ignoring the religious ideas underlying and motivating that history.

Germany, and an apparently increasing reluctance on the part of the church authorities to suppress this trend.

The present work represents an attempt to consolidate and expand our understanding of the intellectual origins of the European Reformation of the sixteenth century. There has been a growing recognition on the part of Reformation scholars that neither the events nor the ideas of the sixteenth century may be properly understood unless they are seen as the culmination of developments in the fourteenth and fifteenth centuries.[2] Although there has been an understandable desire on the part of historians of the Reformation to treat the pivotal intellectual developments of the sixteenth century as complete in themselves, requiring little contextualization other than that provided by the early years of that century, certain assumptions underlying this approach have recently been called into question. For example, it is evident that both Protestant and Roman Catholic theologians regard the sixteenth century as defining the point of departure for their present doctrinal positions, and they thus tend to approach the period in the light of this assumption.[3] Whilst this may be perfectly acceptable for their somewhat limited purposes, it is most emphatically not acceptable to the historian of ideas, whose task and concern it is to account for the origins of the ideas which assumed such significance in the sixteenth century.

A further difficulty relates to the vexed question of *periodization*. How is the 'period of the Reformation' to be defined? And to what epoch may the Reformation itself be assigned? For example, the Reformation may be viewed as the culmination of the Renaissance emphasis upon *studia humanitatis*[4] – and thus merely as an episode in the general history of learning and scholarship over the period 1300–1600. Alternatively, on the basis of the Marxist interpretation of the place of the Reformation in European history – in which the superstructure of the history of its religious ideas is seen as inextricably linked with the

---

2 See, e.g., Erich Hassinger, *Das Werden des neuzeitlichen Europa 1300–1600* (Braunschweig, 2nd edn, 1966); Jaroslav Pelikan, *The Christian Tradition: A History of the Development of Doctrine. 4. Reformation of Church and Dogma (1300–1700)* (Chicago/London, 1984).

3 This point is brought out by Heiko A. Oberman, 'Reformation: Epoche oder Episode', *ARG* 68 (1977), pp. 56–111, especially pp. 56–64, who draws attention to the influence of interests upon the definition of epochs. See further Paul Ourliac and Henri Gilles, *La période post-classique, 1378–1500: la problématique de l'époque* (Paris, 1971); Franklin H. Littell, 'The Periodization of History', in *Continuity and Discontinuity in Church History*, ed. F. Forrester Church and Timothy George (Leiden, 1979), pp. 18–30.

4 See Oberman, 'Reformation: Epoche oder Episode', pp. 74–88.

substructure of the class struggle – the movement is viewed as a significant epoch in the development of the European bourgeois revolution.[5] A further possibility is to view the Reformation as a significant episode in the transition of European countries from territorial states to sovereign powers in the period 1450–1660.[6] The danger is clearly that such periodization is imposed upon, rather than discerned within, the historical process itself.

The assumption underlying the present study is that the Reformation represents a significant episode in the intellectual, institutional, social and political history of Europe, capable of being accommodated within a number of schemes of periodization on account of its multifaceted character. For the present purposes, however, the Reformation will be viewed primarily as an intellectual phenomenon. This is not to deny that it possessed other dimensions, nor even to assert that the intellectual element of the Reformation must be regarded as taking precedence over others. It is simply to observe that there was an irreducible intellectual element to the movement, which exercised considerable influence over it, and which thus both merits and demands serious study by all concerned with the Reformation. The Reformation occupies, and must continue to occupy, a legitimate and significant place in the history *of ideas*. The significance of the period to the self-understanding of the major western Christian traditions obviously lends added weight to these considerations.

While not necessarily suggesting that certain periods in history are genuinely more significant than others, the full significance of any such period – and the Reformation is clearly a case in point – can only be established through comparison with those that preceded it, and those that followed. It is for this reason that it is so important to establish the areas of continuity and discontinuity between the religious thought of the Reformation and that of the late medieval period, in that it is only through this process that the innovative character and originality of the Reformation may be identified and established. It will therefore be clear that an essential part of the present

5 See, e.g., Abraham Friesen, *Reformation and Utopia: The Marxist Interpretation of the Reformation and its Antecedents* (Wiesbaden, 1974), especially pp. 189–205; Thomas Nipperdey, 'Die Reformation als Problem der marxistischen Geschichtswissenschaft', in *Reformation, Revolution, Utopie: Studien zum 16. Jahrhundert* (Göttingen, 1975), pp. 9–34. Interestingly, on the basis of this understanding of the significance of the Reformation, it still proves possible to treat Huss as a 'Forerunner of the Reformation': see Robert Kalivoda, *Revolution und Ideologie: Der Hussitismus* (Cologne/Vienna, 1976), especially p. 254.

6 For example, Josef Engel, *Die Entstehung des neuzeitlichen Europa* (Stuttgart, 1971), pp. 1–443.

task will be the elucidation of both the relationship of the emerging Lutheran and Reformed theologies, in their formative periods, to the religious ideas of the later Middle Ages, and the sources and methods employed in their establishment and articulation.

A further point must, however, be noted. The analysis of the points of continuity between late medieval and Reformation thought cannot end with the death of Calvin (1564), even though this event is often treated as heralding the end of the first phase of the Reformation. It is becoming increasingly clear that the development of Reformed theology in the period between the death of Calvin and the outbreak of the Thirty Years War in 1618 was subject to a remarkable extent to influence from methodological presuppositions similar to those underlying medieval scholasticism. The first age of the Reformation may be regarded as functioning as a period of transition between two related, though quite distinct, forms of scholasticism – those of the medieval period, and of Protestant Orthodoxy. It is therefore necessary to include this later period in an analysis of the continuities and dis- continuities between the religious thought of the Reformation and the late medieval period, in an attempt to account for the remarkable rise of Protestant scholasticism in the second half of the sixteenth century.

At this point, the distinction should be clarified between 'Lutheran' and 'Reformed' as epithets applied to the two main confessions that developed within the Reformation.[7] In the early period of the Reformation, the Reformers regarded themselves as evangelicals committed to a common programme of theological education and reform. By the second half of the century, however, it was evident that a major bifurcation had occurred within the movement (if, indeed, it had not always been there from the beginning). One section of the movement, broadly corresponding to the German territories, regarded Luther, his catechisms and the Augsburg Confession as theological authorities, whereas the cities of the Rhineland and Switzerland recognized the rival authority of Calvin and his *Institutio*, and the Heidelberg Catechism. Although it is evident that the two movements still regarded themselves as heirs to a common tradition,[8] political

---

7 For a perceptive introduction to the terms, see Josef Bohatec, '"Lutherisch" und "Refor- miert"', *Reformiertes Kirchenblatt für Österreich* 28 (January, 1951), pp. 1–3.

8 Thus they are more accurately referred to as 'Evangelical-Lutheran' and 'Evangelical- Reformed': see Bohatec, '"Lutherisch" und "Reformiert"', p. 2.

and ecclesiological developments, particularly the rise of confession-
alism, led to an emphasis upon their divergence, rather than upon
their convergence upon matters once held to be fundamental to the
Reformation. The developments leading to the introduction of the
term 'Calvinism' illustrate this point.

In the sixth decade of the sixteenth century, a new theological term
entered the polemical literature of the churches of the Reformation.
'Calvinism' appears to have been introduced by the Lutheran polemi-
cist Joachim Westphal to refer to the theological, and particularly the
sacramental, views of the Swiss Reformers in general, and John Calvin
in particular.[9] Once introduced, the term rapidly passed into general
use within the Lutheran church. In part, this rapid acceptance of
the new term reflected intense disquiet within the Lutheran camp
concerning the growing influence of Reformed theology in regions
of Germany hitherto regarded as historically Lutheran.[10] Elector
Frederick III's open support for the Reformed theology in the
Palatinate, especially his introduction of the celebrated Heidelberg
Catechism in 1563, was the cause of particular concern. The defection
of the Elector from the Lutheran to the Reformed party was widely
regarded as an open infringement of the Peace of Augsburg,[11] and
a destabilizing influence in the region. The introduction of the term
'Calvinist' appears to have been an attempt to stigmatize Reformed
theology as a foreign influence in Germany: Calvin himself was
alarmed at the use of the term, which he rightly regarded as a thinly
veiled attempt to discredit the Elector's espousal of the Reformed
faith.[12] By then, however, Calvin had only months to live, and his
protest was ineffective. The term 'Calvinism' thus came to be used
to refer to the theological views of the Reformed church *by its opponents*,
and the modern student of the Reformation period thus finds himself

9 For example, his *Farrago confusanearum et inter se dissidentium opinionum de coena Domini ex sacra-
mentariorum libris congesta* (Magdeburg, 1552). See Ernst Bizer, *Studien zur Geschichte des Abend-
mahlstreirs im 16. Jahrhundert* (Gütersloh, 1940); Jean Cadier, *La doctrine calviniste de la sainte cène*
(Montpellier, 1951).
10 See further Hans Leube, *Kalvinismus und Luthertum im Zeitalter der Orthodoxie I: Der Kampf
um die Herrschaft im protestantischen Deutschland* (Leipzig, 1928).
11 For its terms, see C. W. Spieker, *Geschichte des Augsburger Religionsfriedens von 26. September
1555* (Schleiz, 1854); G. Wolf, *Der Augsburger Religionsfriede* (Stuttgart, 1890).
12 See the dedicatory epistle to the Jeremiah commentary, dated 23 July 1563, CR (Calvin)
20.73 'Dum ergo *Calvinismum* obiciendo aliqua infamiae nota tua, Celsitudinem aspergere
conantur, nihil aliud quam suam privitatem cum stultitia frustra et magno suo cum dedecore
produnt.'

an unwilling heir to this most dubious bequest of early Protestant internecine politics. The precise relationship between Calvin and Reformed theology, particularly in the period after the death of Calvin, is considerably more complex than might be expected, and the use of the term 'Calvinism' to refer to that theology is to be discouraged.

The present study is conceived as an investigation and interpretation of the relationship between the Reformation and the two great intellectual movements of the late medieval period – scholasticism and humanism – with a view to clarifying the intellectual origins of the European Reformation. This analysis involves both a general overview of the relation between the Reformation and these intellectual movements, as well as a sustained examination of the Reformers' appropriation of the understandings of theological sources and methods associated with these movements. The study opens with a survey of religious thought in the two centuries immediates preceding the Reformation, documenting the inherent doctrinal pluralism which proved to be so effective a breeding ground for the ideas of the Reformers, and allowing the traditional concept of the 'Forerunners of the Reformation' to be critically evaluated. In the two major chapters that follow, the broad outlines of the relation of the Reformation to both humanism and late medieval scholasticism are delineated, taking full note of the developments in our understanding of the nature of both these movements which have been gained in the last quarter century, and which have necessitated modification of many traditional interpretations of their relation. These broad outlines are then further developed by five subsequent chapters, dealing with the basis of all theological speculation – the understanding of the sources and the methods to be used. On the basis of this analysis, the clear divergence between the early Lutheran and Reformed churches' relation to humanism and late medieval scholasticism becomes evident. The remarkable parallels between late Renaissance humanism and late medieval scholasticism are noted in the final of these chapters, as the vitality of the early Reformed church gave way to the scholasticism of the later sixteenth century.

Although the work ends with a conclusion, it must be made clear from the outset that the complexity of the questions under consideration in the present volume make their succinct summarization an impossibility. The generalizations of popular historiography are ill-suited to the analysis of the mutual relationship of three movements so complex and heterogeneous as humanism, late medieval scholasticism and the Reformation. The conclusions of the present work are inter-woven with analysis in the body of the text of this study, and the conclusion is intended merely to provide a broad overview of some of the questions considered.

1

The Shape of Late Medieval Religious Thought

The intellectual, social and spiritual upheavals of the fourteenth and fifteenth centuries define the context within which the development of the Reformation of the sixteenth century must be approached. Although it has often been suggested in the past that the late Middle Ages was merely a period of disintegration,[1] it is now appreciated that it was also a period of remarkable development which sets the scene for the Reformation itself.[2] In this chapter, I propose to present a general survey of the religious situation in the fourteenth and fifteenth centuries, as a prelude to an analysis of areas of continuity between the late medieval and Reformation periods.

It is now clear that the fourteenth and fifteenth centuries did not witness the general decline in interest in the Christian religion in western Europe which was once thought to have taken place.[3] A careful examination of parameters such as church attendance or religious bequests and endowments – not to mention the new interest in pilgrimages and personal devotion – points to the vitality of Christian life in pre-Reformation Europe.[4] Although it is clear that

1 See, e.g., Armand Maurer, *Medieval Philosophy* (New York, 1962), p. 265; Gordon Leff, *The Dissolution of the Medieval Outlook: An Essay on Intellectual and Spiritual Change in the Fourteenth Century* (New York, 1976).

2 See Heiko A. Oberman, 'Fourteenth Century Religious Thought: A Premature Profile', *Speculum* 53 (1978), pp. 80–93.

3 On Germany, see G. Ritter, 'Why the Reformation occurred in Germany', *Church History* 27 (1958), pp. 99–106; Berndt Moeller, 'Frömmigkeit in Deutschland um 1500', *ARG* 61 (1965), pp. 5–31; Karl Schlemmer, 'Gottesdienst und Frömmigkeit in Nürnberg vor der Reformation', *Zeitschrift für bayerische Kirchengeschichte* 44 (1975), pp. 1–27. On England, see C. Haigh, 'Some Aspects of Recent Historiography of the English Reformation', in *The Urban Classes, the Nobility and the Reformation*, ed. W. J. Mommsen (London, 1980), pp. 88–106.

4 See R. Crofts, 'Books, Reform and the Reformation', *ARG* 71 (1980), pp. 21–35; J. J. Scarisbrick, *The Reformation and the English People* (Oxford, 1985), pp. 1–39.

there was a growing anti-clericalism in many European cities,[5] the development of this phenomenon was not solely a reflection of growing irritation with clerical privilege.[6] The rise in piety and theological awareness on the part of the laity – particularly evident in the manner in which speculative theology was subordinated to Marian devotion in popular literature[7] – inevitably led to a growing dissatisfaction with the role allocated to the clergy in the order of salvation. The close relationship between education and lay piety in the later Middle Ages is indicated by the fact that the remarkable growth of interest in education in the fifteenth century was primarily associated with monastic houses, particularly those of the *devotio moderna*.

Although the early *devotio moderna* was not primarily concerned with popular education, but rather with the reformation of monasteries,[8] it rapidly assumed a major pedagogical role in the fifteenth century. The student hostels attached to the major monasteries of the Brethren of the Common Life extended their interest in the pastoral welfare of their pupils to include their education. Inevitably, the piety of the *devotio moderna* was transmitted in this education process. The monastic educational programme resulted in an increasing consciousness of the

---

5 For examples of the impact of this phenomenon on late medieval city life, see N. Birnbaum, 'The Zwinglian Reformation in Zürich', *Past and Present* 15 (1959), pp. 27–47; R. M. Kingdom, 'Was the Protestant Reformation a Revolution?', in *Transition and Revolution: Problems and Issues of European Renaissance and Reformation History*, ed. R. M. Kingdom (Minneapolis, 1974), pp. 53–107; R. W. Scribner, 'Civic Unity and the Reformation in Erfurt', *Past and Present* 66 (1975), pp. 29–60; Steven E. Ozment, *The Reformation in the Cities: The Appeal of Protestantism to Sixteenth-Century Germany and Switzerland* (New Haven, Conn., 1975). Ozment's psychological and social account of the origins and success of the Reformation is open to serious criticism: see Thomas A. Brady, *Ruling Class, Regime and Reformation at Strasbourg* (Leiden, 1978), pp. 9–10. For a careful and well-documented study of the discontent evident in popular German religious thought between c. 1438 and 1519, see Gerald Strauss, *Manifestations of Discontent in Germany on the Eve of the Reformation* (Bloomington, Ind., 1971).

6 For a well-documented study of the social status and activities of the inferior clergy in the later Middle Ages, see Dietrich Kurze, 'Der niedere Klerus in der sozialen Welt des späten Mittelalters', in *Beiträge zur Wirtschafts- und Sozialgeschichte des Mittelalters*, ed. Knut Schultz (Cologne/Vienna, 1976), pp. 273–305. This question is set in a broader context in the invaluable survey of Karl Trödinger, *Stadt und Kirche im spätmittelalterlichen Würzburg* (Stuttgart, 1978).

7 See Peter Kern, *Trinität, Maria, Inkarnation: Studien zur Thematik der deutschen Dichtung des späteren Mittelalters* (Berlin, 1971). It is also important to appreciate that the ability to read manuscript text became increasingly common among the laity in the fifteenth century: see Paul Saenger, 'Silent Reading: Its Impact on Late Medieval Script', *Viator: Medieval and Renaissance Studies* 13 (1982), pp. 367–414, especially pp. 408–13.

8 This point has been emphasized by R. R. Post, *The Modern Devotion: Confrontation with Reformation and Humanism* (Leiden, 1968), p. 97, against the earlier views of Albert Hyma, *The 'Devotio Moderna' or Christian Renaissance (1380–1520)* (Grand Rapids, Mich., 2nd edn, 1975).

rudiments of a well-established spiritual tradition, as well as the elements of Latin grammar, in the laity of the later medieval period. The connection between the *devotio moderna* and individuals such as Erasmus,[9] and institutions such as the universities of Paris[10] and Tübingen,[11] serves to indicate how piety and pedagogy were intermingled in the period. Although there are indications that the educational standards of the clergy were themselves improving towards the end of the fifteenth century, the new educational movements were steadily eroding the advantage the clergy once enjoyed over the laity. All the indications are that piety and religion, if not theology itself, were becoming increasingly laicized towards the end of the medieval period.

The impact of the rising professional groups in cities throughout Europe in the late fifteenth century was considerable. No longer could a priest expect to satisfy his urban congregation by reading a Latin sermon as an adjunct to the reading of the mass – an intelligent and fresh sermon was required, if the priest was to be seen to justify his position within society. No longer could he expect to justify his privileged position in urban society merely with reference to his calling.[12] At a time of economic depression, there was widespread criticism of priests, who were both supported by the public, and exempt from their taxes. This increasing anticlericalism must not, however, be seen as a reaction against the Christian religion, but merely as a growing dissatisfaction with the role and status of the clergy within an increasingly professional urbanized, yet still Christian, society. Similarly, the rising hostility towards scholasticism in theology must not be thought to imply a decline in popular interest in religion,[13] but actually reflects both a growing theological competence on the part of some of the laity (and Erasmus may serve as an example), and increasing interest in non-academic forms of religion (often expressed in sentimental or external forms) on the part of others. To dismiss this latter form of religious expression as 'superstition' is for the

---

9 See, e.g., James D. Tracy, *Erasmus: The Growth of a Mind* (Geneva, 1972), pp. 21–9.

10 See Augustin Renaudet, *Préréforme et humanisme à Paris pendant les premières guerres d'Italie (1494–1517)* (Paris, 2nd edn, 1953), pp. 172–81.

11 Heiko A. Oberman, *Werden und Wertung der Reformation: Vom Wegestreit zum Glaubenskampf* (Tübingen, 1977), pp. 56–71.

12 Heiko A. Oberman, *Forerunners of the Reformation: The Shape of Late Medieval Thought Illustrated by Key Documents* (Philadelphia, 1981), pp. 7–9.

13 As Oberman notes, late medieval Germany was characterized by, if anything, an excess of piety: *Werden und Wertung der Reformation, pp. 10–11.*

historian to impose improperly a modern *Weltanschauung* upon the period.

The advent of printing led to works of popular devotion becoming accessible to the intelligent and literate laity, and appears to have contributed considerably to the promotion of popular piety. The remarkable success of Erasmus' *Enchiridion Militis Christiani* in the first decades of the sixteenth century unquestionably reflects the fact that it was addressed to precisely such an articulate lay piety, expressing that piety in an intelligent and intelligible form.[14] Thus Erasmus' criticisms of scholastic theology were directed against the form in which it was expressed – particularly the inelegant Latin employed by the scholastic theologians – rather than against the religious ideas thus articulated.[15] The remarkable impact of the *Hortulus Animae* at Strasbourg – which went through 25 editions in the 19 years following its publication in 1498 – is a typical testimony to the vitality of the interiorized piety characteristic of the urban professional classes of the later medieval period.[16] It is also clear that there was an essential continuity between the piety of the *devotio moderna* and that of the Reformation,[17] thus indicating the fertile ground upon which the new religious outlook associated with the sixteenth century movement would fall.

THE CRISIS OF AUTHORITY WITHIN THE CHURCH

While the challenge to the authority of the church posed by the rise of the lay religious consciousness must not be underestimated, a more serious challenge to that authority had arisen within the church itself. The late medieval period witnessed a crisis in ecclesiastical authority,

---

14 On the *Enchiridion*, see Robert Stupperich, 'Das Enchiridion Militis Christiani des Erasmus von Rotterdam nach seiner Entstehung, seinem Sinn und Charakter', *ARG* 69 (1978), pp. 5–23.
15 For Erasmus' comments upon the questions debated by the scholastic theologians at Paris, see *Opera Omnia*, ed. J. Leclerc (Leiden, 1703–6), vol. 6, pp. 926D–927B. Similar criticisms of the unintelligibility of the Latin of the scholastics were made by Melanchthon: *De corrigendis adolescentiae studiis*; *Werke*, ed. H. Engelland and R. Nürnburger, (3 vols: Tübingen, 1952–61) vol. 3, p. 45.
16 See René Bornert, *La réforme Protestante du culte à Strasbourg au XVIe siècle (1523–1598)* (Leiden, 1981), pp. 25–8.
17 For an excellent analysis, see Robert Stupperich, *Das Herforder Fraterhaus und die Devotio Moderna: Studien zur Frömmigkeitsgeschichte Westfalens an der Wende zur Neuzeit* (Münster, 1975). On the situation in Germany and Bohemia, see Franz Machilek, 'Die Frömmigkeit und die Krise des 14. und 15. Jahrhunderts', *Medievalia Bohemica* 3 (1970), pp. 209–27.

which would ultimately find its expression in the astonishing doctrinal diversity of the fifteenth century. The fourteenth century opened without any real awareness of what the future held in this respect. The Jubilee of 1300 constituted a splendid backdrop to the publication of *Unam sanctam* in 1302, marking the zenith of medieval papal ecclesiastical ambitions.[18] The apparent moral victory which the pope had secured over the French monarch was, however, shown to be hollow through the humiliation of Anagni, and the establishment of the Avignon papacy in 1309.[19] The fact that the theological authority of the Avignon popes was largely based upon that of the theology faculty at Paris serves to demonstrate the severe restrictions placed upon him in this respect. Although the theology faculty supported the condemnation of William of Ockham in 1339,[20] in 1333–34 it had forced upon an unwilling John XXII a humiliating alteration of his pronouncement on the beatific vision.[21] The condemnation of Ockham is faintly ironical, in that one of Ockham's chief targets in his *Tractatus contra Johannem* was none other than John XXII's pronouncement on the beatific vision.[22] Ockham has, however, added significance on account of his theory of the sources of Christian doctrine. In his *Opus nonaginta dierum*, Ockham developed a theory of doctrinal authority which denied the pope (or, indeed, an ecumenical council) any right to legislate in matters of faith.[23] There were thus

18 On which see J. Rivière. *Le problème de l'Eglise et de l'Etat au temps de Philippe le Bel* (Louvain/ Paris, 1926), pp. 79–91; 150–5; 394–404. It is possible to suggest that the claims to absolute temporal and spiritual power made by *Unam sanctam* may be traced back to Innocent III: see Brian Tierney, '"Tria quippe distinguit iudicia . . ." A Note on Innocent III's Decretal *Per venerabilem*', *Speculum* 37 (1962), pp. 48–59. The suggestion that such views were foreshadowed in the works of the Franciscan Francis de Meyronnes has been successfully challenged: see F. Baethgen, 'Dante und Franz von Mayronis', *Deutsches Archiv für Erforschungen des Mittelalters* 15 (1959), pp. 103–36.

19 G. Mollat, *Les papes d'Avignon 1305–1378* (Paris, 10th edn, 1965); Y. Renouard, *La papauté à Avignon* (Paris, 1954).

20 *Chartularium Universitatis Parisiensis*, ed. H. Denifle and E. Châtelain (4 vols: Paris, 1889–97), vol. 3, no. 1023, p. 485. Ockham had earlier been condemned at Avignon: see A. Pelzer, 'Les 51 articles de Guillaume Ockham censurés en Avignon en 1326', *Revue d'Histoire Ecclésiastique* 18 (1922), pp. 240–70; C. K. Brampton, 'Personalities at the Process against Ockham at Avignon 1324–26', *Franciscan Studies* 26 (1966), pp. 4–25.

21 *Chartularium*, vol. 3, nos. 779–87; pp. 414–42.

22 Ockham, *Tractatus contra Johannem*, cap. 15, in *Guillelmi de Ockham Opera Politica* (3 vols: Manchester, 1940–56), vol. 3, pp. 67–72.

23 *Opus nonaginta dierum*, cap. 123, in *Opera Politica*, vol. 2, pp. 832–46. As Lagarde notes, Ockham allows the pope spiritual *potestas*, rather than jurisdiction: Georges de Lagarde, *La naissance de l'esprit laïque au declin du moyen-âge* (6 vols: Paris, 1940–6), vol. 5, p. 183. See further Brian Tierney, 'Ockham, the Conciliar Theory, and the Canonists', *Journal of the History of Ideas* 15 (1954), pp. 40–70.

no means by which the pope might resolve the contemporary diversity of belief concerning the eucharist or the assumption of the Virgin,[24] other than those available to the common believer.

The death of the last Avignonese pope (Gregory XI) led to the Great Schism of 1378–1417, culminating in the recognition of three rival claimants to the papacy in the aftermath of the Council of Pisa (1409).[25] It is difficult to overestimate the impact of the 'Babylonian Captivity' of the papacy at Avignon and the ensuing schism upon the medieval church. To whom should believers look for an authoritative, or even a provisional, statement concerning the faith of the church? In a period of unprecedented expansion in theological speculation in the universities and religious houses of western Europe, guidance was urgently required as to the catholicity of the new methods and doctrines which were emerging. The traditional method of validation of such opinions was by reference to the teaching of the institutional church, objectified in the episcopacy and papacy – yet the institution of the church itself appeared to many to be called into question by the events of the Great Schism, and the period immediately preceding it. Furthermore, Ockham had called into question the role of both the papacy and ecumenical councils in such a process of validation, and thus initiated a debate continued by Pierre d'Ailly, Jean Gerson and Johannes Breviscoxa.[26] The development of the astonishing doctrinal diversity of the late fourteeth and fifteenth centuries is probably largely due to the apparent suspension of the normal methods of validation of theological opinions, together with an apparent reluctance (or inability) on the part of the ecclesiastical authorities to take decisive action against heterodox views as and when they arose.[27] The weakening in the fifteenth century of the means by which orthodoxy

24 Ockham, *De corpore Christi* cap. 5; ed. T. B. Birch (Burlington, 1930), pp. 182–4; cap. 36, p. 444.

25 The Pisa claimant was notable for his strong affinities with the theology of the *via moderna*: see F. Ehrle, *Der Sentenzenkommentar Peters von Candia des Pisaner Papstes Alexanders V: Ein Beitrag zur Scheidung der Schulen in der Scholastik des vierzehnten Jahrhunderts und zur Geschichte des Wegestreits* (Münster, 1925).

26 See Heiko A. Oberman, *The Harvest of Medieval Theology: Gabriel Biel and Late Medieval Nominalism* (Cambridge, Mass., 1963), pp. 378–90.

27 Ecclesiastical inactivity in the fifteenth century in relation to matters of doctrine is evident from the growth of heresy at the time: see John N. Stephens, 'Heresy in Medieval and Renaissance Florence', *Past and Present* 54 (1972), pp. 25–60. For the worsening of the situation in the sixteenth century, see the invaluable study of Gerhard Müller, *Die römische Kurie und die Reformation 1523–1534: Kirche und Politik während des Pontifikates Clemens VII* (Gütersloh, 1969).

might be enforced became more pronounced in the first half of the sixteenth century, as factors such as the continued rise of nationalism in northern Europe, the Franco-Italian war, and the Hapsburg–Valois conflict, combined to make the suppression of heterodoxy by force considerably more difficult. The nationalist overtones of the early reforming movements and growing independence of the Swiss and southern German cities, to name no other factors, considerably diminished the ability of the curia to respond to the growing ideological and political threat from north of the Alps. Furthermore, Hadrian VI (1522–3) failed to press for the convening of diocesan and provincial synods in northern Europe during the years when the possibility of suppressing the new movements was greatest. The factors leading to the erosion of such centralized power as had previously existed at this crucial period in history are not fully understood: what *is* evident, however, are the consequences of this erosion of power, in that the new reforming movements were allowed to develop with minimal hindrance.

The Great Schism was ended by the Council of Constance (1414–17), which elected Martin V as pope on 11 November 1417.[28] The circumstances under which this council was convened, however, were to occasion a further crisis of authority within the church. In that there were several claimants to the papacy, it was widely held that the only manner in which the matter might be settled was through the convening of an ecumenical council. The fifth session of the Council enacted the decree *Haec sancta*, which affirmed that its authority was derived directly from Christ, and was to be respected even by popes. Although it was on the basis of this presupposition that the election of Martin V took place, the assumption that such authority was invested in a council (rather than the pope) led to disagreement concerning its ecumenicity.[29] The subsequent undermining of the

28 For recent works on this council, see Remigius Bäumer, 'Die Reformkonzilien des 15. Jahrhunderts in der neueren Forschung', *Annuarium Historiae Conciliorum* 1 (1969), pp. 153–64.
29 Odilo Engels, 'Zur Konstanzer Konzilsproblematik in der nachkonziliaren Historiographie des 15. Jahrhunderts', in *Von Konstanz nach Trient: Beiträge zur Kirchengeschichte von den Reformkonzilien bis zum Tridentinum*, ed. R. Bäumer (Paderborn, 1972), pp. 233–59. Disagreement about the status of Constance and Basle is also evident in the numeration of the ecumenical councils in contemporary sources: see Remigius Bäumer, 'Die Zahl der allgemeinen Konzilien in der Sicht von Theologen des 15. und 16. Jahrhunderts', *Annuarium Historiae Conciliorum* 1 (1969), pp. 288–313.

conciliarist position,[30] culminating in Pius II's bull *Execrabilis* (1460), did not defuse the crucial theological question arising from the Conciliar Movement: who had the authority to validate theological opinions – the pope, a council, or perhaps even a professor of theology? It was this uncertainty which contributed to no small extent to the remarkable doctrinal diversity of the late medieval church.

The doctrinal diversity so characteristic of the later medieval period cannot be explained on the basis of any single development. Of the various factors contributing to this development, in addition to the absence of magisterial pronouncements, however, a number may be singled out as being of particular importance. First, it is clear that a number of quite distinct theological schools emerged during the late thirteenth and early fourteenth centuries, with differing presuppositions and methods. These schools tended to be based upon, or at least associated with, specific religious orders. As a result, a number of quite distinct approaches to theology, with differences both in substance and in emphasis, may be discerned within the late medieval period. Second, there was considerable disagreement upon the nature of the sources of theology, and their relative priority. Of particular interest in this respect is the absence of general agreement concerning the status and method of interpretation of both scripture and the writings of Augustine.[31] Third, the tension between the logico-critical and historico-critical method became increasingly significant in the later fourteenth century, with a concomitant polarization in areas of doctrine sensitive to methodological presuppositions (such as Christology, and the doctrine of justification). Fourth, the rise of lay piety – an important phenomenon for many reasons – proved a near-irresistible force for development in certain areas of theology, particularly Mariology, as an expression of the beliefs and attitudes underlying popular piety. Fifth, in certain areas of doctrine – most notably the doctrine of justification – there appears to have been considerable confusion during the first decades of the sixteenth century concerning the offical teaching of the church, with the result that doctrinal diversity arose through uncertainty over whether a given opinion corresponded to the teaching

30 The defection of Nicholas of Cusa from a conciliar to a papal stance appears to have occasioned a crisis in humanist circles at the time: see James E. Biechler, 'Nicholas of Cusa and the End of the Conciliar Movement: A Humanist Crisis of Identity', *Church History* 44 (1975), pp. 5–21.
31 See Hermann Schüssler, *Der Primat der Heiligen Schrift als theologisches und kanonistisches Problem im Spätmittelalter* (Wiesbaden, 1977).

of the church or not. Some of these factors may conveniently be considered at this point, before being developed further in later chapters.

Although the development of theological schools may be traced to the establishment of Tours, Reims, St Gall, Reichenau and Laon as centres of learning in the ninth century,[32] the rise of the great theological schools is associated with the late eleventh and twelfth centuries, in the aftermath of the Gregorian reforms. By the end of the twelfth century, Paris had become established as the theological centre of Europe. Its theological schools propagated both the views of, and the disagreement among, masters such as Peter Abailard, Gilbert of Poitiers, Peter Lombard and Hugh of St Victor. It was, however, events of the thirteenth century which are of decisive importance for present purposes. The Dominicans and Franciscans arrived at Paris in the second decade of the thirteenth centuries, and gradually wrested three chairs of theology from the control of secular masters to that of their orders.[33] The opinions of the first Dominican and Franciscan professors (Roland of Cremona O.P. and John of St Giles O.F.M., respectively) came to be perpetuated in the teachings of the early Dominican and Franciscan schools, culminating in the teachings of Thomas Aquinas and Bonaventure respectively.[34] A distinct school appears to have developed slightly later within the Augustinian Order, based upon the writings of Giles of Rome.[35] The impact of the teaching of Duns Scotus, and subsequently that of William of Ockham *cum suis*, in the early fourteenth century led to further diversification within these schools, with the rise of the later Franciscan school, the *via moderna* and the *schola Augustiniana moderna*, to name but the most significant. Although these schools tended to be linked with specific religious orders, it is clear that there was considerable diversity of belief within such orders.

32 See, e.g., J. J. Conteni, *The Cathedral School of Laon from c. 850–c. 1000* (Munich, 1978); John Marenbon, *From the Circle of Alcuin to the School of Auxerre: Logic, Theology and Philosophy in the Early Middle Ages* (Cambridge, 1983).

33 For details of the controversy leading to these developments, see M.-M. Dufeil, *Guillaume de Saint-Amour et la polémique universitaire parisienne 1250–1259* (Paris, 1972), especially pp. 146–282.

34 I have documented these developments in the case of the doctrine of justification: see Alister E. McGrath, *Iustitia Dei: A History of the Christian Doctrine of Justification* (2 vols: Cambridge, 1986), vol. 1, pp. 155–63.

35 See Adolar Zumkeller, 'Die Augustinerschule des Mittelalters', *Analecta Augustiniana* 27 (1964), pp. 167–262; A. E. McGrath, '"Augustinianism?" A Critical Assessment of the so-called "Medieval Augustinian Tradition" on Justification', *Augustiniana* 31 (1981), pp. 247–67.

Although Carl Stange argued, in a study dating from the beginning of the present century, that late medieval theology was essentially a theology of religious orders – so that Dominicans followed the teaching of Thomas Aquinas, Franciscans that of Bonaventure, and Augustinians that of Giles of Rome or Gregory of Rimini[36] – subsequent studies indicated that this was not entirely accurate. For example, the influence of local universities could not be discounted. Thus Hermelink pointed out how the Dominicans at Cologne were heavily influenced by the *via antiqua*, and those at Vienna and Erfurt by the *via moderna* – these differences corresponding to the school dominant in the local university faculty of arts.[37] Robert Holcot O.P. well exemplifies the tendency for Dominicans to be influenced by currents of thought (in this case, the *via moderna*) originating from outside their order.[38] A similar observation might be made on the influence of the *via moderna* upon the Augustinian priory at Erfurt in the final decade of the sixteenth century.[39] Furthermore, it is clear that there was considerable tension within the later medieval Franciscan Order concerning the relative status of Bonaventure and Duns Scotus, each of whom could lay claim to the title of doctor of that order. This became particularly apparent at the Council of Trent, where the evident differences between the two doctors on points of importance could no longer be ignored.[40] Indeed, there are reasons for supposing that the chief contribution of the Franciscans to the intellectual life of

36 Carl Stange, 'Über Luthers Beziehungen zur Theologie seines Ordens', *Neue kirchliche Zeitschrift* 11 (1900), pp. 574–85.

37 H. Hermelink, *Die theologische Fakultät in Tübingen vor der Reformation 1477–1534* (Tübingen, 1906).

38 See Heiko A. Oberman, '*Facientibus quod in se est Deus non denegat gratiam*: Robert Holcot O.P. and the Beginnings of Luther's Theology', *HThR* 55 (1962), pp. 317–42; Fritz Hoffmann, *Die theologische Methode des Oxforder Dominikanerlehrers Robert Holkot* (Münster, 1972).

39 This point is usually emphasized in the course of discussing the *initia theologiae Lutheri*: See, e.g., Alister E. McGrath, *Luther's Theology of the Cross: Martin Luther's Theological Breakthrough* (Oxford, 1985), pp. 27–71, especially pp. 69–70. On the *via moderna* at Erfurt, see W. Urban, 'Die "via moderna" an der Universität Erfurt am Vorabend der Reformation', in *Gregor von Rimini: Werk und Wirkung bis zur Reformation*, ed. H. A. Oberman (Berlin/New York, 1981), pp. 311–30.

40 Note the comments of Bonaventura Pius de Costacciaro, made at Trent on 28 December 1546: *Concilium Tridentinum diarorum, actorum, epistularum, tractatuum nova collectio*, ed. Societas Goeresiana (Freiburg, 1901–), vol. 5, p. 741, lines 28–32. In fact, as Heynck has pointed out, there was considerable disagreement within the Franciscan contingent at Trent as to precisely what Scotus' views on certain matters of significance were: Valens Heynck, 'A Controversy at the Council of Trent concerning the Doctrine of Duns Scotus', *FcS* 9 (1949), pp. 181–258.

late medieval period was its spirituality,[41] rather than any coherent theological system. It will therefore be clear that there was potentially a remarkably broad spectrum of theological opinions current within the universities and religious orders of Europe on the eve of the Reformation, simply on account of the diversity of theological schools and the absence of well-defined and strictly limited spheres of influence (such as specific countries, universities or religious orders) by which their teachings might be restricted or controlled.

A further contributing factor to the development of endemic doctrinal plurality in the later medieval period was the controversy between the *via antiqua* and *via moderna* concerning the role of the logico-critical method in theology. This conflict – exemplified in microcosm in the fourteenth century disputes within the Augustinian Order[42] – was pregnant with theological significance in relation to numerous areas of doctrine, including Christology and the theology of justification. The use of the dialectic between the two powers of God by theologians of the later Franciscan school, the *via moderna* and the *schola Augustiniana moderna*, called into question the foundations of certain traditional doctrines. The appeal to the dialectic between the two powers of God was based upon the distinction between the ordained (*potentia Dei ordinata*) and absolute (*potentia Dei absoluta*) powers of God.[43] A dialectic was set up between things as they might have been, and things as they actually are, corresponding to the absolute and ordained powers of God respectively. In view of the widespread misunderstanding of the nature and purpose of this dialectic, a brief

41 For a careful study of such a spirituality towards the end of our period, see André Godin, *L'homélaire de Jean Vitrier: spiritualité franciscaine en Flandre au XVIe siècle* (Geneva, 1971). Although the Franciscans were considerably more successful in their popular ministry than the Dominicans, certain difficulties are known to have remained: Paul L. Nyhus, *The Franciscans in South Germany 1400–1530: Reform and Revolution* (Philadelphia, 1975).
42 See Damasus Trapp, 'Augustinian Theology of the Fourteenth Century', *Augustiniana* 6 (1956), pp. 146–274. The terms *antiqui* and *moderni* assume a range of meanings in contemporary sources, in that they were employed in a variety of contexts, and for a variety of purposes, in addition to distinguishing the views of Thomas Aquinas and Duns Scotus from those of William of Ockham and Gabriel Biel: see Elizabeth Gössmann, *Antiqui und Moderni im Mittelalter: Eine geschichtliche Standortsbestimmung* (Munich/Paderborn, 1974).
43 See K. Bannach, *Die Lehre von der doppelten Macht Gottes bei Wilhelm von Ockham: Problemgeschichtliche Voraussetzungen und Bedeutung* (Wiesbaden, 1975); Berndt Hamm, *Promissio, pactum, ordinatio: Freiheit und Selbstbindung Gottes in der scholastischen Gnadenlehre* (Tübingen, 1977), pp. 340–90. It should be noted that the principle was originally intended to function primarily as a defence of the divine freedom in the face of thirteenth-century Averroist determinism: M. Grabmann, *Der lateinische Averroismus des 13. Jahrhunderts und seine Stellung zur christliche Weltanschauung* (Munich, 1931).

account is called for, before moving on to consider its implications for doctrinal pluralism.

The essential point made by those who appealed to the dialectic between the powers of God was that the present created order, including the order of salvation, did not result from God acting out of necessity. Out of the initial set of potentialities open to actualization by God, only a subset was thus actualized. The argument runs thus. Before his decision concerning which potentialities should be actualized, God was at liberty to select any, subject solely to the condition that this should not involve contradiction. The fact that it is impossible to construct a triangle with four sides is thus not understood to involve a restriction upon God's course of action. Once God has determined which potentialities shall be actualized, and executed this decision, however, he is under a self-imposed restriction in regard to his actions. In other words, once God has created a certain order, he is under an obligation to himself to respect this order. Scotus thus points out that the present established created order is essentially an expression of the divine wisdom and benevolence, rather than the result of a necessity imposed upon God from outside.[44] As Ockham emphasizes, however, the dialectic between the two powers of God does not imply that there are two present modes of action open to God,[45] but simply that God has now committed himself to a specific course of action, so that he cannot now act *inordinate*. Ockham is therefore able to highlight the contingent, rather than necessary, character of this order (in that God could have created a different order, had he so desired). The effect of this was to draw attention to the weakness of the foundations of certain significant doctrines. Consideration of two such doctrines will illustrate this point.

44 'Aliquid autem est possibile deo dupliciter: vel secundum eius potentiam absolutam, qua potest omne id, quod non includit contradictionem; aut secundum eius potentiam ordinatam, secundum quam fit omne aliud, quod consonat legibus divinae iustitiae et regulis sapientiae eius, quod si fieret aliter et secundum alias leges statutas et ordinatas a divina voluntate, non inordinate fieret, set ita ordinate sicut modo secundum ista': *Reportatio Parisiensis* IV dist. i q. 5 n. 2, as cited by Werner Dettloff, *Die Lehre von der acceptatio divina bei Johannes Duns Scotus mit besonderer Berücksichtigung der Rechtfertigungslehre* (Werl, 1954), p. 206, n. 7.
45 'Haec distinctio non est sic intelligenda quod in Deo sint realiter duae potentiae quarum una sit ordinata et alia absoluta, quia unica est potentia in Deo ad extra, quae omni modo est ipse Deus. Nec sic est intelligenda quod aliqua potest Deus ordinate facere et aliqua potest absolute et non inordinate. Sed est intelligenda quod "posse aliquid" quandoque accipitur secundum leges ordinatas et institutas a Deo; et illa dicitur Deus posse facere de potentia ordinata'. *Quodl.* VI q. 1; *Opera Theologica* (9 vols: New York, 1966–) vol. 9, pp. 585–6.

The theologians of the thirteenth century were virtually unanimous in their opinion that justification involved created habits of grace.[46] This opinion was substantiated on the grounds that such a created habit was necessary, on account of the nature of sin and grace – in other words, that such a habit was necessary *ex natura rei*. The appeal to the dialectic between the two powers of God called this 'necessity' into question: had God so desired, a completely different means of justifying man could have been devised. While not actually calling into question the *de facto* necessity of such habits, the original grounds upon which their necessity had been deduced were discredited.[47] As a result, the main theological schools of the fourteenth century – such as the modern Franciscan school, the *via moderna* and the *schola Augustiniana moderna* – regarded the divine acceptation itself, rather than created habits of grace, as the immediate cause of justification. God was free to do directly (such as justify man) what he might otherwise do through created intermediates (such as habits of grace). This significant shift in opinion is important for two reasons. First, it indicates how the new logico-critical method posed a powerful challenge to received doctrines, and thus contributed significantly to the doctrinal pluralism of the fourteenth and fifteenth centuries. Second, it suggested that the present order of salvation was merely one of a number of possibilities, thus undermining its permanent significance. This impression was confirmed by Ockham's analysis of the incarnation, which recognized the possibility that God could have become incarnate as a stone, a block of wood, or an ass – rather than as man.[48] To many critics, the application of the logico-critical method seemed simply to result in the disintegration of the traditional structure of Christian doctrine, resulting in a Nestorian Christology and a Pelagian soteriology.[49] The rise of the logico-critical method thus led not merely to a diversification in late medieval theological opinions, but also to an implicit challenge to the foundations of much traditional theology.

---

46 McGrath, *Iustitia Dei*, vol. 1, pp. 100–9; 158–63.

47 McGrath, *Iustitia Dei*, vol. 1, pp. 145–54. The older study of Paul Vignaux, *Justification et prédestination au XIVe siècle* (Paris, 1934), is still valuable in documenting this controversy.

48 There was, in fact, a serious purpose to this apparently pointless speculation: see Alister E. McGrath, '*Homo assumptus?* A Study in the Christology of the *Via Moderna*, with Particular Reference to William of Ockham', *EThL* 60 (1985), pp. 283–97.

49 Thus Borchert speaks of the fourteenth century being characterized by 'Trennungstendenzen und häretischen Lehranschauungen eines abgewandelten Nestorianismus': Ernst Borchert, *Der Einfluß des Nominalismus der Spätscholastik nach dem Traktat de communicatione idiomatum des Nikolaus Oresme* (Münster, 1940), p. 151.

It was clear that plurality in certain areas of doctrine was inevitable. For example, the Great Schism gave rise to a range of ecclesiologies, as the church's theologians attempted to grapple with the theoretical difficulties arising from the evident disunity within the church.[50] Even in those areas of theology where greater doctrinal coherence might have been expected, however, considerable diversity developed.[51] Although practically every late medieval theologian recognized the authority of Augustine of Hippo – a consideration which might at first sight suggest a basis for theological coherence – there was actually little agreement at the time on how he might be interpreted. The rise of the historico-critical method within the Augustinian Order in the fourteenth century is of particular importance in this respect, as it marked a recognition of the need to establish reliable Augustinian texts as a necessary prelude to their interpretation.[52] The remarkable number of pseudo-Augustinian texts in circulation at the time greatly hindered the establishment of Augustine's views,[53] particularly in the area of soteriology. The pseudo-Augustinian treatise *Hypomnesticon* is of particular significance, on account of its strongly Massilian tone. The general tendency among theologians of the period to use collections of *sententiae*, rather than consulting original works at first hand, inevitably led to Augustinian citations being used out of context, and occasionally quite inappropriately. An excellent example of this phenomenon may be seen in the case of the late fifteenth century theologian Gabriel Biel. While considering the relation between grace and free will in justification, Biel alludes to Augustine's image of a horse and its rider as an illustration. By confusing this image with a similar image, to be found in the pseudo-Augustinian *Hypomnesticon*, a total inversion of Augustine's meaning results.[54] It is quite probable that Biel derived both this illustration and its quite inappropriate interpretation at second hand from Duns Scotus.[55] Nor was it merely doctors of antiquity who proved difficult to interpret, as the

50 Jaroslav Pelikan, *The Christian Tradition: A History of the Development of Doctrine. 4. Reformation of Church and Dogma (1300–1700)* (Chicago/London, 1984), pp. 69–126.
51 Pelikan, *Reformation of Church and Dogma*, pp. 10–68.
52 Trapp, 'Augustinian Theology of the Fourteenth Century', passim.
53 M. de Kroon, 'Pseudo-Augustin im Mittelalter: Entwurf eines Forschungsberichts', *Augustiniana* 22 (1972), pp. 511–30.
54 Oberman, *Harvest of Medieval Theology*, pp. 160–5, especially 163–4.
55 See J. Auer, *Die Entwicklung der Gnadenlehre in der Hochscholastik* (2 vols: Freiburg, 1942–51), vol. 2, p. 200.

controversy surrounding the teachings of Thomas Aquinas in the early years of the fourteenth century was to prove.[56]

The rising influence of lay piety is particularly marked upon the Mariological controversies of the late medieval period. The maculist position was regarded as firmly established within the High Scholasticism of the thirteenth century. The veneration of the Virgin within popular piety, however, proved to have an enormously creative power which initially challenged, and subsequently triumphed over, the academic objections raised against it by university theologians.[57] Significantly, it was the theologians of the Franciscan Order who supported the new doctrine in the face of opposition from the Dominicans: the former are known to have had deep popular roots denied to their more academic Dominican opponents. The early fourteenth century saw increasing support for the immaculists, initially within the Franciscan Order,[58] and subsequently within the universities and elsewhere. Of especial interest is the rapid acceptance of the doctrine of the immaculate conception within the Augustinian Order. The earlier Augustinians, such as Giles of Rome, Albert of Padua, Augustinus Triumphus of Ancona and Gregory of Rimini, were strongly maculist.[59] In the middle of the fourteenth century, however, a remarkable shift in opinion took place, with theologians such as Johannes Hiltalingen of Basel, Henry of Friemar,[60] and Thomas of Strasbourg, and continuing into the fifteenth and sixteenth centuries, with Jacobus Perez of Valencia, Johannes de Paltz[61] and Johannes von Staupitz[62] adopting the immaculist opinion. The fourteenth century thus witnessed remarkable fluidity in this matter.

---

56 Franz Ehrle, 'Der Kampf um die Lehre des hl. Thomas von Aquin in den ersten fünfzig Jahren nach seinem Tod', *ZKTh* 37 (1913), pp. 266–318.

57 See Paulus Rusch, 'Mariologische Wertungen', *ZKTh* 85 (1963), pp. 129–61, especially pp. 129–50.

58 F. de Guimarens, 'La doctrine des théologiens sur l'Immaculée Conception de 1250 à 1350', *Etudes Franciscaines* 3 (1952), pp. 181–203; 4 (1953), pp. 23–51; 167–87; Ignatius Brady, 'The Development of the Doctrine on the Immaculate Conception in the Fourteenth Century after Aureoli', *FrS* 15 (1955), pp. 175–202. Similar developments may be documented within the Augustinian Order in the later medieval period: G. Tumminello, *L'immacolata concezione di Maria et la scuola Agostinian del secolo XIV* (Rome, 1942).

59 Oberman, *Harvest of Medieval Theology*, pp. 286–92.

60 Wilfrid Werbeck, *Jacobus Perez von Valencia: Untersuchungen zu seiner Psalmenkommentar* (Tübingen, 1959), pp. 214–15.

61 R. Weijenborg, 'Doctrina de Immaculata Conceptione apud Ioannem de Paltz OESA, Magistrum Lutheri Novitii', *Virgo Immaculata* 14 (Roma, 1957), pp. 160–83.

62 David C. Steinmetz, *Misericordia Dei: The Theology of Johannes von Staupitz in its Late Medieval Setting* (Leiden, 1968), pp. 146–7.

The development of this doctrine also emphasized the prevailing uncertainty in matters of authority, on account of the declaration of the thirty-sixth session of the Council of Basle (September 1439), which declared that the immaculate conception was a 'pious doctrine, in conformity with the worship of the church, the catholic faith, right reason and Holy Scripture'.[63] By that point, however, the Council was in serious disagreement with the pope, with the result that this decision was not treated as canonically binding. It is, however, clear that at least some later fifteenth century theologians regarded this conciliar decision as magisterial, and appealed to it in their defence of the doctrine.[64]

It is now clear that the late medieval period saw considerable confusion develop concerning the official teaching of the church. Although there was a widespread consensus that it was necessary that there should be agreement – indeed, that no deviation could be permitted – concerning the fundamentals of the faith, expressed in the Apostle's Creed,[65] it was also generally recognized that there was a need to distinguish these fundamentals from theological *opinions*, which could be debated in academic situations. These 'opinions' were to be tolerated, in that they did not pose a threat to the unity of the church. By the end of the fifteenth century, however, it was becoming increasingly clear that the distinction between 'explicit catholic doctrine' and 'theological opinion' was becoming confused, with widespread uncertainty concerning to which of the two categories in question the wide range of theological views in circulation should be assigned. The introduction of the new methodologies of the *via moderna*, particularly the logico-critical method, gave rise to a plethora of new theological ideas, which rapidly achieved a wide circulation in northern Europe – but it was far from clear what status these views enjoyed. In such an age of confusion, it was inevitable that doctrinal plurality should flourish, and the distinction between 'opinion' and 'catholic truth' become blurred. Indeed, it could be argued that Luther's theological protest against the church of his day was the consequence of his improper identification of the theological *opinions* of the *via moderna*

---

63 *Monumenta conciliorum generalium seculi decimi quinti*, ed. F. Palacky et al. (3 vols: Vienna/Basle, 1857-1932), vol. 3, p. 362. For the broader issues, see Ernst Reiter, 'Rezeption und Beachtung von Basler Dekreten in der Diözese Eichstätt unter Bischof Johann von Eych (1445–1464)', in *Von Konstanz nach Trient*, pp. 215–32.
64 See Pelikan, *Reformation of Church and Dogma*, p. 50.
65 See Pelikan, *Reformation of Church and Dogma*, pp. 59–61.

concerning man's justification before God (opinions which he came to regard as Pelagian) with the official teaching of the church. For Luther, it seemed that the entire church of his day had fallen into Pelagianism, and thus required doctrinal reformation as a matter of urgency – a judgement based upon the confusion of 'opinion' and 'dogma'.

The uncertainty in the early decades of the sixteenth century in relation to the official teaching of the church on a number of matters is particularly evident in relation to the doctrine of justification, thus lending some weight to Luther's misgivings. The Pelagian controversy had been brought to an end with the decisions of the Council of Carthage (418), which were subsequently clarified by the pronouncements of the Second Council of Orange (529). Between this date and that of the sixth session of the Council of Trent (1546) – a period of more than a millenium – the church made no magisterial statement concerning the doctrine of justification. Furthermore, the decisions of Orange II were not available to the theologians of the Middle Ages: from the tenth century until the opening of the Council of Trent, the existence of the council, as well as its decisions, appear to have been unknown.[66] The theologians of the medieval period thus based their doctrines of justification upon the decisions of the Council of Carthage, which proved incapable of bearing the conceptual strain which came to be placed upon them. In a period of intense speculation, such as the fourteenth and fifteenth centuries, the orthodoxy of a new approach to man's justification – such as that of the *via moderna* – had to be determined with reference to the Council of Carthage, which used terms such as 'grace' in a less precise sense.[67] As a result, a wide spectrum of theologies of justification, all of which could be regarded as legitimated by the standards of the Council of Carthage, passed into general circulation. Had the pronouncements of Orange II been available, a much more restricted range of such theologies would have resulted.

Two examples may be given to illustrate this confusion. In 1510, a group of young Italian humanists, intensely concerned with their salvation, adopted two very different courses of action. One, led by

66 As first pointed out by Henri Bouillard, *Conversion et grâce chez Thomas d'Aquin* (Paris, 1944), pp. 99–123. See further M. Seckler, *Instinkt und Glaubenswille nach Thomas von Aquin* (Mainz, 1961), pp. 90–133.
67 See A. E. McGrath, 'The Anti-Pelagian Structure of "Nominalist" Doctrines of Justification', *EThL* 57 (1981), pp. 107–19.

Paolo Giustiniani, felt that the only hope for their justification lay in a monastic life of extreme austerity and piety; the other, led by Gasparo Contarini, felt that it was possible to be justified by remaining in secular life.[68] But which corresponded to the teaching of the church? In a period of doctrinal confusion, a definitive answer to this question was not forthcoming. Our second example is provided by Erasmus of Rotterdam, in his controversy with Martin Luther over the question of the freedom of the human will. In his *Hyperaspistes*, Erasmus showed himself unaware of *any* official teaching of the church concerning the question of what man must do if he is to be saved[69] – a fact that must be taken into account when assessing the 'catholicity' of Erasmus' views on justification.

Such was the confusion concerning what constituted the official teaching of the *magisterium* and what was merely theological opinion, that an astonishing diversity of views on the justification of man before God were in circulation at the opening of the sixteenth century. Those in the *via moderna* espoused a theology of justification which approached, although cannot be said to constitute, Pelagianism, whilst their counterparts within the *schola Augustiniana moderna* developed a strongly – occasionally ferociously – anti-Pelagian theology of justification. For the theologians of the *via antiqua*, still influential in the later medieval period, the formal cause of justification was the intrinsic denomination of a created habit of grace; for the theologians of the *via moderna* and *schola Augustiniana moderna*, the formal cause of justification was the extrinsic denomination of the divine acceptation. There was no agreement on the cause of man's predestination, nor upon the nature of the human and divine role in justification. In short, an astonishingly broad spectrum of theologies of justification existed in the later medieval period, encompassing practically every option which had not been specifically condemned as heretical by the Council of Carthage. In the absence of any definitive magisterial pronouncement concerning which of these options (or even what range of options) could be considered authentically catholic, it was left to each theologian to reach his own decision in this matter. A self-perpetuating doctrinal pluralism was thus an inevitability.

68 See Hubert Jedin, 'Ein Turmerlebnis des jungen Contarinis', in *Kirche des Glaubens – Kirche der Geschichte: Ausgewählte Aufsätze und Vorträge I* (Freiburg, 1966), pp. 167–90; McGrath, *Luther's Theology of the Cross*, pp. 9–10.
69 See Harry J. McSorley, *Luther – Right or Wrong? An Ecumenical-Theological Study of Luther's Major Work, The Bondage of the Will* (Minneapolis, 1969), pp. 288–93.

This point is of importance for a number of reasons. First, it can be shown that Luther's theological breakthrough involved his abandoning one option within this broad spectrum of theologies of justification, and embracing another within that spectrum. In other words, Luther's initial position of 1513–14, and his subsequent position (probably arrived at in 1515), were both recognized contemporary theological opinions, legitimate by the standards of the time. Luther does not appear to have appreciated this point, apparently confusing the theological opinions of the *via moderna* (which he would reject) with the official teaching of the catholic church (which he would also reject, apparently on the assumption that it had universally lapsed into a form of Pelagianism, such as that which Luther saw in the teachings of the *via moderna*.) Why, it may reasonably be asked, was Luther unaware of this point? And why, it must be asked, should Luther's changed views on justification have led to a doctrinal Reformation? (If, indeed, they did lead to such a Reformation – the relationship between the *initia theologiae Lutheri* and the *initia Reformationis* is far from clear at present.) After all, Luther's 'new' views on justification were still well within the spectrum of contemporary catholic theological opinion: even if Luther did not recognize this point, there must have been others at the time who did.

Second, when the Council of Trent met to define the catholic position on justification in relation to that of the Protestant churches, it found itself in the position of having to legitimize a wide range of theologies of justification, rather than defining *one* specific theology. In fact, it is quite misleading to refer to '*the* Tridentine doctrine of justification', in that there is no such single doctrine, but a broadly defined range of such theologies (note the deliberate use of the plural). The Council of Trent was not concerned with resolving the theological disputes between the *via antiqua* and *via moderna*, nor between Thomists or Scotists, but with drawing a line of demarcation between catholic and Protestant teachings. In effect, Trent was obliged to acknowledge and endorse the doctrinal pluralism of the late medieval period.

Although a similar doctrinal diversity and confusion may be demonstrated in the case of doctrines other than that of justification, this particular doctrine is clearly of outstanding importance in relation to this present study. There is still every reason to suggest that the theological issue over which the Lutheran Reformation began was that of justification, and the doctrinal diversity within the late medieval church in relation to this doctrine, when linked to the apparent inability to distinguish catholic dogma from theological opinion, may be regarded as the backdrop to Luther's reforming vocation. Although, as will be emphasized later in this chapter, it is improper to extrapolate from Luther's personal concerns to those of the Reformation as a whole, it is nevertheless significant that the intellectual origins of the Lutheran Reformation appear to be linked with the doctrinal pluralism of the later Middle Ages.

Briefly stated, then, the later medieval period may be regarded as characterized by a two-fold crisis of authority. First, a lack of clarity concerning the nature, location and exercise of *theological* authority at a time of rapid intellectual development led to considerable diversification of theological opinions, and confusion concerning the precise status of these opinions. The views of the Reformers initially appear to have paralleled views entertained elsewhere in the period, and thus not to have attracted attention until the situation had developed to a point at which forcible suppression of their views was necessary. Second, it is clear that the church, whether through inability or disinclination, did not move to suppress the views of the Reformers during the period when such suppression was a real possibility. The provincial and diocesan synods, established by the Fourth Lateran Council as the means of enforcing theological orthodoxy, appear to have failed to exercise such authority when it was most required.

FORERUNNERS OF THE REFORMATION

The search for the intellectual origins of the Reformation has traditionally been conducted in terms of the framework of 'Forerunners of the Reformation'. This tendency may be traced back to the work of Karl Heinrich Ullmann,[70] who identified Johannes Pupper of Goch, Johannes Ruchrat of Wesel and Wessel Gansfort as chief among such Forerunners. Inevitably, Ullmann's understanding of the nature of the Reformation is heavily influenced by his Lutheran presuppositions. The search for such 'Forerunners' has, in fact, met with little success.[71] There has, for example, been a tendency to treat the Reformation as a homogeneous phenomenon, essentially defined by

---

70 Karl H. Ullmann, *Reformatoren vor der Reformation vornehmlich in Deutschland und den Niederlanden* (2 vols: Hamburg, 1841–2).
71 Oberman, *Forerunners of the Reformation*, pp. 32–43.

by Luther's doctrine of justification. 'Forerunners of the Reformation' are thus defined as medieval thinkers who anticipated one or more aspects of Luther's theology of justification.[72] It is, however, quite unacceptable to limit such an inquiry in this way. In particular, two objections may be made. First, why should the inquiry be restricted to Luther's *doctrine of justification*? Second, why should the inquiry be restricted to *Luther*? The relation between the *initia theologiae Lutheri* and the *initia Reformationis* is now appreciated to be of such complexity[73] that it is quite improper to regard Luther's personal theological preoccupations as identical with, or even coterminous with, those of the Lutheran Reformation as a whole.

It is clear that the search for 'Forerunners of the Reformation' owed its origins to polemical, rather than scholarly, considerations. In condemning Luther's early theological theses in the sixteenth century, the University of Paris attempted to establish the essential continuity between earlier heresies and those now being expounded by Luther. Luther's ideas were not original, but were essentially the republication of older heresies. Thus Luther was a Hussite in his theology of contrition, a Wycliffite in his doctrine of confession, and a Manichaean in his theology of grace and free will.[74] According to the University of Paris, there were 'Forerunners of the Reformation' only in the sense that the Reformation represented a reappearance of older heresies: the polemical rhetorical device of *reductio ad haeresim* was sufficient to establish the heretical lineage of the movement.

The Lutheran apologists, on the other hand, attempted to establish continuity between the Reformation and the *testes veritatis* – the authentic Christian tradition, which had survived in the medieval period, despite the corruptions of scholasticism.[75] The charge to which the Lutheran Reformers were particularly sensitive was that of doctrinal innovation, and the most persuasive means of countering this charge was to demonstrate the continuity of the theology of the Reformers and the fathers *via* the representatives of the *testes veritatis* in

---

72 In fact, it proves difficult to identify such 'Forerunners': see Alister E. McGrath, 'Forerunners of the Reformation? A Critical Examination of the Evidence for Precursors of the Reformation Doctrines of Justification', *HThR* 75 (1982), pp. 219–42.

73 See Heiko A. Oberman, 'Headwaters of the Reformation: *Initia Lutheri – Initia Reformationis*', in *Luther and the Dawn of the Modern Era*, ed. H. A. Oberman (Leiden, 1974), pp. 40–88.

74 For the text of the Parisian *Determinatio*, see *Collectio Iudicorum de Novis Erroribus*, ed. C. du Plessis d'Argentré (Paris, 1724), vol. 1, cols. 358–74.

75 See McGrath, 'Forerunners of the Reformation?', pp. 219–22; 228–30.

the medieval period. The most significant exposition of this continuity was Flacius Illyricus' *Ecclesiastica Historia secundum singulas centurias*,[76] better known as the *Magdeburg Centuries*. Based on Flacius' earlier work *Catalogus testium veritatis*,[77] the *Centuries* developed its method in an increasingly sophisticated direction. The *Catalogus* was primarily concerned with identifying those who had opposed papal claims, or suffered as a result of them, in the past; the *Centuries* emphasized the positive criterion of theological continuity between the Reformers and their Forerunners, with such effect that it was dubbed *pestilentissimum opus* by the opponents of the Reformation. In that it was the Lutheran Reformation which was subjected to the most persistent and penetrating critique by contemporary catholic academics, it was inevitable that the question of the theological antecedents of the Reformation should be discussed solely with reference to it. The question of the antecedents of the Reformed church appears to have been regarded as insignificant at the time.

The historian cannot, however, be satisfied with such a basis for the thesis of the 'Forerunners of the Reformation', whether this is interpreted negatively (that is, the Lutheran Reformation as the revitalization of old heresies) or positively (that is, the Lutheran Reformation as the restitution of the *testes veritatis*). There has been a regrettable tendency, undoubtedly reflecting both the nationality and the confessional bias of scholars working in the field, to deal with the question of 'Forerunners of the Reformation' solely in terms of the *German Lutheran* Reformation. The question of the origins of the leading ideas associated with the Reformed church cannot be excluded from this analysis. In fact, the limitations of the thesis of 'the Forerunners' are largely due to its historical origins as a sixteenth century polemical device in the disputes over the 'catholicity' of the Lutheran Reformation. Modern scholarship, not wishing to be impeded by such considerations, is at liberty either to modify the concept, or to abandon it altogether. The polemical intentions of the thesis of the 'Forerunners', stated in its original form, make it unsuitable for the purposes of this study. It will, however, be clear that this does not invalidate the thesis of theological continuity between the Reformation and the late

---

76 *Ecclesiastica historia secundum singulas centurias per aliquot studiosos et pios viros in urbe Magdeburgi* (Basle: 1559-74). See Heinz Scheible, *Die Entstehung der Magdeburger Zenturien* (Gütersloh, 1966). The older study of A. Jundt, *Les Centuries de Magdebourg* (Paris, 1883), is still a valuable introduction.

77 *Catalogus testium veritatis, quae ante nostram aetatem reclamarunt Papae* (Basle, 1556).

medieval period: it simply means that this thesis cannot be investigated on the basis of such questionable sixteenth century presuppositions. In particular, it is no longer possible to overlook the enormously significant question of the intellectual origins of the Reformed church, which was generally overlooked on account of the polemical intentions of both the critics and defenders of early Lutheranism. It is on the basis of considerations such as these that the concept of the 'Forerunners' must be recognized to require modification.

It is becoming increasingly clear that, if there exist 'Forerunners of the Reformation', these are not to be identified with specific individuals within the late medieval church, but *with trends within the late medieval church as a whole*. It was the methodological and doctrinal pluralism of the later Middle Ages which gave birth to both the German and Swiss Reformations, in that the distinctive ideas associated with the Reformation in its various manifestations arose within the vortex of late medieval religious thought. The diversity of opinion concerning the sources and methods of theological speculation, the confusion concerning the *locus* of authority within the church, and other factors such as those which already noted in this chapter, combined to create a significant degree of theological instability in northern Europe, which seems to have gone largely unnoticed in Italy. From this matrix would emerge the ideas and methods which would shape the intellectual foundations of the Reformation, and rupture the unity of the European church. The present study is conceived as an investigation into the continuities and discontinuities between the thought of the Reformation *as a whole* and that of the later medieval period, in an attempt to cast light upon both the intellectual origins and character of this movement, which has exercised so great an influence over the shaping of modern Europe.

2

Humanism and the Reformation

It is now becoming increasingly clear that the intellectual environment of the early sixteenth century is sufficiently complex to inhibit generalizations concerning the precise relationship between humanism and scholasticism, or humanism and the Reformation.[1] In particular, the tendency of certain older scholars to identify 'humanism' with the personal interests, concerns and beliefs of Erasmus of Rotterdam is now regarded as both improper and misleading. This chapter is concerned with the identification of the interests and methods of the humanists, in order to cast light upon the relationship of humanism and the Reformation.

THE PROBLEM OF DEFINITION

At least four views of the nature and aims of the humanism of the Italian Renaissance have gained some support in the present century.[2] First, there is the view based upon the writings of Jacob Burckhardt,

---

1 For useful analysis and comments, see Jacques Etienne, *Spiritualisme érasmien et théologiens louvainistes: un changement de problématique au début du XVIe siècle* (Louvain/Gembloux, 1956); Charles G. Nauert, 'The Clash of Humanists and Scholastics: An Approach to Pre-Reformation Controversies', *Sixteenth Century Journal* 4 (1973), pp. 1–18.

2 Helmar Junghans, 'Der Einfluß des Humanismus auf Luthers Entwicklung bis 1518', *Luther-Jahrbuch* 37 (1970), pp. 37–101, especially 45–51; Donald Weinstein, 'In Whose Image and Likeness? Interpretations of Renaissance Humanism', *Journal of the History of Ideas* 33 (1972), pp. 165–76.

On the concept of the 'Renaissance', see Delio Cantimori, 'Sulla storia del concetto di Rinascimento', *Annali della scuola normale superiore di Pisa: lettere, storia e filosofia*, 2nd series, 1 (1932), pp. 229–68. The debate between Trier and Stackelberg also casts valuable light on the relationship between the Renaissance and classical antiquity: J. Trier, 'Zur Vorgeschichte des Renaissance-Begriff', *Archiv für Kulturgeschichte* 33 (1955), pp. 45–63; J. von Stackelberg, 'Renaissance: "Wiedergeburt" oder "Wiederwunsch"? Zur Kritik an J. Triers Aufsatz über die Vorgeschichte des Renaissance-Begriffs', *BHR* 22 (1960), pp. 406–20; Trier, 'Wiederwuchs', *Archiv für Kulturgeschichte* 43 (1961), pp. 177–87.

which regards the Renaissance as marking the birth of the modern consciousness: humanists may be viewed as the advocates of individualism, secularism and moral autonomy.[3] Second, there is the rival view based upon the writings of Giuseppe Tofannin, viewing Italian humanists as exponents of an authentically Christian culture, in the face of heterodoxy and paganism.[4] Third, there is the view based upon the works of Hans Baron, according to which Florentine humanists were exponents of republicanism, who studied the classics in order to benefit from their political and moral insights.[5] Fourth, there is the more restrained view of Paul Oskar Kristeller, which envisages humanism as a cultural and educational movement, primarily concerned with written and spoken eloquence, and only secondarily concerned with matters of philosophy and politics.[6] In fact, the Italian Renaissance is such a multifaceted phenomenon that most generalizations concerning its essence are prone to reductionist tendencies. For reasons outlined below, there are excellent grounds for preferring Kristeller's view.

According to Baron, humanism prior to 1400 was still an essentially medieval movement. The emancipation of humanism from this medieval context took place within Florence, through the influence of Leonardo Bruni. A new sense of history developed, with republican Florence being regarded as the heir of the Roman tradition. A new appreciation of Cicero appears to have developed more or less simultaneously, reflecting the new interest in the political ideas of the Roman republic.[7] But, as others have pointed out,[8] the Florentine humanism of the period appeared to be characterized more by rhetoric than by the positive defence of republican civil ideals. Indeed, Cicero appears to have been studied by the humanists of the *Quattrocento* as an orator,

3 See Wallace K. Ferguson, *The Renaissance in Historical Thought: Five Centuries of Interpretation* (Boston, Mass., 1948), pp. 195–252.

4 Giuseppe Toffanin, *Storia dell'umanesimo II: l'umanesimo italiano* (Bologna, 1964).

5 Hans Baron, *The Crisis of the Early Italian Renaissance: Civic Humanism and Republican Liberty in an Age of Classicism and Tyranny* (Princeton, NJ, revised edn, 1966).

6 P. O. Kristeller, *Renaissance Thought and Its Sources* (New York, 1979).

7 See G. Radetti, 'Le origini dell'umanesimo civile fiorentino nel 1400', *Giornale critico della filosophia italiana*, 3rd series, 12 (1959), pp. 98–122; G. Cervani, 'Il Rinascimento italiano nella interpretazione di Hans Baron', *Nuova rivista storica* 39 (1955), pp. 492–503.

8 Jerrold E. Seigel, '"Civic Humanism" or Ciceronian Rhetoric? The Culture of Petrarch and Bruni', *Past and Present* 34 (1966), pp. 3–48. For the subsequent debate, see Hans Baron, 'Leonardi Bruno: "Professional Rhetorician" or "Civic Humanist"?', *Past and Present* 36 (1967), pp. 21–37; David Robey, 'P. P. Vergerio the Elder: Republicanism and Civic Values in the Work of an Early Humanist', *Past and Present* 58 (1973), pp. 3–37.

rather than as a political thinker. The attractiveness of Kristeller's view of humanism lies in the fact that it is able to account for the remarkable diversity of outlooks evident within the Renaissance. The humanists do not appear to have adopted a coherent position on matters of substance: thus both Burckhardt and Tofannin can point to strands within Renaissance thought which support their very different approaches to the movement. Nor was the Renaissance characterized by a coherent philosophical outlook, which distinguishes it from that of scholasticism. Although it is unquestionably true that the period witnessed a wide and significant revival of various forms of Platonism,[9] the fact remains that a significant number of humanists consciously adopted Aristotelianism,[10] not least on account of its perceived importance in the fields of ethics and logic. Indeed, there are excellent reasons for suggesting that the rise of scholasticism within Reformed theology is ultimately due to the influence of Paduan Renaissance Aristotelianism (see chapter 8). Ermolao Barbaro's lectures on the *Nicomachean Ethics*, delivered during the academic year 1474–5 at Padua, illustrate the attraction Aristotle's ethics exercised over many late Renaissance thinkers.[11] Similarly, the *Heptadogma* of Robert Goulet – basically an introduction to the curriculum at the university of Paris in the late Renaissance – indicates the importance of Aristotle in relation to logic.[12] Perhaps more significantly, there appears to have been a degree of indifference to such matters within the Renaissance: of the published works dating from the Renaissance period, the relatively small number devoted

9 Raymond Klibansky, *The Continuity of the Platonic Tradition during the Middle Ages* (Munich, 1981). Marsilio Ficino is perhaps the most noted Christian Platonist of the period: see Michael J. B. Allen, 'Marsilio Ficino on Plato, the Neoplatonists and the Christian Doctrine of the Trinity', *Renaissance Quarterly* 37 (1984), pp. 555–84.

10 E. Garin, 'Le traduzioni umanistische di Aristotele nel secolo XV', *Atti e memorie dell'Accademia fiorentini di scienze morali 'La Colombaria'* 16 (1951), pp. 55–104; Toffanin, *Cinquecento*, pp. 447–520; P. O. Kristeller, 'Renaissance Aristotelianism', *Greek, Roman and Byzantine Studies* 6 (1965), pp. 157–74; Kristeller, *La tradizione aristotelica nel Rinascimento* (Padua, 1972); Kristeller, *Aristotelismo e sincretismo nel pensiero di Pietro Pomponazzi* (Padua, 1983). Earlier, Hans Baron drew attention to the important role of Aristotle's *Ethics* in the development of 'civic humanism': 'Franciscan Poverty and Civic Wealth as Factors in the Rise of Humanistic Thought', *Speculum* 13 (1938), pp. 1–37.

11 Antonio Poppi, 'Il problema della filosophia morale nella scuola padovana del Rinascimento: Platonismo e Aristotelismo nella definizione del metodo dell'ethica', in *Platon et Aristote à la Renaissance* (XVIe Colloque Internationale de Tours: Paris, 1976), pp. 105–46.

12 Michel Reulos, 'L'enseignement d'Aristote dans les collèges au XVIe siècle', in *Platon et Aristote à la Renaissance*, pp. 147–62. Note also the stipulation (p. 149) that Cicero is to be studied as an *orator*.

to philosophical or political discussions – often characterized by their amateurishness – are far outnumbered by those devoted to the 'pursuit of eloquence'. It seems that the humanists were primarily men of letters, concerned with written and spoken eloquence.[13]

This point may be illustrated from the inaugural orations of Bartolommeo della Fonte (1446–1513), a minor humanist and professor of poetry and oratory at the university of Florence in the penultimate decade of the *Quattrocento*.[14] In the *Oratio in laudem oratoriae facultatis*, delivered on 7 November 1481, as a prelude to the study of Cicero's *Orationes*, della Fonte argues that the characteristic mark of man, distinguishing him from the animals, is the capacity to express his thoughts in words. Rhetoric is thus the discipline which brings out the distinctively human dimension to man, in addition to elevating him above his fellows.[15] That this view of humanism embraces both pagan and Christian is evident from his assertion that the apostle Paul, Chrysostom, Jerome and Augustine were not merely men of outstanding piety, but also men who excelled in the elegance of their speech and writing (*dicendi quoque ac scribendi elegantia praestiterunt*).[16] In other words, humanism is essentially conceived as a cultural and educational programme, based upon written and spoken eloquence, to which men of any religious, political or philosophical persuasion may subscribe without compromising their convictions. It is perhaps on account of the fact that humanism did not embrace any specific opinions on any of these matters, confining itself to the pursuit of eloquence, that the movement made such deep inroads into all sections of Italian society in the period of the Renaissance.

A further point that should be noted is the alleged tension between northern European and Italian humanism. Although an earlier generation of historians felt able to construct a model of humanism in Europe, which contrasted a Christian humanism north of the Alps with an essentially profane and secular humanism in Italy, modern scholarship has called this model into question. Although it is clear that some contemporary northern European humanists recognized a tension

13 Hannah Holborn Gray, 'Renaissance Humanism: The Pursuit of Eloquence', in *Renaissance Essays*, ed. P. O. Kristeller and P. P. Wiener (New York, 1968), pp. 199–216.
14 Charles Trinkaus, 'A Humanist's Image of Humanism: The Inaugural Orations of Bartolommeo della Fonte', *Studies in the Renaissance* 7 (1960), pp. 90–147.
15 Wolfenbüttel Cod. 43 Aug. Fol., ff. 141v–142v, cited in Trinkaus, 'Bartolommeo della Fonte', p. 97 n. 26.
16 Wolfenbüttel Cod. 43 Aug. Fol., ff. 142v–143r, cited in Trinkaus, 'Bartolommeo della Fonte', p. 98 n. 27.

between their own views and those of certain Italian humanists, this serves merely to confirm the fundamental diversity of Renaissance humanism. The profane and the Christian existed side by side in the Renaissance, both laying claim to be 'humanist'.

The importance of Kristeller's definition of humanism lies in the fact that it still permits us to regard humanism as a coherent movement, with certain minimal characteristics, while simultaneously recognizing that its complex network of intellectual interests defies simplistic reduction in terms of an underlying philosophical unity. Without the recognition of the polymorphism of the movement, it is quite possible that the term 'humanism' would cease to function as a meaningful designation in intellectual history. In the Renaissance, a *humanista* was a professional teacher of the *studia humanitatis*, and the temptation to impose the modern secular nuances of the term upon its Renaissance equivalent must be resisted. Far too many modern students tend to approach the question of the relation between humanism and the Reformation on the basis of the assumption that humanists were predisposed *against* Christianity in general, and the catholic church in particular.

Although it is clear that Renaissance humanism was characterized by no distinctive philosophical or ideological stance, the fact remains that, virtually without exception, the humanists were Christians, men who saw themselves as operating within the context of the church. There has been an increasing reaction against the Enlightenment tendency, still evident in some quarters, to regard the humanists as precursors of the Enlightenment critique of religion. The humanists were regarded by the Enlightenment as prophets of the free human spirit, working towards their emancipation from the narrow confines of the world of medieval religion, in much the same way as the Reformation was regarded as primarily concerning the right to exercise unrestricted private judgement.[17] Perhaps the most important consideration leading to the discrediting of this view of humanism concerns the obsession of certain humanists with magic and the cabala.[18] As the interest (or obsession, as some scholars would have it) in the

---

17 Heinrich Bornkamm, *Luther im Spiegel der deutschen Geistesgeschichte* (Heidelberg, 1955), pp. 14–15.
18 See, e.g., François Masai, *Plethon et la Platonisme de Mistra* (Paris, 1956); D. P. Walker, *Spiritual and Demonic Magic from Ficino to Campanella* (London, 1958); Frances Yates, *Giordano Bruno and the Hermetic Tradition* (London, 1967).

Faust legend indicates,[19] many humanists had more in common with the spirit of Romanticism than with the sober rationalism of the Enlightenment.[20] Furthermore, successive studies of Pico della Mirandola,[21] Valla[22] and Erasmus[23] – to name but some of the more important figures associated with the movement – have indicated the continuity of humanism with the medieval catholic spiritual tradition. Humanism was an important element in the flux of late medieval religious life and thought, being particularly influential among the intellectual elite, and thus inevitably possessing a significant potential influence upon late medieval piety, religion and theology. The crucial question with which the historian is particularly concerned is the identification of the nature and extent of such influence.

A further point that should be noted is the cosmopolitan character of humanism. Although various movements which could conceivably be designated as 'proto-humanist' may be identified in fifteenth century northern Europe,[24] it seems that the development of northern European humanism was both stimulated and informed by the diffusion of the ideals of the Italian Renaissance. Three main channels of diffusion have been identified.[25] First, through the exchange of

19 See D. Harmening, 'Faust und die Renaissance-Magie: Zum ältesten Faust-Zeugnis (Johannes Trithemius an Johannes Viridung, 1507)', *Archiv für Kulturgeschichte* 55 (1973), pp. 56–79.

20 As sugegsted by Heinz Otto Burger, *Renaissance, Reformation, Humanismus* (Bad Homburg, 1969). Goethe's reworking of the Faust legend is significant in this connection.

21 E. Monnerjahn, *Giovanni Pico della Mirandola: Ein Beitrag zur philosophischen Theologie des Humanismus* (Wiesbaden, 1960).

22 Franco Gaeta, *Lorenzo Valla: filologia e storia nell'umanesimo* (Naples, 1955); Salvatore I. Camporeale, *Lorenzo Valla: umanesimo e teologia* (Florence, 1972).

23 Thus Auer demonstrated that Erasmus' ethical bias reflected the influence of the Greek fathers, rather than that of rationalism: Alfons Auer, *Die vollkommene Frömmigkeit eines Christen* (Düsseldorf, 1954). Erasmus' continuity with the earlier catholic tradition is brought out by John B. Payne, *Erasmus: His Theology of the Sacraments* (Richmond, Va, 1970).

24 On German humanism, see G. Ritter, 'Die geschichtliche Bedeutung des deutschen Humanismus', *Historische Zeitschrift* 127 (1922–3), pp. 393–453; H. Entner, 'Der Begriff "Humanismus" als Problem der deutschen Literaturgeschichtsschreibung', *Klio* 40 (1962), pp. 260–70; R. Newald, *Probleme und Gestalte des deutschen Humanismus* (Berlin, 1963); Lewis W. Spitz, *The Religious Renaissance of the German Humanists* (Cambridge, Mass., 1963); Entner, 'Probleme der Forschung zum deutschen Frühhumanismus 1400–1500', *Wissenschaftliche Zeitschrift der Ernst-Moritz-Arndt-Universität Greifswald* 15 (1966), pp. 587–90. On the Low Countries, see Jozef IJsewijn, 'The Coming of Humanism to the Low Countries', in *Itinerarium Italicum*, ed. H. A. Oberman with Thomas A. Brady (Leiden, 1975), pp. 193–304.

25 P. O. Kristeller, 'The European Diffusion of Italian Humanism', in *Renaissance Thought II: Papers on Humanism and the Arts* (New York, 1965), pp. 69–88, especially pp. 71–83. This essay may be supplemented by other works. For example, attention has been drawn to the role of northern European printing houses as channels for the diffusion of Italian humanism: see Friedrich Luchsinger, *Der Baslerbuchdruck als Vermittler italienischer Geistes* (Basle, 1953).

persons between northern Europe and Renaissance Italy. Thus northern European students might study at Italian universities before returning to assume influential teaching positions in northern universities. Second, through the extensive foreign correspondence of the Italian humanists, the full extent of which is only gradually becoming apparent through the process of cataloguing. Third, through the dissemination of manuscripts, and particularly through printed works. Athough printing was a German invention, many of the more important late fifteenth century presses were situated in northern Italy. The strongly cosmopolitan aura of humanism is, of course, particularly well instanced in the case of Erasmus, who regarded himself as a citizen of the world,[26] and treated languages other than Latin with disdain. His momentary lapse into his native Dutch on his deathbed should not be permitted to obscure the fact that Erasmus, unlike many strongly nationalist humanists, regarded national boundaries and languages as impediments in the path of humanist ideals.[27] The strongly national overtones associated with local humanist circles – such as that to which Zwingli belonged[28] – contrast strongly with Erasmus' indifference to local cultures and political situations. Erasmus had no time for the nationalist pride evident in Vadian's dedicatory poem to Glarean's hexameters in praise of Switzerland, in which he asserts that the intellectual minority of Switzerland has been ended through the efforts of Glarean and Myconius, the muses of Apollo now having climbed the Swiss Alps.[29]

CHARACTERISTIC FEATURES OF NORTHERN EUROPEAN HUMANISM

In dealing with the question of the intellectual origins of the European Reformation, we are primarily concerned with the characteristics of the ideals, methods and presuppositions of northern European humanism. Broadly speaking, three quite distinct, although related,

26 Note the famous remarks to Zwingli: 'Ego mundi civis esse cupio, communis omnium, vel peregrinis magis. Utinam contingat ascribi civitati coelesti'. CR (Zwingli) 7.580.
27 See J. Huizinga, 'Erasmus über Vaterland und Nationen', in *Gedenkschrift zum 400. Todestage des Erasmus* (Basle, 1936), pp. 34–49.
28 CR (Zwingli) 5.250.8–11. See W. P. Stephens, *The Theology of Huldrych Zwingli* (Oxford, 1986), pp. 7–8. Erasmus distanced himself from such matters: see CR (Zwingli) 8.37.8–9.
29 H. Glareanus, *Descriptio de situ Helvetiae et vicinus gentibus* (Basle, 1519). Vadian's assertion that Swiss national freedom must be defended *armis animisque* is sharply at odds with Erasmus' cosmopolitan vision of humanism.

such characteristics may be identified. These are a literary or cultural programme, directed towards the ideal of *bonae litterae*; a religious programme directed towards the ideal of *Christianismus renascens*; and a political programme, primarily directed towards the establishment of peace in Europe.

The rise of classical scholarship is one of the most distinctive features of the Italian Renaissance, and its influence upon northern European humanism, such as that of Erasmus, is beyond dispute.[30] It must, of course, be appreciated that the intense study of ancient literature and philology was not generally seen as an end in itself, but as a means towards the attainment of eloquence, both written and spoken. The negative attitude adopted towards the vernacular by many humanists, such as Erasmus, reflected their conviction that *eloquentia* could only be achieved through the medium of Ciceronian Latin. The humanist emphasis upon the significance of language is, however, of greater significance than might at first be thought. The new interest in classical rhetorical theory and sources, such as Aristotle's *Posterior Analytics* and Cicero's *Topica*, was linked with an emphasis upon the unique and particular elements of literature and history – the irreducible particularity of human reality was widely recognized as being more suited to historical description, rather than logical analysis.[31] Thus the New Testament was read, not as the basis of an intellectually comprehensive and logically consistent theological system, but as the record of the early Christian experience given in a specific literary and historical form. Those who see the origins of modern historicism as lying in the Renaissance period have good reason for doing so.[32] The early

---

30 The rise of classical scholarship is well documented in the following studies: G. Billanovitch, 'Petrarch and the Textual Tradition of Livy', *Journal of the Warburg and Courtauld Institute* 14 (1951), pp. 137–208; Winifried Trillitzsch, 'Erasmus und Seneca', *Philologus* 109 (1965), pp. 270–93; Sesto Prete, 'Leistungen der Humanisten auf dem Gebiete der lateinischen Philologie', *Philologus* 109 (1965), pp. 259–69; Vittore Branca, 'Ermolao Barbaro and Late Quattrocento Venetian Humanism', in *Renaissance Studies*, ed. J. R. Hale (Totowa, NJ, 1973), pp. 218–43; Antony Grafton, 'On the Scholarship of Politian and its Context', *Journal of the Warburg and Courtauld Institute* 40 (1977), pp. 150–88; Charles G. Nauert, 'Humanists, Scientists and Pliny: Changing Approaches to a Classical Author', *American Historical Review* 84 (1979), pp. 72–85.
31 See George M. Logan, 'Substance and Form in Renaissance Humanism', *Journal of Medieval and Renaissance Studies* 7 (1977), pp. 1–34.
32 The emphasis upon the importance of particular circumstances, rather than universal categories, has been well documented in the cases of Bruni, Budé and Poggio: see Nancy L. Struever, *The Language of History in the Renaissance* (Princeton, NJ, 1970); Donald Kelley, *The Foundations of Modern Historical Scholarship* (New York, 1970).

humanist concern with the *text* of the New Testament, particularly
evident with Valla, is ultimately an expression of the conviction that
this text may, through literary and historical analysis, yield moral
and doctrinal insights of importance to the specific historical situation
of the interpreter. Although many of the humanists commended the
eloquentia of the New Testament, particularly the Pauline writings,
it is clear that this text was recognized as an intellectually modest source
incapable of bearing the dialectical weight imposed upon it through
the theological speculation of the schoolmen.

The appeal to the New Testament and the fathers[33] as the sources
of a reformed and renewed church was an appeal to return *ad fontes*.
This celebrated slogan must not be misunderstood: the New Testament, and writers such as Vergil and Galen, had been known for
centuries – what was new was not so much these sources themselves,
as both the method and the spirit by and in which they were
approached. Commentaries and glosses were to be by-passed, in order
to engage directly with the text itself – whether the text in question
was the Justinian *Pandects* or the New Testament. The importance
of this point will be further emphasized in chapter 4. The new spirit
in which these classical sources were read must not be overlooked.
Vergil was read with the idea of imitating Aeneas by setting out by
sea, to voyage to distant lands (it need hardly be added that the
discovery of the Americas in the final decade of the fifteenth century
made a deep impression upon the contemporary European consciousness). Galen was read with the idea of carrying out experiments
by which medical and scientific knowledge might be confirmed and
enlarged. The New Testament was read with the idea of encountering
the risen Christ (*Christus renascens*) through faith, and recapturing the
vitality of the experience of the early church.[34] The slogan *ad fontes*
was more than simply a call to return to ancient sources – it was a
call to return to the essential realities of human existence as reported
in these literary sources. The new literary and philological techniques
enabled the reader to return to and reinterpret his own experience
e fontibus. Far from being merely a purely literary or cultural programme,

---

33 A distinction is frequently made between *doctores* (e.g., Augustine) and *patres* (e.g., Origen)
in sixteenth century sources: see, e.g., CR (Zwingli) 1.366.24–5. The term 'fathers' is used
in the present study simply to designate an ecclesiastical writer, whether Greek- or Latin-speaking,
of the first five centuries.
34 It is thus significant that Vadian's first major exegetical work was his commentary on the
Acts of the Apostles, which highlighted the experiential aspects of the early church.

the recall *ad fontes* was a search for experience and meaning, which recognized in classical sources the means towards this end. Literary and philological techniques allowed the reader to break out of the literary situation of these works, and encounter something deeper. For the Reformers, the new techniques allowed the reader to break out of the specific historical situation of the New Testament writings, and hear in them nothing other than the Word of God.

The humanist literary programme encapsulated in the slogan *ad fontes* has immediate affinities with the theological concerns of the Reformation. Reformer and humanist alike wished Christian doctrine and practice to be established *e fontibus*, upon the basis of the New Testament and the fathers, rather than upon biblical glosses or commentaries, or the complex matrix of presuppositions underlying scholastic theology. Particularly in the early phase of the Reformation, there appears to have been a 'productive misunderstanding' between humanists and Reformers, the former apparently assuming that the latter were committed to essentially the same programme as themselves.[35] It is easy to see how this impression could arise. Both humanist and Reformer were hostile towards scholastic theology; both wished to return to the bible, particularly the New Testament, as the source of Christian doctrine; both greatly valued the fathers as witnesses to the vitality and character of early Christianity. This appeared to indicate that both movements possessed a common theological programme, and many at the time appear to have assumed that this was the case. It was the humanists who, by their uncritical support for Luther in the period 1518–21, transformed a minor controversy within the theological faculty of the University of Wittenberg into a major controversy with ramifications for both church and society. What was initially a purely local controversy was, through the cosmopolitanism of its humanist observers, debated by intellectuals throughout much of Europe. Nevertheless, the fact remains that superficial similarities between the reforming programmes of the humanists and the early evangelicals served only to conceal profound differences.

Both humanists and Reformers were hostile towards scholastic theology.[36] The humanists objected to the scholastic concern with

---

35 See Berndt Moeller, 'Die deutschen Humanisten und die Anfänge der Reformation', *ZKG* 70 (1959), pp. 46–61; p. 54. This point is returned to in a later section of this chapter.
36 See Etienne, *Spiritualisme érasmien et théologiens louvainistes*; Nauert, 'Clash of Humanists and Scholastics'.

universal and religious truths, preferring to deal with specific concrete historical situations. Furthermore, the degenerate Latin and arcane terminology employed by the schoolmen in their dialectical disputations were the subject of derision: for the humanists, there was no reason why matters of ethics or doctrine could not be expressed eloquently and simply. For the Reformers, particularly Luther, the schoolmen were not to be criticized on account of their style or vocabulary, but on account of the theology for which these were vehicles. A reformation of doctrine, rather than one of style or vocabulary, was the real issue at stake.

Similarly, the humanists regarded scripture, and particularly the New Testament, as the *fons et origo* of Christianity, valuing it both on account of its antiquity and literary significance. For Erasmus, the importance of the New Testament relates to the teaching of Jesus, the *lex Christi*, so that the New Testament was regarded as the primary instrument in an educative and formative process. It was, however, only one of several such sources, and could not be regarded as the sole authoritative source of doctrine and ethics. For the Reformers, scripture was the sole means by which access might be had to the Word of God, so that the slogan *sola scriptura* was interpreted in an exclusive sense.[37]

Finally, the humanists valued the fathers as representatives and exponents of a simple and comprehensible form of Christianity. Their authority was vested in both their antiquity and their eloquence, rather than in their theological opinions.[38] For the Reformers, however, the fathers were to be valued as expositors of scripture, representing a form of Christianity which had since become corrupted and distorted through the questionable presuppositions and methods of medieval theologians.[39] Augustine was to be regarded as pre-eminent among the fathers on account of his theological opinions. For the humanists, Augustine could not be singled out in this manner: indeed, for Erasmus it was Jerome who was *summus theologus*.[40] The question of whether a patristic writer's importance was determined by his theology, or his eloquence and scholarship, served to distinguish humanist and Reformer, although this point was not fully appreciated in the heady days of the early Reformation.

37 See Moeller, 'Die deutschen Humanisten', pp. 53–4.
38 Moeller, 'Die deutschen Humanisten', p. 53.
39 See the careful study of Pierre Fraenkel, *Testimonia Patrum: The Function of the Patristic Argument in the Theology of Philip Melanchthon* (Geneva, 1961).
40 H. A. Oberman, *Werden und Wertung der Reformation* (Tübingen, 1977), pp. 93–5.

Later chapters will consider the importance of humanist literary scholarship and techniques in relation to theological sources and methods. Attention should now turn to the interaction of humanism and the two main elements of the Reformation.

HUMANISM AND THE ORIGINS OF THE REFORMED CHURCH

In recent years, there has been a growing tendency among scholars of the Swiss Reformation to recognize the political origins of the Reformed church in the so-called 'First Zurich Disputation' of 29 January 1523.[41] The *sola scriptura* principle had been introduced in Zurich in the late autumn of 1520, making scripture the sole basis for preaching, and its application had proved to be a cause for popular dissension. Zwingli's attacks of 1522 on clerical celibacy and the intercession of the saints – both of which challenged the authority of the church on the basis of that of scripture – had aroused considerable feeling, to which the council was obliged to respond. In the disputation (which the city council appears to have regarded as a purely judicial proceeding, designed to establish whether Zwingli had conformed to earlier decisions of that council),[42] the *sola scriptura* principle was re-affirmed, and the legality of Zwingli's preaching upheld. The disputation proved to be the prototype of a whole series of similar disputations in the period 1523–36, defining the characteristics of the Reformed church.[43] Although it must be emphasized that the disputation merely confirmed an earlier decision of the city council, to encourage preaching based upon scripture alone, the outcome of the disputation proved to have considerable impact upon the nascent Reformation in Switzerland and south Germany, in that the *sola scriptura* principle quickly became accepted as normative.[44] Zwingli had turned an academic disputation into an occasion of public

41 See Berndt Moeller, 'Zwinglis Disputationen: Studien zu den Anfängen der Kirchenbildung und des Synodalwesens im Protestantismus', *Zeitschrift der Savigny-Stiftung für Rechtsgeschichte*, Kanonische Abteilung, 56 (1970), pp. 275–324; 60 (1974), pp. 213–364.
42 It was not a 'disputation' in the strict academic sense of the term. For a full discussion and analysis, see Oberman, *Werden und Wertung der Reformation*, pp. 237–66.
43 Berndt Moeller, 'Die Ursprünge der reformierten Kirche', *Theologische Literaturzeitung* 100 (1975), 642–53.
44 See the classic study of Emil Egli, 'Zur Einführung des Schriftprinzips in der Schweiz', *Zwingliana* 1 (1903), pp. 332–9.

decision, and, as events would show, into a formidable weapon of reformation. Although it is possible to argue that the city council was actually strengthening its own position (in that it was the council, rather than scripture itself, which was to be recognized as the arbiter of what was formally consistent with scripture), the decision was widely regarded as establishing the theological basis of the emerging Reformed church.

This discussion, however, is primarily concerned with the intellectual origins of the Reformed church, rather than the means by which its theological programme came to be legitimized and propagated – in other words, with the question of *how* the thinkers of the early Reformed church came to hold their distinctive ideas. It is therefore necessary to consider the background of its leading figures, and attempt to assess the influence of humanism upon their intellectual development.

It is now clear that the second decade of the sixteenth century witnessed the emergence of a distinctively Swiss form of humanism, which may be contrasted with the cosmopolitanism of Erasmus.[45] The efforts of Vadian in Vienna, Glarean in Paris, Myconius and Xylotectus in Lucerne and Zwingli in Einsiedeln during this period were not concerned with the creation of a cosmopolitan republic of letters, but with establishing the literary and cultural identity of the Swiss nation.[46]

The importance of the University of Vienna in relation to this circle of Swiss humanists should be noted.[47] Through the university reforms introduced by Heinrich von Langenstein in 1386, Vienna had become a centre for the *via moderna*. By the final decade of the fifteenth century, however, the confrontation between humanism and scholasticism so characteristic of many late medieval universities had become a major factor at Vienna. The arrival of Konrad Celtis in the final years of the century catalysed this confrontation, and led to Vienna becoming increasingly recognized as a centre for humanist

45 See Hans von Greyerz, 'Studien der Kulturgeschichte der Stadt Bern am Ende des Mittelalters', *Archiv des Historischen Vereins des Kantons Bern* 35 (1940), pp. 175–491; W. Näf, 'Schweizerische Humanismus: Zu Glareans "Helvetiae Descriptio"', *Schweizerische Beiträge zur allgemeinen Geschichte* 5 (1947), pp. 186–98; Näf, *Vadian und seine Stadt St Gallen* (2 vols: St Gallen, 1944–57), vol. 1, pp. 335–60; vol. 2, pp. 55–121.
46 For the influence of patriotism upon the young Zwingli, see Stephens, *Theology of Huldrych Zwingli*, pp. 7–8.
47 See Conradin Bonorand, 'Die Bedeutung der Universität Wien für Humanismus und Reformation, insbesondere in der Ostschweiz', *Zwingliana* 12 (1964–8), pp. 162–80.

studies.[48] In the first two decades of the sixteenth century, Vienna was the most sought-after university in eastern Europe.[49] The arrival of Zwingli at Vienna in 1498 coincided with that of Celtis: although little is known of Zwingli's interests and concerns at that time,[50] it is significant that he became associated with a humanist circle with strong links with the university.[51] One of the leading figures within this circle was Joachim Vadian, who was at Vienna in the period 1501–18.[52]

The leading features of Swiss humanism in the first two decades of the sixteenth century broadly parallel those of northern European humanism in general,[53] although with strongly nationalist overtones. The geographical location of Switzerland facilitated contact with both Italian and northern European intellectual movements, and these contacts were further strengthened by the tendency, particularly evident in the final decade of the fifteenth century, of Swiss students to study abroad. Major printing presses were established in leading Swiss cities (such as those of Froben, the brothers Amerbach and Cratander in Basle and Froschauer in Zurich), thus facilitating the establishment of a *respublica litteraria* in the region.[54] The same vision of *Christianismus renascens* which so excited other northern European humanists was an essential aspect of the Swiss movement.[55] Vadian's

48 Gustav Bauch, *Die Rezeption des Humanismus in Wien* (Breslau, 1903). For a valuable analysis of the situation at the turn of the century, see Elisabeth Brandstätter and Hans Trümpy, ed. *Arbogast Strub* (Vadian-Studien 5: St Gallen, 1955), pp. 5–12. On the rhetorical tradition at Vienna, see Matthäus Gabathuler, ed. *Joachim Vadian: Lateinische Reden* (Vadian-Studien 3: St Gallen, 1953), pp. 17*–23*.

49 Bonorand gives the following (p. 166) for the matriculation figures at various universities for the summer term of the academic year 1515–16: Vienna – c. 355; Cologne – c. 200; Freiburg im Breisgau – 54; Rostock – 114; Ingolstadt – c. 210; Leipzig – c. 210; Heidelberg (for the entire year 1516) – 140; Wittenberg – 90; Tübingen – 52; Basle – 32.

50 The little monograph of Erwin Liefert, *Zwingli in Wien* (Vienna, 1984), summarizes the present state of research.

51 See Conradin Bonorand, *Aus Vadians Freundes- und Schülerkreis in Wien* (Vadian-Studien 8: St Gallen, 1965), pp. 17–87, for further details.

52 See the summary of Heinz Haffter, 'Vadian und die Universität Wien', *Wiener Geschichtsblätter* 20 (1965), pp. 385–90. (The author's name is incorrectly spelled as 'Hafter' therein). Other notable humanists include Georg Collimitius, centre of the *Sodalitas Collimitiana*, and Johannes Cuspinian: see H. Ankwick-Kleehoven, *Der Wiener Humanist Johannes Cuspinian, Gelehrter und Diplomat zur Zeit Kaiser Maximilians I* (Graz, 1959); Bonorand, *Vadians Freundes- und Schülerkreis*, pp. 80–7.

53 See Kurt Maeder, *Die via media in der schweizerischen Reformation: Studien zum Problem der Kontinuität im Zeitalter der Glaubensspaltung* (Zurich, 1970), pp. 37–53.

54 See Eduard Buechler, *Die Anfänge des Buchdrucks in der Schweiz* (Berne, 2nd edn, 1951).

55 Maeder, *Die via media*, pp. 47–9.

first major religious work was his commentary on the Acts of the Apostles, in which he contrasted the vitality of the early church with the stagnation being experienced within the contemporary church, as well as breaking new ground in literary analysis by drawing on classical geographical sources (such as the Ulm edition of Ptolomaus' *Geographia*) in the course of his exposition of his text.[56] The strongly political cast of the Swiss humanist movement was particularly evident in the widespread dissatisfaction with the role forced upon Switzerland during the Franco-Italian war. Zwingli's writings from his early Glarus period indicate his reaction against this war,[57] as do other humanist accounts of its brutalities.[58] One of the more significant features of Swiss humanism in the period 1516–19 is the growing interest in pacifism and the establishment of a distinct Swiss national identity, evident in Myconius' dialogue *Philirenus* (1519).[59]

The growing interest in humanism on the part of Swiss students has been carefully documented by Hans Trümpy, in a study of the universities attended by students from Glarus in the period 1475–1520.[60] Before 1507, such students tended to study at German universities, such as Freiburg and Heidelberg.[61] Between 1507 and 1521, however, in the period during which Swiss humanism began to flourish, a marked shift is evident: of the 28 students documented, all but three attended universities established as centres of humanism. Thus four studied at Vienna; twelve studied at Basle, the centre of a humanist circle including Heinrich Lupulus (Wölfli), Melchior Volmar, Jakob Fullonius (Walker), Valerius Anshelm, Michael Rubellus (Röttli) and Thomas Wyttenbach, which gained an international reputation among humanists,[62] such as Erasmus. Eight

56 Conradin Bonorand, *Vadians Weg vom Humanismus zur Reformation und seine Vorträge über die Apostelgeschichte* (Vadian-Studien 7: St Gallen, 1962), pp. 91–100.
57 See, e.g., CR (Zwingli) 1.10-22, in which the ox represents the Swiss, and the cats foreign powers exploiting them.
58 See Conradin Bonorand, *Vadian und die Ereignisse in Italien im ersten Drittel des 16. Jahrhunderts* (Vadian-Studien 13: St Gallen, 1985), pp. 43–54.
59 Erasmus' *Querela Pacis* was published at Basle in 1517. For its influence upon Zwingli, see Joachim Rogge, *Zwingli und Erasmus: Die Friedensgedanken des jungen Zwinglis* (Stuttgart, 1962). For Zwingli's favourable comments on Myconius' work, see CR (Zwingli) 7.231.11–13.
60 Hans Trümpy, 'Glarner Studenten im Zeitalter des Humanismus', *Beiträge zur Geschichte des Landes Glarus: Festgabe des Historischen Vereins des Kantons Glarus* (Glarus, 1952), pp. 273–84.
61 Of the 13 students documented, the following analysis is given by Trümpy (p. 281): Basle – 1; Freiburg – 2; Heidelberg – 6; Cologne – 1; Leipzig – 1; Tübingen – 1; Vienna – 1.
62 Guido Kisch, 'Forschungen zur Geschichte des Humanismus in Basel', *Archiv für Kulturgeschichte* 40 (1958), pp. 194–221. The conflict between *mos gallicus* and *mos italicus* illustrates

studied at Glarean's academy in Paris, dedicated to the propagation of humanist ideals.[63] (The trauma of the 1520s, when the Turks stood at the gates of Vienna, effectively bringing the work of that university to an end, and political disturbances at Basel reduced the student enrolment there from 60 in 1521 to one in 1528, and none at all in 1529, was not forseen in these heady days.) The student figures for the canton of Glarus are clearly highly suggestive, indicating considerable interest in humanist learning among Swiss students in the first two decades of the sixteenth century. That interest was certainly shared by Huldrych Zwingli, the pastor of Glarus from 1506 to 1516, and formerly a student at both Vienna (1498–1502) and Basle (1502–6).

Zwingli's relation to both Erasmus and Luther is difficult to assess, in that he appears defensively to minimize his obligations to both for domestic political reasons.[64] Nevertheless, the considerable influence of both Erasmus in particular, and humanist editorial and textual undertakings in general, upon the development of his thought is well established. Zwingli embraced the humanist principle that historical and textual research – similar to that of Valla, which demonstrated the inauthenticity of the *Donation* of Constantine – should be freely employed in relation to ecclesiastical sources and traditions. Thus he argued that the tradition of priestly celibacy had been falsified at points,[65] and undertook historical inquiries which demonstrated that Swiss congregations had occasionally demanded – and been granted! – the right of their clergy to marry.[66] Similarly, his researches into local liturgical practices indicated that the people of Glarus had earlier been permitted to received communion in both kinds.[67] Here we

---

the tensions at the university in the late medieval period: see Kisch, *Humanismus und Jurisprudenz: Der Kampf zwischen mos italicus und mos gallicus an der Universität Basel* (Basle, 1955); Peter Bietenholz, *Der italienische Humanismus und die Blütezeit des Buchdrucks in Basel* (Basle, 1959). Later, of course, the strongly Erasmian Oecolampadius settled at Basle: J. J. Herzog, *Das Leben Johannes Oekolampads und die Reformation der Kirche zu Basel* (2 vols: Basle, 1843); E. Staehelin, *Das theologische Lebenswerk Johannes Oekolampads* (Leizig, 1939). On Capito's time at Basle, see James M. Kittelson, *Wolfgang Capito: From Humanist to Reformer* (Leiden, 1975), pp. 23–51.

63 Albert Büchi, 'Glareans Schüler in Paris', in *Festschrift für Robert Durrer* (Stans, 1928), pp. 372–421. On his earlier and later periods, see Marc Sieber, 'Glarean in Basel, 1514–1517 und 1522–1529', *Jahrbuch des Historischen Vereins des Kantons Glarus* 60 (1963), pp. 53–75.

64 See Wilhelm H. Neuser, *Die reformatorische Wende bei Zwingli* (Neukirchen, 1977), pp. 38–74. For the autobiographical passages in question, see Ulrich Gäbler, *Huldrych Zwingli im 20. Jahrhundert: Forschungsbericht und annotierte Bibliographie 1897–1972* (Zurich, 1975), pp. 41–4.

65 CR (Zwingli) 1.236–7.

66 CR (Zwingli) 1.247.5–23.

67 CR (Zwingli) 2.132–5.

find an essentially neutral humanist tool (historical inquiry) functioning as a weapon in a Reformer's armoury.

The influence of humanism upon Zwingli is, however, by no means restricted to historical or textual inquiry. Zwingli's personal library contained a substantial number of works by both Erasmus and Luther: while the former were heavily annotated, the latter appear to have been used but little.[68] Zwingli made his first trip to Basle to visit Erasmus in 1516, shortly after the publication of the *Novum Instrumentum* on Froben's press, and his letter to the great humanist of 29 April 1516 – written shortly after his visit – clearly indicates how he had been won over to a programme embracing humanist cultural and educational ideals.[69] Furthermore, his letters dating from the remainder of the decade frequently make reference to his intention to go back to Basle. Although Zwingli learned Greek in 1513, with the express purpose of studying scripture, it was through Erasmus' *Novum Instrumentum* of 1516 that this project was realized.[70] From his comments upon the inaccuracies of the Vulgate text, it is clear that Zwingli recognized the theological implications of the new sacred philology.[71] Indeed, Bullinger informs us that Zwingli was able to commit the entire Greek New Testament to memory while at Einsiedeln.[72] Although some have argued that a clear divergence is evident between the manner in which Erasmus and Zwingli regarded or appropriated biblical scholarship in the Einsiedeln years (1516–18),[73] the evidence for this is less than convincing. In several important areas, particularly in relation to biblical exegesis, the 'spiritual' (in other words, internalized) understanding of religion and the concept of *imitatio Christi*,

---

68 For an analysis of the 23 works by Erasmus, see Walther Köhler, *Huldrych Zwinglis Bibliothek* (Zurich, 1921), pp. 14–16. Ten other works by Erasmus were known to Zwingli, although not in his possession. A comparison with Vadian's library is instructive: see Verena Schenker-Frei, *Bibliotheca Vadiana: Die Bibliothek des Humanisten Joachim von Watt nach dem Katalog des Josua Kessler von 1553* (Vadian-Studien 9: St Gallen, 1973).

69 Interestingly, Zwingli's personal edition of the *Novum Instrumentum* is that of 1519, not 1516: Köhler, *Zwinglis Bibliothek*, n. 106.

70 See the comments of J. F. Gerhard Goeters, 'Zwinglis Werdegang als Erasmianer', in *Reformation und Humanismus: Robert Stupperich zum 65. Geburtstag*, ed. M. Greschat and J. F. G. Goeters (Witten, 1969), pp. 255–71; pp. 268–9.

71 His acid comments concerning the Vulgate translator's audacity may be noted: CR (Zwingli) 3.682.25–7.

72 *Heinrich Bullingers Reformationgeschichte*, ed. J. J. Hottinger and H. H. Vögeli (2 vols: Frauenfeld, 1838–40), vol. 1, p. 8.

73 For example, Gottfried W. Locher, 'Zwingli und Erasmus', *Zwingliana* 13 (1969), pp. 37–61. See James M. Stayer, 'Zwingli before Zürich: Humanist Reformer and Papal Partisan', *ARG* 72 (1981), pp. 55–68.

Zwingli clearly follows Erasmus, and frequently emphasized the importance of Erasmus' philological techniques to his expository work. The evidence certainly suggests that the Zwingli who began his ministry in Zurich on 1 January 1519 was an Erasmian, albeit with political convictions reflecting those of a narrower Swiss humanism.

An important consideration in establishing the origins of Zwingli's religious ideas is his soteriology: whereas for Luther, the question of how a gracious God might be found led to his intense personal pre-occupation with the doctrine of justification, Zwingli's concerns appear to have been primarily with the reform and revitalization of the church – in other words, with the humanist vision of *Christianismus renascens*. Far from regarding the doctrine of justification as the centre of the gospel, and the foundation of a programme of theological reform, Zwingli appears to have adopted a form of moralism, demonstrating affinities with Erasmus' *philosophia Christi*.[74] Zwingli's programme of reform initially corresponds to that of the circle of Swiss humanists to which he belonged; his divergence from that programme is probably to be dated from 1520.[75] Prior to that point, Zwingli appears to have been convinced that his humanist programme of preaching was having its desired effect: in a letter to Myconius, dated 31 December 1519, Zwingli exults over the success of his programme, which had already engendered more than two thousand 'more or less enlightened' people.[76] Six months later, however, Zwingli appears to have conceded the inadequacy of his initial expectations. In a letter of 24 July 1520, Zwingli makes clear his disenchantment with the humanist educational programme, embodied in Erasmus' *philosophia Christi*. It seems that Zwingli recognized that the reforming battle in which we was engaged could only be won with divine assistance, rather than Quintillian's pedagogical insights.[77] At any rate, from this point onwards, Zwingli's theology exhibits a mixture of humanist and Reformed elements,[78] humanist insights being retained alongside an

74 See A. E. McGrath, 'Humanist Elements in the Early Reformed Doctrine of Justification', *ARG* 73 (1982), pp. 5–20; McGrath, *Iustitia Dei: A History of the Christian Doctrine of Justification* (2 vols: Cambridge, 1986), vol. 2, pp. 32–3.
75 For the question of the date of Zwingli's inception as a theological Reformer, see Neuser, *Die reformatorische Wende bei Zwingli*, pp. 38–74. The main lines of evidence are summarized on pp. 38–9.
76 CR (Zwingli) 7.245.14–15.
77 This may be seen as marking the break with Erasmus: see Arthur Rich, *Die Anfänge der Theologie Huldrych Zwinglis* (Zurich, 1949), pp. 96–104; 119–23.
78 This is a common feature of the religious thought of many Reformers of the period, such as Zwingli's colleague Leo Jud: Karl-Heinz Wyss, *Leo Jud: Seine Entwicklung zum Reformator 1519–1523* (Berne/Frankfurt, 1976), pp. 80–3.

increasing emphasis upon the priority of divine action in moral action and the interpretation of scripture.

The ambivalent influence of Erasmus upon Zwingli's later religious thought is best seen from the latter's *Commentarius de vera et falsa religione*, which left the presses of Froschauer in March 1525.[79] Writing to Vadian on 28 May of that same year, Zwingli reported that Erasmus suggested that the work was derivative, reflecting his own views.[80] Such convergence is immediately evident in the dedicatory epistle to Francis I (an interesting choice, incidentally, suggesting Zwingli was aware of the changing religious situation in France), in which the theologians of the Sorbonne are ridiculed.[81] The work opens with a definition of *religio* which is obviously humanist in provenance, being taken directly from Cicero: 'omnia, quae ad cultum deorum pertinerent, diligentes retractarent et tanquam relegerent, sunt dicti religiosi ex relegendo.'[82] Similarly, following Cicero, it is asserted that the existence of God can readily be ascertained by human reason: 'deum . . . esse, vulgo consensus est apud omnes gentes.'[83] Zwingli develops this idea to the point where he approaches the *logos spermatikos* of the second-century apologists, evident in Erasmus' *Enchiridion*: in that God is truth, signs (*semina*) of his divinity may be found in both nature and in man, and discerned by all. Nevertheless, it is clear that Zwingli's appeal to scripture indicates that he regards these *imagines divini et vestigia* as inadequate for any reliable knowledge of God, developing a position which would be expanded and developed by Calvin in the opening of his 1559 *Institutio* (see below). Perhaps the most striking remaining affinities with Erasmus lie in Zwingli's 'spiritualism' – in other words, with his emphasis upon the interior character of religion. Religion is primarily concerned with internal attitudes, rather than with external religious observances or ecclesiastical structures. The emphasis both humanist and Reformer place upon the interior dimension of religion – evident in Zwingli's affirmation that 'the Christian religion is nothing other than a firm hope in God through Jesus Christ and a blameless life fashioned after the example

---

79 See Richard Stauffer, 'Einfluß und Kritik des Humanismus in Zwinglis 'Commentarius de vera et falsa religione', *Zwingliana* 16 (1983), pp. 97–110.
80 CR (Zwingli) 8.333.26–9 'Erasmus Roterodamus ubi commentarium nostrum in manum cepit, ut familiaris quidem eius prodit, dixit: O bone Zwingli, quid scribis, quod ipse prius non scripserim!'.
81 Stauffer, 'Einfluß und Kritik des Humanismus', pp. 99–102.
82 cf. Cicero, *De natura deorum*, ii, 28.
83 CR (Zwingli) 3.641.

of Christ'[84] – suggests a disinterest in matters of church structure and ceremonies. While this is certainly true of Erasmus, who often treated such matters as *adiaphora*, it is evident that Zwingli had quite definite views, particularly in relation to the sacraments, which he felt could not be compromised. Although there are clearly similarities between Erasmus and Zwingli at this point, they should not be exaggerated.[85]

Alongside these clear convergences with Erasmianism, distinct divergences are evident within the *Commentarius*. The most significant of these is Zwingli's critique of Erasmus' concept of the *liberum arbitrium* (which, incidentally, dates from several months before Luther's savage attack on Erasmus' *de libero arbitrio*).[86] The deeply pessimistic view of man which Zwingli now adopts contrasts sharply with his own earlier views, as well as those of Erasmus. Linked with this pessimistic theological anthropology is a strong doctrine of providence, developed in the sermon *De providentia Dei*, by which man's fate is understood to be determined by divine predestination.[87] Curiously, however, Zwingli supports this theology with a sustained appeal to Seneca,[88] causing more than one commentator to suggest that Zwingli's thought is fundamentally Stoic at this point – and hence pointing to humanist influence at an unexpected point in his theology. A second point in the *Commentarius* at which divergence from Erasmus is evident is the scepticism Zwingli expresses concerning the means by which the humanists propose to reform the church. The vision of *Christianismus renascens* requires more than half-measures if it is to be actualized, and Zwingli effectively argues that the measures proposed by the humanists are incapable of achieving their stated

84 CR (Zwingli) 3.705.7–10.

85 An uncritical assessment of the *Commentarius* greatly reduces the value of the study of Dorothy Clark, 'Erasmus and Zwingli's *On the True and False Religion*', in *Prophet, Pastor, Protestant: The Work of Huldrych Zwingli after Five Hundred Years*, ed. E. J. Furcha and H. Wayne Pipkin (Allison Park, Pa, 1984), pp. 23–42. As Stauffer suggests, Erasmus' remark reported by Zwingli is best understood if the humanist read no futher than the dedicatory epistle to the work, with its scathing references to scholastic theology.

86 Stauffer, 'Einfluß und Kritik des Humanismus', pp. 105–8; Stephens, *Theology of Huldrych Zwingli*, pp. 148–9.

87 The possible impact of Zwingli's near-fatal illness in 1519, during which an autobiographical text (the *Pestlied*) indicates a growing awareness of divine providence, is of interest here: Rich, *Anfänge der Theologie Huldrych Zwinglis*, pp. 104–119.

88 CR (Zwingli) 6 iii.92.19–114.9. For comparable statements in the *Commentarius* (although without the sustained appeal to Seneca), see CR (Zwingli) 3.647.7–16. It must be appreciated that the sixteenth century witnessed a considerable revival in interest in Stoicism (and hence both Seneca and Cicero): see Léontine Zanta, *La renaissance du stoïcisme au XVIe siècle* (Geneva, 1975).

objective.[89] The humanist vision of the reform of man and the church through a programme of education is now regarded by Zwingli as unrealistic; what is required is a divine reformation of both the individual and the church in which God, rather than man, is regarded as the chief agent. The growing radicalism of Zwingli in this respect appears to have led to his being regarded as a religious fanatic by some of his former humanist colleagues.

The second major Reformed theologian to be considered is Martin Bucer, whose full influence over the development of both Lutheran and Reformed theology is only now being appreciated. The origins of Bucer's theology are unquestionably to be traced to humanism.[90] His education at the Schlettstadt humanist school, his intensive study of the works of Erasmus,[91] and his correspondence with significant humanists (such as Beatus Rhenanus),[92] indicate his early humanist leanings. In 1518, Bucer was present at the Heidelberg disputation, and within days wrote to Beatus Rhenanus concerning his impressions of the Reformer.[93] This letter is of considerable importance, in that it indicates how seriously Bucer misunderstood Luther's theological concerns. For Bucer, Luther merely stated explicitly what Erasmus hinted at – and it is clear that Bucer regards Luther as differing from Erasmus only in the forthrightness with which he stated his views. In this letter, Bucer tends to omit, or gloss over, Luther's views where they could not be accommodated to those of Erasmus; the remainder of Luther's theses were interpreted within an Erasmian framework.[94] In other words, he appears to have 'productively misunderstood' the Reformer, in common with so many others at the time. Indeed, even when Bucer committed himself publicly to Luther, it seems that this

89 Stauffer, 'Einfluß und Kritik des Humanismus', pp. 108–9.
90 The two studies of Martin Greschat are invaluable: 'Die Anfänge der reformatorischen Theologie Martin Bucers', in *Reformation und Humanismus: Robert Stupperich zum 65. Geburtstag*, ed. M. Greschat and J. F. G. Goeters (Witten, 1969), pp. 124–40; 'Der Ansatz der Theologie Martin Bucers', *Theologische Literaturzeitung* 103 (1978), 81–96. The older study of Henri Strohl, 'Théologie et humanisme à Strasbourg au moment de la création de la Haute-Ecole', *Revue d'histoire et de philosophie religieuse* 17 (1937), pp. 435–56, is still important.
91 See Martin Greschat, 'Martin Bucers Bücherverzeichnis', *Archiv für Kulturgeschichte* 57 (1975), pp. 162–85.
92 See R. Raubenheimer, 'Martin Bucer und seine humanistischen Speyerer Freunde', *Blätter für pfälzische Kirchengeschichte und religiöse Volkskunde* 32 (1965), pp. 1–52.
93 The best text of this letter, dated 1 May 1518, is to be found at WA 9.160–9: see Greschat, 'Ansatz der Theologie Martin Bucers', 94, n. 53.
94 This was first clearly shown by Karl Koch, *Studium Pietatis: Martin Bucer als Ethiker* (Neukirchen, 1962), pp. 10–15.

commitment was primarily a personal affair, stemming from the personality of the Reformer and his programme for reform, rather than the specific religious ideas underlying them. As has often been shown, Bucer remained an Erasmian in his theology in the 1520s.[95]

Erasmus' influence upon Bucer is at its most evident in his moralism. Thus Bucer, following Erasmus, places considerable emphasis upon the tropological sense of scripture – in other words, upon the ethical application of the scriptural text to the specific historical situation of the reader.[96] Old and New Testament are *idem in substantia*, and both may be designated as *lex*. For Bucer, as for Erasmus, scripture bears witness to the *lex Christi*, understood as an ethical pedagogical principle. 'Nam et sacra doctrina proprie moralis est, ars nimirum recte et ordine vivendi.'[97] The obvious difficulty in accommodating sentiments such as these with Luther's doctrine of justification (which seemed to the humanists to destroy the foundations of morality) led to Bucer's radically modifying that doctrine, resulting in a strongly ethical conception of justification which prefigures that of later Pietism.[98] This point is of considerable importance, for a number of reasons. First, it indicates Bucer's failure to understand Luther's theology of justification, or sympathize with it. The origins of Bucer's theology are not to be sought in relation to the doctrine of justification, nor the agonizing over man's status *coram Deo* so evident in Luther's early theological reflections. Second, Bucer's concerns were, and appear to have remained, primarily ethical, his support for Luther apparently reflecting the 'productive misunderstanding' of the great Reformer so widespread among humanists in the period 1517–21. The origins of Bucer's reforming theology are to be sought in the complex milieu of humanist ethical, spiritual and political expectations, which are so pervasive a feature of the intellectual life of southern Germany, the Rhineland and Switzerland in the first quarter of the sixteenth century, and which play so important a role in relation to the origins of the Reformed church.

95 This point is not affected by the increasing personal alienation between Bucer and Erasmus: see the highly perceptive comments of Robert Stupperich, *Der Humanismus und die Wiedervereinigung der Konfessionen* (Leipzig, 1936), p. 23.
96 Johannes Müller, *Martin Bucers Hermeneutik* (Gütersloh, 1965), pp. 142–50. This point will be further developed in chapter 6.
97 Koch treats this maxim as the key to Bucer's theology: *Studium Pietatis*, p. 8.
98 F. Krüger, *Bucer und Erasmus: Eine Untersuchung zum Einfluß des Erasmus auf die Theologie Martin Bucers* (Wiesbaden, 1975); McGrath, 'Humanist Elements in the Early Reformed Doctrine of Justification', pp. 10–14; McGrath, *Iustitia Dei*, vol. 2, pp. 34–6.

The most significant theologian of the Reformed church is, of course, John Calvin. Calvin is, however, a second-generation reformer, whose importance lies not in relation to the *origins*, but in the consolidation and later expansion of the Swiss reforming movement in the period 1536–64. Thus the 1536 *Institutio*, modelled upon Luther's catechisms, is essentially pedagogical in content and style, concerned with educating and informing its reader. It is significant that the term *Institutio* would probably have been understood as 'education', 'instruction', or even 'primer' by its sixteenth century readers – Erasmus' *Institutio principis Christiani* of 1516 had established this sense as normative (Budé's *Institution du Prince* also follows this model). It will thus be clear that Calvin, despite his importance for the history and thought of the Reformation, assumes a minor place in any discussion of the intellectual origins of the Reformation. Indeed, there are reasons for suggesting that Calvin's transition from humanist to Reformer parallels that of others (such as Zwingli), with perhaps the chief difference being the enigma which scholars have come to attach to the question of the date and nature of Calvin's 'conversion'.[99] As far as can be determined, the young Calvin was a humanist, with a knowledge of, but – like Erasmus – little enthusiasm for, scholastic theology. Calvin's first published work was a commentary on Seneca's *De clementia*, and is thoroughly humanist in character.[100] Although containing no significant indications of the manner in which his thought would develop, the text indicates that Calvin was already in possession of the literary and textual exegetical techniques which he would later so successfully apply to the text of scripture. Just as his commentary on Seneca attempted to clear away all obstacles (such as contemporary allusions or modes of speech) preventing the reader from engaging directly with the thought of this rhetorician and politician, so Calvin would later attempt to permit the reader to engage directly with the world of the New Testament. At this point (1532), we find Calvin in the process of moving away from the study of law to that of *bonae litterae*[101] – but not towards becoming a Reformer.

99 The debate within the literature is sterile and inconclusive, and points to a date in 1533: beyond this, little may be said, in that documentary evidence is wanting. See P. Sprenger, *Das Rätsel um die Bekehrung Calvins* (Neukirchen, 1960); Jean Cadier, 'Le conversion de Calvin', *Bulletin de la societé de l'histoire du protestantisme français* 116 (1970), pp. 142–51; Harro Höpfl, *The Christian Polity of John Calvin* (Cambridge, 1985), pp. 219–26.
100 The work is best studied in the modern edition of F. L. Battles and A. M. Hugo, *Calvin's Commentary on Seneca's 'De Clementia'* (Leiden, 1969).
101 See Quirinius Breen, *John Calvin: A Study in French Humanism* (Hamden, 2nd edn, 1968).

The most important recent contribution to the discussion concerning Calvin's shift from a humanist to an evangelical position has come from Alexandre Ganoczy, who argued that the documentary sources up to the year 1539 simply do not support the idea of a 'sudden conversion (*subita conversio*)', referred to in the much later (1557) semi-autobiographical preface to the Commentary on the Psalms.[102] Furthermore, the use of the term 'conversion' is itself open to question, in that the penitential aspects of the concept, as it is normally understood, are conspicuously absent. Rather, the 1530s witnessed the gradual unfolding of Calvin's 'reforming vocation (*vocation réformatrice*)', in which Calvin steadily moved from a position initially characterized by Fabrisian humanism to one subsequently overtly evangelical. Unfortunately, there is no evidence of any direct link between Calvin and the reforming humanism of Lefèvre,[103] so this suggestion must remain purely conjectural. Nevertheless, Ganoczy, by drawing attention to the inadequacy of the contemporary sources, has highlighted how little we know about Calvin's *subita conversio*, whether it actually was *subita* – or even a *conversio* in any meaningful sense of the word.

The most careful study of Calvin's relation to humanism to date suggests that Calvin's thought after his 'conversion' demonstrates both continuity and discontinuity with the humanist tradition.[104] The continuity relates primarily to Calvin's continued use of classical culture as a resource which he might exploit in the interests of both scholarship, preaching and apologetics,[105] while the discontinuity relates to

---

102 Alexandre Ganoczy, *Le jeune Calvin: genèse et évolution de sa vocation réformatrice* (Wiesbaden, 1966), pp. 271–300.

103 Richard Stauffer, *Problèmes et méthodes d'histoire des religions* (Paris, 1968), pp. 262–4. It is, of course, far from clear how Lefèvre's humanism relates to the onset of the Reformation: see Stauffer, 'Lefèvre d'Etaples, artisan ou spectateur de la Réforme?', *Bulletin de la société de l'histoire du protestantisme français* 113 (1967), pp. 405–23; Henry Heller, 'The Evangelicalism of Lefèvre d'Etaples: 1525', *Studies in the Renaissance* 19 (1972), pp. 42–77.

104 François Wendel, *Calvin et l'humanisme* (Paris, 1976). The older study of Josef Bohatec, *Budé und Calvin: Studien zur Gedankenwelt des französischen Frühhumanismus* (Graz, 1950) remains valuable as an account of Calvin's relation to early French humanism.

105 See Jean Boisset, *Sagesse et sainteté dans la pensée de Jean Calvin* (Paris, 1959); Charles Partee, *Calvin and Classical Philosophy* (Leiden, 1977). The suggestion that Calvin was influenced by Stoicism (rather than merely using it as a means towards his own ends), may be regarded as lacking substantiation: Zanta, *Renaissance du stoïcisme*, pp. 47–73; Jean Cadier, 'Le prétendu stoïcisme de Calvin', *Etudes théologiques et religieuses* 41 (1966), pp. 217–26.

the radical dichotomy which Calvin recognizes between divine revelation and classical wisdom.[106] This dichotomy may be illustrated by Calvin's discussion of the theological significance of a natural knowledge of God.

The first five chapters of the 1559 *Institutio* represent a critical evaluation of a natural knowledge of God, in which Calvin's object of criticism is Cicero's *de natura deorum*.[107] Cicero, in his exposition of the Epicurean natural theology,[108] asserts that nature herself has imprinted the existence of the gods upon man.[109] 'Quae est enim gens aut quod genus hominum, quod non habeat sine doctrina anticipationem quandam deorum?' Calvin follows this line of reasoning exactly, arguing from the existence of *religionis semen* to that of God. 'Quendam inesse humanae menti, et quidem naturali instinctu, divinitatis sensum, extra controversiam ponimus.'[110] Although Cicero argues from such natural intuitions of divinity to the existence of the gods, and Calvin to the existence of *one God*, their starting points and conclusions are convergent. Furthermore, both Cicero and Calvin conclude that a natural knowledge of God includes not merely the fact of his existence, but also insights into his nature. For Cicero, such insights include the immortality and blessedness of the gods: 'Quae enim nobis natura informationem ipsorum deorum dedit, eadem insculpsit in mentibus ut eos aeternos et beatos haberemus.'[111] Calvin's analysis of the natural experience of God proceeds along similar lines, allowing him to deduce that God is omnipotent and eternal.[112] Although Calvin might appear to derive such insights on the basis of scriptural texts, a closer examination of his argument indicates that he formally establishes two essentially independent and distinct, although convergent, routes by which these insights may be derived – scripture and experience. Both Cicero and Calvin are further

---

106 Even here, of course, it is necessary to observe that some contemporary humanists recognized precisely such a dichotomy. Budé's *De transitu hellenismi ad christianismum* (1535), dating from the same period as Calvin's 'conversion', may be studied in this connection.

107 Egli Grislis, 'Calvin's Use of Cicero in the Institutes I:1–5 – A Case Study in Theological Method', *ARG* 62 (1971), pp. 5–37.

108 For a discussion, see Knut Kleve, *Gnosis Theon: Die Lehre von der natürlichen Gotterserkenntnis in der epikureischen Theologie* (Oslo, 1963).

109 *De natura deorum* I.xvi.43. See further the references collected by Grislis, 'Calvin's Use of Cicero', pp. 5–6.

110 *Institutio* I.iii.1. See further Grislis, 'Calvin's Use of Cicero', pp. 6–9.

111 *De natura deorum* I.xvii.45.

112 See Grislis, 'Calvin's Use of Cicero', pp. 13–14.

agreed, however, that man's natural knowledge of God is fragmentary and at times contradictory, and thus leads only to relatively certain statements concerning the nature of God. It is at this point that the radical differences between Cicero and Calvin – and the reasons why the latter chose to criticize the former – become evident.

For Cicero, the fact that man possesses inconclusive, fragmentary and inconsistent knowledge of God is to be regarded as a liability, calling into question the basis of his theological statements. For Calvin, this fact is a distinct advantage, as it points to the fundamental principle that man requires a more reliable source for such knowledge. In effect, Calvin exploits the inadequacy of natural revelation by pointing to the inherently more reliable statements concerning God made by scripture. The *sensus divinitatis* known to man is shown to be consistent with what is found in scripture – and the scriptural statements concerning the nature and identity of God are shown to correspond to, but to far surpass in reliability, consistency and certainty, those which may be had from nature.[113] Calvin's purpose in engaging in dialogue with Cicero at the opening of the 1559 *Institutio* is too easily overlooked, in that it indicates the manner in which Calvin's humanism is made subservient to his evangelicalism. For Calvin, the wisdom of the ancient classical tradition concerning the knowledge of God, to which humanism made its appeal, may be seen at its best in Cicero – and that knowledge is shown to be fragmentary and lacking in certainty. It is, however, consistent with what may be known of God the creator from scripture, which establishes substantially the same truths in a more certain manner, in addition to revealing an aspect of the knowledge of God of which nature knows nothing –the *cognitio Dei redemptoris*.[114] In this way, Calvin is able to demonstrate the inherent harmony of the classical tradition and Christianity, while at the same time indicating the superiority of the latter over the former, and laying the foundation for his *theologia verbi divini*. For Calvin, classical wisdom has its place in Christian theology, in that it demonstrates the necessity of, and partially verifies the substance of, divine revelation.

A second aspect of Calvin's theology in which an unequivocal divergence from the humanist tradition (especially Erasmianism) may

---

113 See Edward A. Dowey, *The Knowledge of God in Calvin's Theology* (New York, 1952), pp. 50–147.4
114 Dowey, *Knowledge of God*, pp. 148–242.

be detected is his theology of justification. Following the Reformed tradition, Calvin accords the doctrine no place of special importance, and it is clear that he, like other early Reformed theologians, was not concerned with the existential aspects of the doctrine which had so preoccupied Luther before him. In this respect, there is a certain degree of continuity between Calvin, the earlier Reformed tradition and Erasmian humanism. Erasmus and Bucer developed an essentially moral theology of justification which is Christocentric in the sense that it embodies the principle of *imitatio Christi*; Calvin develops a doctrine of justification which is Christocentric in the sense that a fundamental change in the believer is understood to arise through his *insitio in Christum*.[115] Whereas both Erasmus and Bucer tend to make justfication dependent upon man's *imitatio Christi*, Calvin understands both justification and sanctification to be subsequent aspects of his *insitio in Christum*. In this way, Calvin is able to avoid making justification contingent upon prior ethical regeneration, while simultaneously maintaining a Christologically orientated theology of justification.

If Calvin's criticism of the classical tradition (here exemplified by Cicero) and Erasmian moralism represents one aspect of his relation to humanism, his literary, philological and textual tools must be conceded to represent another, considerably more positive, aspect of that relation. Of particular importance is Calvin's exploitation of the classical rhetorical tradition as a vehicle – in both his sermons and the *Institutio* – for his theology.[116] Although it is not clear whether Calvin subordinates theology to rhetoric, as does Melanchthon (see below), it is certainly true that rhetoric influences the manner in which Calvin articulates his theological convictions.[117]

In considering the extent of humanist influence upon Reformed theology it is not enough, however, merely to consider the origins of that theology. Chapter 8 will indicate that the Aristotelian insights into methodology developed at the University of Padua in the late fifteenth and early sixteenth centuries were destined to exercise a considerable influence upon the development of Reformed theology

---

115 See McGrath, 'Humanist Elements in the Early Reformed Doctrine of Justification', pp. 14–17.
116 See the somewhat breezy study of Quirinius Breen, 'John Calvin and the Rhetorical Tradition', *Church History* 26 (1957), pp. 3–21; Rodolphe Peter, 'Rhétorique et prédication selon Calvin', *Revue d'histoire et de philosophie religieuses* 55 (1975), pp. 249–72 (more valuable).
117 Compare Peter, 'Rhétorique et prédication', with Benoît Girardin, *Rhétorique et théologique: Calvin, le commentaire de l'epître aux Romains* (Paris, 1979).

in the period immediately after the death of Calvin. One of the most curious aspects of the relationship between the Reformation and Renaissance is that it is the latter, rather than the scholasticism of the medieval period, which appears to have given rise to the rebirth of scholasticism in a movement which was initially implacably opposed to precisely this phenomenon. Although the documentation and analysis of this development properly belongs to a later chapter, it should be noted here in order to draw attention to the dangers of making uncritical generalizations concerning the relation of humanism and the Reformation.

HUMANISM AND THE ORIGINS OF THE LUTHERAN CHURCH

The origins of the Lutheran Reformation are quite distinct from those of its Reformed counterpart. Whereas the Reformed theology originated in humanist circles, and developed in the cities of Switzerland and the Rhineland, Lutheranism originated within, and initially developed within, the theological faculty of an obscure German university. Furthermore, whereas Reformed theology owed its origins to a group of individual thinkers, undergoing considerable development during its initial period, Lutheranism was shaped to a remarkable extent by the personal theological insights of one individual – Martin Luther.

It is clear that Luther regarded the humanist movement as having placed at his disposal the textual and philological techniques necessary for his programme of theological reform. Fundamental to Luther's reforming vocation was the conviction that the aspect of the Christian church requiring reform was not her morals, but her theology.[118] For Luther, the possibility of reforming the theology of the church through the new techniques of 'sacred philology', pioneered by Valla in the *Quattrocento*, was nothing less than providential, allowing him access to *die Sprachen* through which a programme of reform might be developed.[119] Whatever disagreements Luther might have with

---

118 WATr 1.624 'Doctrina et vita sunt distinguenda. Vita est mala apud nos sicut apud papistas; non igitur de vita dimicamus et damnamus eos'. WATr 4.4338 'Sed doctrina non reformata frustra fit reformatio morum.'
119 See Bengt Hägglund, 'Martin Luther über die Sprache', *Neue Zeitschrift für systematische Theologie und Religionsphilosophie* 26 (1984), pp. 1–14, for an analysis of the importance of *die Sprache* for Luther's theology.

Erasmus, he was initially unhesitant in recognizing the importance of the latter's textual and philological achievements in relation to the New Testament.[120] Luther's knowledge of the Hebrew language was the result of humanist enterprise, as were the editions of Augustine and other fathers which he employed in the course of his theological reflections. The texts – scripture and the fathers in their original languages – on which Luther's reformation at Wittenberg would depend were only available through the activity of humanist editors and publishers, such as Erasmus and the brothers Amerbach. In this sense, Luther's debt to humanism was considerable. Events within the Wittenberg theological faculty in the first two decades of its existence, particularly the years 1516–19, will be considered to illustrate this point.

Although the personal influence of Christoph Scheurl upon the development of the university curriculum at Wittenberg in the final years of the first decade of the sixteenth century should not be overlooked,[121] it seems that the driving force behind the introduction of what many regarded as a 'humanist' curriculum came from the faculty of theology in the years 1517–19. It is, however, clear that the motivation underlying the reform of the theological curriculum owed little to the spirit of humanism, even though many humanists failed to appreciate this – once more, it is necessary to draw attention to the 'productive misunderstanding' of the Reformers' theological programme on the part of most humanists. The emergence of the *vera theologia* within the theological faculty at Wittenberg necessitated a direct engagement with the original text of scripture and of Augustine, and thus led to the espousal of a programme which appeared to

---

120 See the letter to Oecolampadius of 20 June 1523, WABr 3.98.18–25 'Ipse fecit, ad quod ordinatus fuit: linguas introduxit et a sacrilegis studiis avocavit. Forte et ipse cum Mose in campestribus Moab morietur, nam ad meliora studia (quod in pietatem pertinet) non provehit. Vellemque mirum in modum abstinere ipsum a tractandis scripturis sanctis et paraphrasibus suis, quod non sir par istis officis et lectores frustra occupat et moratur in scripturis discendis. Satis fecit, quod malum ostendit, bonum ostendere (ut video) et in terram promissionis ducere non potest.'

121 Alister E. McGrath, *Luther's Theology of the Cross: Martin Luther's Theological Breakthrough* (Oxford, 1985), pp. 27–32. The study of Junghans, 'Der Einfluß des Humanismus auf Luthers Entwicklung bis 1518', *Luther-Jahrbuch* 37 (1970), pp. 37–101, contains valuable insights, further developed in his major study *Der junge Luther und die Humanisten* (Göttingen, 1985), which contains a particularly valuable study of Luther's relation to the Erfurt humanism associated with Nikolaus Marschalk. More generally, see Maria Grossmann, *Humanism in Wittenberg 1485–1517* (Nieuwkoop, 1975).

coincide with that of the humanists. The origins of this programme may be traced to the autumn of 1516.

On 25 September 1516, Luther presided over an academic disputation on the occasion of the promotion of Bartholomaus Feldkirchen to the degree of Bachelor of Divinity. Feldkirchen was Luther's protégé, and it is generally considered that the theses he chose to defend on this occasion had been drawn up by Luther himself.[122] In the course of this disputation, Feldkirchen argued that the treatise *de vera et falsa poenitentia* should not be ascribed to Augustine, and supported this assertion by arguing that Augustine taught that man could not fulfil the commandments of God through his own reason and strength.[123] These assertions outraged Karlstadt, who insisted that both Augustine and the scholastic theologians had been seriously misrepresented during the course of the debate.[124] Luther then proceeded to challenge Karlstadt to confirm his assertions, a challenge which Karlstadt had little option but to accept.[125] Unfortunately, Karlstadt did not have access to an edition of Augustine, and was obliged to travel to the Leipzig book fair on 13 January 1517 – some four months after the disputation – to purchase one. Significantly, Karlstadt, like most theologians of the early sixteenth century, was obliged to read his Augustine at second hand, in the form of collections of 'sentences' extracted from his works, or references made to him in the writings of other theologians (such as those of Thomas Aquinas or Duns Scotus, with whose writings contemporary records indicate he was well acquainted).[126] As chapter 7 will indicate, the

122 See WABr 1.65.18.
123 WABr 1.65.24–66.1.
124 We have Karlstadt's own account of such a disputation: Ernst Kähler, *Karlstadt und Augustin: Der Kommentar des Andreas Bodenstein von Karlstadt zu Augustins Schrift De Spiritu et Litera* (Halle, 1952), 4.13–22 'Exurrexit dei ope quidam de nostris Venerandus Pater Martinus Luther et arcium acutissimus et theologiae doctor acerrimus atque eorundem fratrum per Saxoniam Vicarius, qui meraciores sanctae scripturae litteras perdidicit et earum succum ultra fidem epotavit asserebatque scholasticos doctores et a Christi non solum documentis sed et intelligentia tam Augustini (cuius documenta frequentius citat) tam aliorum similium esse alienissimos. Verumtamen ego de mea intelligentia atque scholasticorum dexteritate confidebam intra me sicut phariseus ille, qui et mussitare et clamore in disputationibus (more solicito), quod deficiente veritate non valui, affirmare cepi.'
125 Kähler, *Karlstadt und Augustin*, 4.22–28 '. . . Sed mihi ita inclamanti prisceque moriae meae laudes profundenti pius Pater respondebat pie: ego te, ait, arbitrium diligenter monumenta ecclesiasticorum rimantem seligo constituoque.'
126 See *Scriptorum insignium qui in celeberrimius praesertim Lipsiensi, Wittenbergensi, Francoforti ad Oderam academiis a fundatione ipsarum usque ad annum Christum 1515 floruerunt centuria*, ed. J. F. L. T. Merzdorf (Leipzig, 1839), pp. 82–3, in which an anonymous peripatetic humanist singles out Karlstadt's learning for particular comment (and, incidentally, makes no reference to Luther).

chief difficulty associated with this second-hand encounter with Augustine arises from the interpretation placed upon the Augustinian 'sentence' by the secondary source: by isolating a sentence from its context, for example, a serious misunderstanding of its meaning could result. Equally, any significant degree of selectivity on the part of the secondary source could lead to a distorted impression of Augustine's views, through the suppression of sentences in which different views are expressed. Karlstadt thus exemplifies the common problem of medieval theologians in relation to their sources: Augustine tended to be encountered at second hand, with no real possibility of verifying the interpretation placed upon him by the secondary source.

Having purchased an edition of Augustine at Leipzig, Karlstadt proceeded to scour it for texts which he could cite against Luther.[127] By April 1517, it is clear that Karlstadt had decided that Luther was right in his interpretation of Augustine, and published 151 theses defending an Augustinian theology over and against that of his former scholastic mentors, particularly Capreolus.[128] In these theses, Karlstadt defended the supreme authority of scripture, and a derivative authority of the fathers, particularly Augustine. In many ways, this may be seen as a humanist programme. Indeed, there are excellent reasons for suggesting that, at this stage, Karlstadt saw himself as developing a theological programme similar to that already associated with Erasmus.[129] On 18 May 1517, in the aftermath of the publication of Karlstadt's theses, Luther wrote in near-ecstasy to his humanist colleague Johannes Lang concerning the changes which were taking place at Wittenberg: 'Theologia nostra et S. Augustinus prospere procedunt. . . Aristoteles descendit paulatim.'[130] The *vera theologia* now gaining the ascendancy was that of the bible and Augustine, and the rival theology, based upon Peter Lombard's *Sentences* and Aristotle, was in irreversible decline. Similarly, in the course of his lectures of 1517–18 on Augustine's work *de spiritu et litera*, Karlstadt pointed out to his students how they now had direct access to the text of the bible and the fathers, and were no longer obliged to depend upon the

127 Kähler, *Karlstadt und Augustin*, 5.4–7. Kähler's suggestion (p. 54 n.1) that Karlstadt purchased the Paris edition of 1515 rests upon a misunderstanding to be discussed in chapter 7: see p. 180.
128 The theses were published on 26 April. For the text, see Kähler, *Karlstadt und Augustin*, pp. 11*–36*. For Luther's favourable comments, see WABr 1.94.15–25
129 Note his favourable references to *noster Erasmus*: e.g., Kähler, *Karlstadt und Augustin*, 100.31–101.1, and particularly his *Epistola adversus ineptam et ridiculam inventionem J. Eckii* (Leipzig, 1519).
130 WABr 1.99.8–13.

schoolmen.[131] In every respect, the theology faculty at Wittenberg appeared to be committed to a programme of theological education which exactly paralleled that of the humanists – a point which was not lost on those humanists with whom Luther and Karlstadt corresponded (such as Christoph Scheurl, Johannes Lang and Georg Spalatin).

This impression was confirmed through the revisions proposed to the theological curriculum at Wittenberg in March 1518.[132] According to Luther, the proposals included the regular teaching of the three sacred languages (Hebrew, Greek and Latin), and lectures on Quintillian (whose educational theories so excited the humanists), and the abolition of lectures on aspects of medieval logic, including some on Aristotle. The position of lecturer in Hebrew attracted considerable attention from humanists – among those short-listed for the post was Johannes Oecolampadius, then still a humanist, and associated with the circle around Christoph Scheurl. It was the need for a lecturer in Greek which attracted perhaps the most significant humanist to Wittenberg – Philip Melanchthon.[133]

By the time of the Leipzig Disputation of 1519, it was clear that the Wittenberg theological faculty as a whole was identified with a programme of theological reform which generated considerable excitement within humanist circles, and apprehension in more traditional ecclesiastical circles.[134] Although Luther's posting of the Ninety-Five Theses on 31 October 1517[135], and the Heidelberg Disputation of April 1518, singled him out as the most significant agitator within the faculty, it is clear that the faculty as a whole was prepared to identify itself with his actions.[136] Writing to Spalatin on 14 October 1518, Luther admitted how his actions had placed Karlstadt, the theological faculty and the university itself at risk. The role of Karlstadt in pioneering the programme of reform is all too easily overlooked. Thus

---

131 Kähler, *Karlstadt und Augustin*, 9.29–10.5
132 For Luther's account of these proposals, see WABr 1.153.3–154.1.
133 For Melanchthon's relation to Tübingen humanism in the period 1512–18, see Oberman, *Werden und Wertung der Reformation*, pp. 17–27; 72–81. On 10 December 1518, Spalatin reported that Melanchthon's lectures on Greek were attended by some four hundred students, roughly two-thirds of the student body and the university: WABr 1.197 n. 10.
134 Luther regarded the entire theological faculty, as well as theuniversity itself, as being committed to this programme: WABr 1.170.22–5.
135 For references and discussion, see McGrath, *Luther's Theology of the Cross*, pp. 15–19.
136 See the important study of Heiko A. Oberman, 'Headwaters of the Reformation: *Initia Lutheri – Initia Reformationis*', in *Luther and the Dawn of the Modern Era*, ed. H. A. Oberman (Leiden, 1974), pp. 40–88.

it was Karlstadt, not Luther, who was initially challenged to public debate by Eck, leading eventually to the Leipzig Disputation of 1519; it was Karlstadt, as well as Luther, who was subsequently excommunicated in the bull of October 1520. Nevertheless, the high standard of Luther's debating skills at Leipzig, together with the positions he defended against Eck, served to concentrate the attention of the outside world on to the Saxon reformer, rather than his more senior (and considerably less charismatic) colleague – despite the fact that Karlstadt had gained recognition as a humanist through his support for Reuchlin.[137] Moreover, it was in the aftermath of the Leipzig Disputation that humanism played its most significant role in furthering the ends of the Lutheran Reformation.

Before 1519, the reforming programme at Wittenberg had attracted little attention, except from those humanists who had personal associations with Wittenberg or members of its theological faculty. The posting of the Ninety-Five Theses attracted considerable sympathy towards Luther from those (not necessarily humanists) hostile towards the indulgence traffic, and the Heidelberg Disputation served to identify (mistakenly, as it happened) Luther as an outspoken Erasmian, through the correspondence of Martin Bucer with Beatus Rhenanus: 'cum Erasmo illi conveniunt omnia, quin uno hoc praestare videtur, quod quae ille duntaxat insinuat, hic [Luther] aperte docet et libere.' The Leipzig Disputation of 1519, however, marks a turning point in the history of the Reformation, in that what had previously been a somewhat arcane academic debate exploded into a *cause célèbre* throughout western Europe. The agency which catalysed this explosion was the humanist movement, which saw in Luther a representative of the 'new learning' engaged in a serious and potentially pivotal conflict with the old order of authoritarian scholasticism. The humanist movement was responsible for turning an essentially private academic debate into a public (indeed, cosmopolitan) political and religious controversy. Through a 'productive misunderstanding', Luther was hailed as the champion of the values of the 'new learning', and came to serve as the focal point of a debate similar to that which had surrounded the person of Johannes Reuchlin a decade earlier. By this time, however, the humanist movement was considerably stronger and more influential, and Luther soon found himself with supporters in humanist circles

---

137 See the letter of 13 February 1514 to Georg Spalatin: Johann Friedrich Heckel, *Manipulus primus epistolarum singularium* (Halle, 1695), pp. 17–20.

in Augsburg, Erfurt, Heidelberg, Leipzig, Nuremberg, Schlettstadt and Strasbourg.[138] Nevertheless, that support appeared to rest upon the mistaken supposition that Luther and Erasmus were engaged upon a common programme – a supposition evident in Albrecht Dürer's suggestion (1521) that Erasmus should assume the leadership of the Wittenberg Reformation in place of the incarcerated Luther.[139]

Nevertheless, despite the clear affinities between the theological programme adopted by the Wittenberg faculty in 1518 and humanist ideals, these affinities served to mask the crucial differences between the *vera theologia* and the *philosophia Christi*. The Wittenberg faculty were concerned with the articulation of a reforming theology which differed from that of scholasticism in terms of its content, rather than its form. Scripture and the fathers, particularly Augustine, were studied in order to establish the content of this *vera theologia*. The emphasis upon Augustine was the consequence of the *theological* judgement (unacceptable to most humanists, who tended to apply the criterion of *eloquentia*) that he represented the most reliable of the fathers, and led to an anthropological pessimism (particularly evident in the writings of Luther) which sharply contrasted with the optimism of Erasmus. The controversy between Luther and Erasmus of 1524–5 over the freedom of the will is already prefigured in their differing attitudes towards theological sources in the period 1515–19. Furthermore, the hermeneutical principles applied to scripture by both Luther and Karlstadt differed considerably from those of Erasmus, as will become clear in a later chapter. Although both the humanists and the Wittenberg Reformers appeared to many to be committed to a similar programme in the period 1515–19, radical differences lay beneath superficial similarities. Luther and his supporters appear to have exploited both the humanist movement and individual humanists in their struggle for the reformation of the doctrine of the church, both through the acquisition of the necessary textual and philological tools, and by gaining political support at a critical juncture in the development of the movement. Without humanism, there would have been no Reformation – because the Reformers needed the scholarly and political support of humanism until it had developed sufficiently to take care of itself.[140]

---

138 See the careful study of Berndt Moeller, 'Luther und die Städte', in *Aus der Lutherforschung: Drei Vorträge* (Opladen, 1983), pp. 9–26, especially pp. 16–24.
139 F. Leitschuh, *Albrecht Dürers Tagebuch der Reise in die Niederlande* (Leipzig, 1884), p. 84.
140 See Moeller, 'Die deutschen Humanisten und die Anfänge der Reformation'.

Confusion has arisen as to the influence of humanism upon the origins of Luther's distinctive reforming theology through misleading definitions of the term 'humanism'. This chapter has sought to emphasize that humanism is not to be identified with the views and preoccupations of Erasmus of Rotterdam, nor with a specific network of philosophical, anthropological or theological doctrines. Kristeller's definition of humanism, alluded to earlier, unquestionably permits Luther to be regarded as a biblical humanist, similar to his Erfurt teacher Nikolaus Marschalk. Nevertheless, Luther's use of humanist tools in his early biblical exegesis (1513–16) must not be allowed to obscure the fact that the hermeneutical principles which Luther brings to bear upon his text appear to owe more to scholasticism than to humanism, nor the uncomfortable fact that Luther appears to employ such methods to engage in a constructive, if highly critical, dialogue with the theology of the *via moderna*. Even after his theological breakthrough (assuming this may be dated in 1515), Luther continued to employ both the theological framework and vocabulary of the *via moderna*.

Luther's correspondence with humanists before 1517 was limited to a few individuals (such as Scheurl), and the initiative in this correspondence generally appears to have been taken by the humanists, rather than by Luther himself, suggesting that Luther did not regard humanism as an important aspect of his theological method. Although Luther appears to have appreciated the importance of rhetorical theory in relation to the theology of the 'Word of God', the correspondence between the humanist analysis of the transrational power of human speech and Luther's concept of the 'Word of God' is at best remote.

Perhaps most significant of all the considerations to be taken into account in evaluating the influence of humanism upon the origins of Luther's theology, however, is the role of humanism in relation to his theological breakthrough. As the following chapter will indicate, the evidence for a decisive influence of humanism in this crucial matter is wanting. Although the relationship between the origins of Luther's personal theological insights and the origins of the Reformation is now recognized to be far too complex to permit their identification,[141] it is clear that humanism was but one of several elements which contributed to shaping the origins of the Lutheran Reformation in the period 1513–19. A catalyst for that Reformation it certainly was – but

141 See Oberman, 'Headwaters of the Reformation', for an important discussion.

the *origins* of the ideas underlying it appear to lie elsewhere.

Although it is possible that humanism exercised a less than decisive influence over the formulation of Lutheran theology, it is clear that its influence over the propagation of that theology was considerable. Humanist and Reformer alike appreciated the importance of rhetoric and pedagogy (particularly the educational theories of Quintillian)[142] in the propagation of the ideas of the Lutheran Reformation. The first work of systematic theology to emerge from the Lutheran Reformation was Melanchthon's *Loci Communes* of 1521. This work clearly betrays the influence of the rhetorical tradition, particularly in terms of the organization of its material.[143] Melanchthon adopts the principle that theology may be organized around a single, saving doctrine, which effectively provides the key to scripture. That key, according to Melanchthon, is not the Erasmian *imitatio Christi*, but Luther's doctrine of justification *sola fide*. The rhetorical origins of Melanchthon's *Loci* are evident in his 1519 treatise on rhetoric,[144] in which he makes reference to the principle of the *locus didacticus*. Although the topical method of expounding theology appears to have been particularly effective in the first phase of the Reformation, it increasingly became recognized as a hindrance to systematic theological exposition. Indeed, it is possible to argue that the weakness of Lutheran theology in the period 1540–75, particularly when viewed in relation to contemporary Reformed theology, lay precisely in the method of organisation bequeathed to Lutheranism by Melanchthon.[145] As the range of *topoi* or *loci* increased, through the rise of controversy between the evangelical factions, Melanchthon's initially elegant system became

---

142 The tension between the ethical and pedagogical optimism evident in humanist educational writings (Erasmus, *Declamatio de pueris instituendis*, ed. Jean-Claude Margolin (Geneva, 1966), for example) and the more pessimistic anthropology of Lutheranism appears to have exercised little influence over the practical affair of education: see further Gerald Strauss, *Luther's House of Learning: Indoctrination of the Young in the German Reformation* (Baltimore, 1978).

143 See Wilhelm Maurer, 'Melanchthons Loci Communes von 1521 als wissenschaftliche Programmschrift: Ein Beitrag zur Hermeneutik der Reformationszeit', *Luther-Jahrbuch* 27 (1960), pp. 1–50.

144 Paul Joachimsen, 'Loci Communes: Eine Untersuchung zur Geistesgeschichte des Humanismus und der Reformation', *Luther-Jahrbuch* 8 (1926), pp. 27–97. For the argument that Melanchthon subordinates both philosophy and theology to rhetoric, see Quirinius Breen, 'The Subordination of Philosophy to Rhetoric in Melanchthon: A Study of His Reply to G. Pico della Mirandola', *ARG* 43 (1952), pp. 13–28.

145 See Alister E. McGrath, 'Reformation to Enlightenment', in *The History of Christian Theology. I. The Science of Theology*, ed. P. D. L. Avis (Basingstoke, 1986), pp. 105–229; 141–5.

increasingly incapable of bearing the pedagogical weight which came
to be placed upon it.

On the basis of the considerations noted in this chapter, it will be
clear that the relationship between humanism and the origins of the
Reformation are complex, reflecting the heterogeneity of both the early
Reforming movement and of humanism itself. It is a truism that
humanism was a contributing factor to the Reformation. In that the
Reformers were dependent upon reliable texts of the bible and the
fathers, the philological and literary techniques to analyse them, and
political support when the occasion demanded it, they were clearly
dependent upon the humanist movement. That does not, however,
permit us to conclude that humanism was the *cause* of the Reformation,
although it was unquestionably an essential catalyst. Although there
is some value in provisionally designating the Reformers as 'biblical
humanists', the tension between humanist and Reformer concerning
both the perceived status of scripture and the spirit in which it should
be approached should be noted. While generalizations are notoriously
unreliable, particularly in so complex a field, it seems that the essential
continuity between humanist and Reformer in relation to scripture
concerns the fields of textual and philological inquiry, with a potential
discontinuity in relation to the hermeneutical principles employed in
its interpretation. So important are these matters that they must be
pursued in later chapters, to which this discussion must be regarded
as an introduction. First, however, attention must now turn to the
other late medieval intellectual movement which had considerable
influence over the Reformation – scholastic theology.

3

Late Medieval Theology and the Reformation

The multifaceted character of late medieval theology is adequately illustrated from the unedifying exchange of views between Philip Melanchthon and the theologians of the Sorbonne in 1521, in the course of which at least eight theological schools were identified: *Albertistae* (following Albertus Magnus), *Egidistae* (following Giles of Rome), *Thomistae* (following Thomas Aquinas), *Scotistae* (following Duns Scotus), *Scotellistae* (following Peter of Aquila), *Modernistae*, *Occamistae* (following William of Ockham), and *Gregoriistae* (following Gregory of Rimini).[1] The fourteenth and fifteenth centuries witnessed the origins and subsequent consolidation of a radical new intellectual movement, initially associated with William of Ockham, which was destined to exercise considerable influence over the faculties of arts in many late medieval universities. In that many of the Reformers (particularly those within the Wittenberg theological faculty in the period 1506–19) were deeply influenced by late medieval theological currents, an analysis of the intellectual origins of the Reformation must include an evaluation of the possible influence of such currents upon the evolution of the new reforming theologies. This movement is still frequently referred to as 'nominalism', despite the potentially misleading nature of the term.[2] In view of the considerable

1 Text as established by Johannes Schilling, 'Determinatio secunda almae facultatis theologiae Parisiensis super Apologiam Philippi Melanchthonis pro Luthero scriptam', in *Lutheriana: Zum 500. Geburtstag Martin Luthers* (Archiv zur Weimarer Ausgabe 5: Vienna, 1984), pp. 351–75; 372.27–31. Developments within the Paris faculty of theology over the period 1500–43 are of relevance to this study, but cannot be pursued here: see J. K. Farge, *Orthodoxy and Reform in Early Reformation France: The Faculty of Theology of Paris, 1500–1543* (Leiden, 1985).

2 For general surveys of the literature, see William J. Courtenay, 'Nominalism and Late Medieval Thought: A Bibliographical Essay', *Theological Studies* 33 (1972), pp. 716–34; Courtenay, 'Nominalism and Late Medieval Religion', in *The Pursuit of Holiness in Late Medieval and Renaissance Religion*, ed. Charles Trinkaus with Heiko A. Oberman (Leiden, 1974), pp. 26–59; Courtenay, 'Late Medieval Nominalism Revisited: 1972–1982', *Journal of the History of Ideas* 44 (1983), pp. 159–64.

influence which this movement is now known to have exercised over the intellectual origins of the Reformation, it is necessary to examine it in some detail, and distinguish the various elements of this complex late medieval intellectual movement. The problem of defining the movement will serve as a starting point.

NOMINALISM: THE PROBLEM OF DEFINITION

The previous chapter considered the difficulties associated with the definition of the term 'humanism', and noted how Kristeller's definition of the term as a broad cultural and educational movement permitted what had appeared to be an increasingly unusable concept (given the intense scholarly activity in the field, which exposed its multifaceted nature) to be retained by historians. In the past half-century, extensive research into the logical, epistemological and theological views of writers usually designated as 'nominalists' has revealed a similar picture: there appears to be little, other than a rejection of realism, in common between the figures in question. Whereas the term 'humanism' has been retained, however, there is an increasing recognition that the term 'nominalism' must be abandoned, in that it appears to be an unusable historical concept.

The origins of late medieval 'nominalism' were once held to lie in the logical terminism of twelfth century figures such as Roscelin or Peter Abailard, according to which universals were concepts created by the mind without extramental referents, and hence without significance as a description of external reality. It was held that fourteenth century figures such as William of Ockham and Gregory of Rimini developed this implicit atomism to the point where the ontological synthesis of High Scholasticism, associated with Albertus Magnus and Thomas Aquinas, was destroyed.[3] This view has been subjected to considerable criticism in recent years, with particular attention being paid to the relation between the 'nominalism' of Abailard and Ockham. In a seminal essay of 1930,[4] Paul Vignaux argued that the correct

---

3 For this view of fourteenth century 'nominalism', see Konstantin Michalski, 'Les courants philosophiques à Oxford et à Paris pendant le XIVe siècle', *Bulletin International de l'Académie Polonaise des Sciences et des Lettres* (Cracow, 1921), pp. 59–88. The same view may be found more recently in David Knowles, *The Evolution of Medieval Thought* (London, 1970).

4 Paul Vignaux, art. 'Nominalisme', in *Dictionnaire de théologie catholique*, vol. II/1, cols. 717–84. Vignaux developed this approach in his later monograph, *Nominalisme au XIVe siècle* (Montreal, 1948).

meaning of the term could only be ascertained by identifying the *differentiae* between the two thinkers: this approach is now being increasingly recognized as fruitful. Jean Jolivet and Martin Tweedale were able to demonstrate the radically different intellectual environments in which Abailard and Ockham developed their theories of the relation of thought, language and entities, and to indicate that Ockham's 'nominalism' was quite distinct from that of Abailard.[5] It is certainly true that Ockham is a 'nominalist' if either or both of the following features are regarded as determinative. First, an epistemological criterion: a universal concept is established on the basis of individual entities, and (at least to some extent) describes them. Second, an ontological criterion: universal concepts signify extramental referents, but are not in themselves extramental. But this does not, as has been pointed out with some force,[6] mean that Ockham regards universals as figments of an overactive human imagination. It is this aspect of Ockham's thought which has forced upon his interpreters the necessity of finding an alternative designation for his epistemology and logic. Perhaps the most satisfactory alternative to 'nominalism' to date is 'realistic conceptualism'.[7]

Ockham appears to have been the first thinker to explore systematically the discrepancy between the conceptual and the ontological, while at the same time recognizing their interdependence. He neither eliminates universals, nor does he accept the *independent* reality of universals. Thus propositions containing universal terms (such as 'white') may be regarded as legitimate inferences based upon the experience of individual extramental entities. The perception that the universal quality 'white' is similar in two distinct individual extramental entities is not to be regarded as a purely intramental construction. Ockham thus appears to succeed in safeguarding concepts from being relegated to the status of purely internal mental constructs.[8] Indeed, it may be suggested that he was the first to combine an epistemology based upon the primacy of individual cognition with an individual ontology which had no place for anything within or beyond the

5 Jean Jolivet, 'Comparaison des théories du language chez Abélard et chez les nominalistes du XIVe siècle', in *Peter Abelard: Proceedings of the International Conference*, ed. E. M. Buytaert (Louvain, 1974), pp. 163–78; Martin Tweedale, *Abailard on Universals* (Amsterdam, 1976).

6 See the particularly important exposition of Stephen F. Brown, 'A Modern Prologue to Ockham's Natural Philosophy', in *Sprache und Erkenntnis im Mittelalter* (Berlin, 1981), pp. 107–29.

7 P. Boehner, 'The Realistic Conceptualism of William Ockham', in *Collected Articles on Ockham*, ed. E. M. Buytaert (New York/Louvain, 1958), pp. 156–74.

8 E. A. Moody, *The Logic of William of Ockham* (New York, 1965), pp. 37–8.

individual which was not itself individual – and in this way is able to avoid the difficulty of seeming to subordinate ontology (being) to epistemology (concepts).

This (admittedly difficult) point is of considerable importance in relation to the general view of nominalism adopted by an earlier generation of scholars, in that it calls into question whether Ockham is a 'nominalist' in any meaningful sense of the term.[9] It is therefore significant that the term 'nominalist' ceased to be used during the thirteenth century, and was only reintroduced in the fifteenth century to refer to a way of teaching logic.[10] The use of the term 'nominalist' in connection with the teaching of William of Ockham is thus an anachronism.

Detailed investigation of the reception of Ockham's thought in the period 1320–50 has also raised serious doubts concerning the coherence of 'nominalism'. Thus most late thirteenth and early fourteenth century thinkers regarded the *species in medio* as essential, in that cognition was understood to involve an abstraction from sense experience. Ockham's radical contribution to this debate was to deny the necessity of such a *species*.[11] Ockham's view, far from being readily received by the Oxford circle associated with him, was subjected to sustained criticism, by figures such as John of Reading, Walter Chatton, Robert Holcot, William Crathorn and Adam Wodeham.[12] On the basis of this striking observation, it may reasonably be concluded that, 'in epistemology at any rate, there seems at Oxford to have been no school of *Ockhamistae*.'[13]

A similar divergence is evident within the so-called 'nominalist' school in relation to the question of the nature of the object of knowledge. For Ockham, the object of knowledge was the proposition, or more accurately, the conclusion of a demonstration. In rejecting this view, Chatton argued that the object of knowledge was actually the thing to which the proposition itself referred. By 1330, William Crathorn had revised this view: the object of knowledge was the entire significate of the proposition (usually known as the *complexe*

---

9 See the seminal study of Erich Hochstetter, 'Nominalismus?', *FcS* 9 (1949), pp. 370–403.
10 Courtenay, 'Nominalism and Late Medieval Religion', p. 52.
11 See the valuable study of Katherine H. Tuchau, 'The Problem of the *species in medio* at Oxford in the Generation after Ockham', *Medieval Studies* 44 (1982), pp. 394–443.
12 Tuchau, 'Problem of the *species in medio*', pp. 404–32.
13 Tuchau, 'Problem of the *species in medio*', p. 443.

significabile).[14] This idea was developed, with important argumentation, by Adam Wodeham, under the phrase *significatum totale conclusionis*.[15] The same phrase and argumentation was later adopted by Gregory of Rimini at Paris,[16] thus establishing a link between the Parisian and Oxford schools. But, as will be evident, the view which finally became adopted was not that of Ockham: the central idea of the *complexe significabile* is due to either Crathorn or Wodeham (depending on the precise dating of Wodeham's comments, which may date from earlier than 1333),[17] and was articulated in conscious opposition to Ockham. The view that 'nominalism' was a radical anti-Ockhamist movement, perhaps centred upon William of Crathorn,[18] indicates how much the traditional view of 'nominalism' requires revision.

The serious limitations which are to be placed upon both the propriety and value of the term 'nominalism' may be illustrated from the astonishingly diverse theological views associated with writers who are unquestionably 'nominalist' in their logic and epistemology, such as Robert Holcot, Pierre d'Ailly, Gregory of Rimini and Hugolino of Orvieto.[19] It will be obvious that the four theologians noted adopt radically different theologies of justification, the first two adopting a theology which approaches (although cannot actually be said to constitute) some form of Pelagianism, while the latter are among the most ferociously anti-Pelagian theologians known in the later medieval

---

14 See the important study of Heinrich Schepers, 'Holkot contra dicta Crathorn', *Philosophisches Jahrbuch* 77 (1970), pp. 320–54; 79 (1972), pp. 106–36.

15 Gedeon Gál, 'Adam of Wodeham's Question on the "complexe significabile" as the Immediate Object of Scientific Knowledge', *FcS* 37 (1977), pp. 66–102. This article solved the long-standing debate over the source of Gregory of Rimini's doctrine of the *complexe significabile*.

16 See Mario Del Pra, 'La teoria del "significato totale" delle propositione nel pensiero di Gregorio da Rimini', *Rivista critica di storia della filosofia* 11 (1956), pp. 287–311. More generally, see F. Hoffmann, 'Der Satz als Zeichen der theologischen Aussage bei Holcot, Crathorn und Gregor von Rimini', in *Der Begriff der Repräsentatio im Mittelalter* (Berlin, 1971), pp. 296–313.

17 See Volker Wendland, 'Die Wissenschaftslehre Gregors von Rimini in der Diskussion', in *Gregor von Rimini: Werk und Wirkung bis zur Reformation*, ed. H. A. Oberman (Berlin/New York, 1981), pp. 241–300; Courtenay, 'Late Medieval Nominalism Revisited', p. 163.

18 The view of Schepers, 'Holkot contra dicta Crathorn', who regards Holcot as a conservative supporter of Ockham against the views of Crathorn.

19 See Adolar Zumkeller, *Hugolin von Orvieto und seine theologische Erkenntnislehre* (Würzburg, 1941); Mario Del Pra, 'Linguaggio e conoscenza assertiva nel pensiero di Roberto Holkot', *Rivista critica di storia della filosofia* 11 (1956), pp. 15–40; E. A. Moody, 'A Quodlibetal Question of Robert Holkot O.P. on the Problem of Knowledge and of Belief', *Speculum* 39 (1964), pp. 53–74; Willigis Eckermann, *Wort und Wirklichkeit: Das Sprachverständnis in der Theologie Gregors von Rimini und seine Weiterwirkung in der Augustinerschule* (Würzburg, 1978).

period.[20] This point has been something of a *crux interpretativum* for those who wish to maintain the viability of the term 'nominalism' to signify a particular school of thought in the later medieval period. In that Gregory of Rimini unequivocally rejects both the Thomist *distinctio realis* and the Scotist *distinctio formalis* in favour of the *complexe significabile*, the traditional identification of Gregory as the 'standard-bearer of the nominalists (*antesignanus nominalistarum*)' is unquestionably correct. Given Gregory's strongly Augustinian views on theological anthropology and the doctrines of predestination, merit and justification, however, which are diametrically opposed to the more genial insights of Holcot and d'Ailly, it became necessary for intellectual historians who wished to retain a meaningful concept of 'nominalism' to treat Gregory as an example of 'nominalistic diversity'.[21] As the views of a circle of thinkers based upon the writings of Gregory (such as Hugolino of Orvieto) became better understood, it became clear that there appeared to be a distinct, coherent school of thought, particularly associated with the Augustinian Order, which adopted a strongly 'nominalist' theory of signification, yet whose theology of grace was diametrically opposed to that of Holcot, d'Ailly or Biel. Furthermore, it became clear that even the older Luther regarded himself as a 'nominalist'.

In a remarkable fragment of his *Table-Talk*, Luther discussed the difference between 'terminism' and 'realism', correctly identifying the latter to include Albertists, Thomists and Scotists (in other words, the *via antiqua*), and the former Ockhamists. According to Luther, the Ockhamists argued that the term *humanitas* named all men individually, and did not refer to a common humanity, existing in all men, as Thomas and the older realists maintained. Although Luther appears slightly confused over Ockham's distinction between *terminus conceptus* and *terminus prolatus* – and we must remember that Luther and his minor Boswells had food and drink as well as epistemology to think about – it is clear that he appreciated the essential difference between 'realism' and 'nominalism' (or 'terminism'), and wished himself to be regarded as *terminista modernus*.[22] Given Luther's views on the

---

20 See Alister E. McGrath, *Iustitia Dei: A History of the Christian Doctrine of Justification* (2 vols: Cambridge, 1986), vol. 1, pp. 166–79 for an analysis.
21 See, e.g., Heiko A. Oberman, *The Harvest of Medieval Theology: Gabriel Biel and Late Medieval Nominalism* (Cambridge, Mass., 1963), pp. 196–206.
22 For the text, see WATr 5.6419; reprinted in Heiko A. Oberman, *Werden und Wertung der Reformation* (Tübingen, 1977), p. 425.

theology of grace at this juncture, it would be an imprudent scholar
who suggested that a 'nominalist' epistemology implied a soteriology
similar to that of Biel!

There has, therefore, been a growing realization of the independence
of many fourteenth century figures who were traditionally grouped
together and designated 'nominalists'. Similarly, it is now appreciated
that there are serious, possibly even insuperable, difficulties attending
the attempt to speak of 'schools' or 'traditions' in the fourteenth century.
Even the modest term 'Ockhamist', once thought an appropriate designation for thinkers such as Holcot, Wodeham and Crathorn, is now
realized to be potentially seriously misleading, for reasons such as
those we have noted above. This is not to say that generalizations
cannot be made, for they clearly can; it is simply to draw attention
to the complexity and diversity of what was once thought to be a
relatively homogeneous movement, and hence to the strength of the
case for ceasing to use the term 'nominalism'.

The present chapter is particularly concerned with two late medieval
theological movements, both of which have been designated as
'nominalism' in the past, despite their radical divergence. These are
the school of thought associated with Pierre d'Ailly and Gabriel Biel,
now usually known as the *via moderna*, and that associated with Gregory
of Rimini and Hugolino of Orvieto, now usually known as the *schola
Augustiniana moderna*. In the following sections, the nature of these
movements will be considered, before their influence upon the intellectual origins of the Reformation is examined in more detail.

VIA MODERNA

In recent years, the late medieval movement traditionally known as
'nominalism' has been subjected to intense scrutiny, resulting in the
recognition of its inherent heterogeneity. It is certainly true that the
later medieval period witnessed a polarization within many university
faculties of arts arising from the rival views of 'realists' and 'nominalists':
the testimony of Philip Melanchthon to the tensions at Tübingen in the
1510s[23] parallels similar tensions evident at fourteenth century Paris[24]

23 See the biography of Joachim Camerarius, *De vita Philippi Melanchthonis*, ed. G. T. Strobel
(Halle, 1777), pp. 22–3.
24 Ruprecht Paqué, *Das Pariser Nominalistenstatut: Zur Entstehung des Realitätsbegriff der neuzeitlichen
Naturwissenschaft (Occam, Buridan und Petrus Hispanicus, Nikolaus von Autrecourt und Gregor von Rimini)*
(Berlin, 1970).

and fifteenth century Heidelberg,[25] to note but two of the better-documented instances of the phenomenon. Nevertheless, it would be a serious error of historical judgement to suppose that the debate over realism defined the universal horizon of intellectual history in the period 1320–1520. There are excellent reasons for suggesting that a number of significant factors conspired to generate a general trend towards a 'non-realist' epistemology in the later medieval period, and that theologians who might otherwise have little in common shared such epistemological presuppositions. We have already noted the radically divergent soteriologies associated with theologians who shared a non-realist epistemology (such as Pierre d'Ailly and Gregory of Rimini). Similarly, epistemological divergences between thinkers were not *a priori* grounds for concomitant theological divergence: Oberman has helpfully pointed out how Conrad Summenhart (representing the *via antiqua*) and Gabriel Biel (representing the *via moderna*) appear content to converge in the field of theological ethics,[26] despite their epistemological differences. Although clearly an important aspect of late medieval thought, particularly in northern European universities, the realist–nominalist debate should not be misunderstood to define *a priori* a parallel dichotomy within the sphere of *religious* thought.

A further point which must be borne in mind when assessing the character and influence of the *via moderna* in the late medieval period relates to local heterogeneity within the movement. However much the historian may desire to simplify complex situations and portray 'nominalism' as an essentially well-defined and relatively homogeneous movement, thus permitting the generalizations of which so much Reformation historiography is made, the evidence suggests that the *via moderna* developed local characteristics associated with the centres upon which it was based. Although William of Ockham may be credited with the initiation of the movement, its specific forms at Oxford, Paris, Heidelberg and Tübingen were established by personalities with differing concerns and emphases. At Paris, the movement was specifically associated with Jean Buridan and Nicolas Oresme; at Heidelberg, with Marsilius of Inghen; at Tübingen with Gabriel Biel and Wendelin Steinbach.

---

25 Gerhard Ritter, *Studien zur Spätscholastik I: Marsilius von Inghen und die okkamistische Schule in Deutschland* (Heidelberg, 1921); Ritter, *Studien zur Spätscholastik II: Via antiqua und via moderna auf den deutschen Universitäten des XV. Jahrhunderts* (Heidelberg, 1922); Maarten van Rhijn, 'Wessel Gansfort te Heidelberg en de strijd tussen de "via antiqua" en de "via moderna"', in *Studiën over Wessel Gansfort en zijn tijd* (Utrecht, 1933), pp. 23–37.
26 Oberman, *Werden und Wertung der Reformation*, p. 35.

Although the movement was often designated as the *via nominalium*[27] or *via modernorum*[28], it was more frequently known after a prominent personality associated with the movement – such as the *via Marsiliana* at Heidelberg (after Marsilius of Inghen)[29] or the *via Gregorii* at Wittenberg (after Gregory of Rimini)[30] – hence raising the question of whether the *via* referred to is the *via moderna* as *exemplified by* or as *modified by* these individuals. Marsilius and Gregory, it need hardly be added, had somewhat different interests and methodologies.

Despite the local variations evident within the *via moderna*, a number of elements common to the various late medieval thinkers associated with the movement may be identified. Two elements of particular interest are the logico-critical tool of the dialectic between the two powers of God, and the voluntarism so characteristic of the movement. These elements will be considered individually.

The dialectic between the two powers of God is one of the most important, and most frequently misunderstood, theological tools of the late medieval period. Through the appeal to this dialectic, the theologians of both the *via moderna* and the *schola Augustiniana moderna* were able to eliminate unnecessary theological concepts and hypotheses. In effect, this dialectic underlies 'Ockham's Razor': quia frustra fit per plura quod potest equaliter per pauciora.[31] This radical elimination of unnecessary theologoumena is of considerable importance to the present study, in that it indicates a revision of the ontological theologies of High Scholasticism in favour of a more conceptually economical deontological theology. The nature and scope of this dialectic should be established first, before further analysis.

Although the origins of the dialectic between the two powers of God is to be sought in the late eleventh or early twelfth centuries, it came to be of major importance in the Parisian Averroist controversy of the thirteenth century.[32] The basic difficulty facing theologians such as Henry of Ghent and Duns Scotus related to the question of how

---

27 For example, at Paris: see R. G. Villoslada, *La Universidad de Paris durante los estudios de Francisco de Vitoria O.P. (1507–1522)* (Rome, 1938), p. 76.

28 For example, at Tübingen: see Rudolph von Roth, ed., *Urkunden zur Geschichte der Universität Tübingen aus den Jahren 1476 bis 1550* (Aalen, 1973), p. 264.

29 Ritter, *Studien zur Spätscholastik I*, p. 46.

30 Walther Friedensburg, *Urkundenbuch der Universität Wittenberg I: (1502–1611)* (Magdeburg, 1926), pp. 53; 56.

31 Ockham, *In II Sent.* qq. 14-15 O.

32 M. Grabmann, *Der lateinische Averroismus des 13. Jahrhunderts und seine Stellung zur christlichen Weltanschauung* (Munich, 1931).

God could be said to act *reliably* without simultaneously implying that he acted *of necessity*. For the Averroists, the claim that God acted reliably was essentially an admission that God's actions were dictated by external constraints which prevented him from acting arbitrarily, and hence that God acted of necessity. The initial difficulty faced by the defenders of the divine freedom was that a conceptual framework was not available by which God's reliability might be upheld, without simultaneously conceding that God acted through the force of external constraints. The dialectic between the two powers of God provided a means of avoiding this dilemma.

The essential distinction underlying the dialectic concerns the *hypothetical* and the *actual*. In that God is omnipotent, he is able to do anything, provided that logical contradiction is not involved (in other words, the fact that God is unable to construct a circular triangle is not seen as compromising his omnipotence). Out of an initial set of possibilities, God was at liberty to actualize any (provided that logical contradiction did not ensue). However, God did not actualize each and every possibility: only a subset of the initial set of possibilities was selected for actualization. A careful distinction must therefore be drawn between two distinct subsets: the subset of actualized possibilities, and the subset of unactualized possibilities which, although hypothetically possible, will never now be actualized. In other words, God must be thought of as possessing the *ability* to do many things which he does not *will* to do, in the past, present or future. God's freedom in relation to the initial set of actualizable possibilities is designated as the sphere of his 'absolute power (*potentia absoluta*)', and in relation to the subset of actualized possibilities his 'ordained power (*potentia ordinata*) – and it is the dialectic between these two powers of God which permits both the divine reliability and freedom to be upheld.

God is free, in that his selection of initial possibilities *de potentia absoluta* was uncoerced – in other words, God was not subject to any external constraints in the selection of the subset of possibilities to be actualized. Once that subset was selected and actualized, however, God was under a self-imposed obligation to respect the established order of actualized possibilities. Although God is under constraint in this matter, it is a self-imposed constraint, arising from the establishment of the ordained order: *de potentia Dei ordinata*, no violation of that order is possible. It will therefore be evident that *potentia Dei absoluta* and *potentia Dei ordinata* are not two different courses of action open to God at any given moment in historical time, the latter being the normal or natural mode of action and the former the miraculous or supernatural, but two quite distinct orders of existence. God is totally reliable, in that having established the ordained order as an act of divine creative will, he remains faithful to that order. To act contrary to it would imply a contradiction within the divine will, which is unthinkable.[33]

Although the dialectic between the two powers of God was employed in the thirteenth century to defend the divine freedom, the fourteenth and fifteenth centuries saw the device become a speculative technique for the elimination of redundant ontological concepts, or the clarification of necessary concepts. The former application of the technique can be illustrated by considering the critique of the role of supernatural habits in justification, and the latter by the analysis of the nature of the incarnation.

Before the theological renaissance of the late eleventh and twelfth centuries, justification tended to be conceived as a personal encounter between God and man, proceeding without the necessity of created intermediates.[34] In the twelfth century, however, the origins of one of the most significant theologoumena of High Scholasticism may be detected: the idea that, as justification involves an *ontological* change in man, an ontological intermediate is required in the process of justification – and this intermediate was to be identified with the created habit of grace or charity. For Peter Aureole, there was an ontologically necessary relation between a created habit and justification, so that, *ex natura rei*, such a habit was implicated in the process of man's justification.[35] In other words, given the nature of divine justification, such a habit is required. For Ockham, however, the reasoning underlying this assertion was fallacious at a crucial point,

33 For an introduction, see McGrath, *Iustitia Dei*, vol. 1, pp. 119–28. The following statement of Ockham, *Quodl.* 6 q.1; *Opera Theologica* 9.585.114–586.24, is definitive: 'Dico quod quaedam potest Deus facere de potentia ordinata et aliqua de potentia absoluta. Haec distinctio non est sic intelligenda quod in Deo sint realiter duae potentiae quarum una sit ordinata et alia absoluta, quia unica est potentia in Deo ad extra, quae omni modo est ipse Deus. Nec sic est intelligenda quod aliqua potest Deus ordinate facere et aliqua potest absolute et non ordinate, quia Deus nihil potest facere inordinate. Sed est intelligenda quod "posse aliquid" quandoque accipitur secundum leges ordinatas et institutas a Deo; et illa dicitur Deus posse facere de potentia ordinata.'
34 For an historical analysis, see McGrath, *Iustitia Dei*, vol. 1, pp. 100–9; 145–54.
35 McGrath, *Iustitia Dei*, vol. 1, pp. 149–50. For an extended discussion, see Paul Vignaux, *Justification et prédestination au XIVe siècle* (Paris, 1934), pp. 43–95.

which he exposed through applying the dialectic of the two powers of God.[36]

For Ockham, the implication of created habits in justification is not a consequence of the nature of the process of justification, but results from a divine decision that they shall be thus implicated. To suggest that habits are involved in justification as a matter of necessity (*ex natura rei*) is to imply that God was subjected to external constraints in establishing the created order, which is unthinkable. *De potentia absoluta*, God could have established an order of being in which created habits are *not* involved in justification, in that there is no logical contradiction involved in this suggestion. Ockham exploits the tension between the absolute and ordained powers to demonstrate the contingency of the role assigned to created habits in justification. The fact that they are involved in the established order is thus the result of God's decision that this shall be the case. In effect, Ockham works with a concept of *covenantal*, rather than *ontological* causality: created habits are involved in the causal sequence of justification, not because of the nature of the entities involved (*ex natura rei*), but on account of the divine will (*ex pacto divino*).

While Ockham does not deny that created habits are involved in justification *de facto*, he demonstrates that there is no necessary reason why they should be. The ontological basis which the High Scholasticism of the thirteenth century established for the implication of created habits in justification was thus shown to be inadequate. Although it is not clear precisely what role the later theologians of the *via moderna* assigned to created habits, it is evident that there was a growing trend in the later medieval period, particularly within the *schola Augustiniana moderna*, to conceive justification in personal or relational terms, and avoid the ontological discussion of the matter so characteristic of the earlier medieval period. As will be indicated later in this chapter, the general trend among the Reformers to deny an ontological dimension to justification represents a continuation of this critique of the conceptual foundations of the *habitus*-theology.

The deontologizing of man's justification is but one consequence of the systematic application of the logico-critical tool of the dialectic of the two powers of God. The deontologizing of man's relation to God, achieved in this manner, is a general feature of the theology

---

36 McGrath, *Iustitia Dei*, vol. 1, pp. 150–1; Vignaux, *Justification et prédestination*, pp. 97–140, especially pp. 99–118.

of both the *via moderna* and *schola Augustiniana moderna*. The Scotist emphasis upon the *acceptatio divina*,[37] developed and consolidated by these theologians of the later medieval period, tended to result in justification being seen as a personal act of divine will, foreshadowing the personalism of the Reformers in this respect. If the humanist movement rejected the ontological theology of High Scholasticism on account of its complexity, the theologians of the *via moderna* were able to eliminate it through demonstrating its redundancy.

The theologians of the *via moderna* developed the concept of the reliability of the *potentia ordinata* with reference to the notion of a 'covenant' or 'contract' (*pactum*) between God and man. It is this *pactum*, established unilaterally by God, which constitutes the turning point of the doctrines of justification associated with the *via moderna*. God is understood to have imposed upon himself a definite obligation, embodied in the *pactum*, to reward the man who does *quod in se est* with the gift of justifying grace. If man meets the minimal precondition for justification (in other words, if he does *quod in se est* – to the meaning of which we shall presently return), God is under a self-imposed obligation to justify him. As Robert Holcot pointed out, God may therefore be said to justify such a man of necessity, provided that this is understood as a 'necessity of consequence (*necessitas consequentiae*)' rather than 'absolute necessity (*necessitas absoluta*)'.[38] Similarly, Gabriel Biel emphasized that God acted in this manner as a deliberate act of will, by which he placed himself under an obligation to man, in that he is now obliged to reward the man who does *quod in se est* with grace. Although God is under no obligation to anyone *ex natura rei*, he has voluntarily placed himself under such an obligation *ex pacto suo*.[39]

---

37 W. Dettloff, *Die Lehre von der Acceptatio Divina bei Johannes Duns Skotus* (Werl, 1954); idem, *Die Entwicklung der Akzeptations- und Verdienstlehre von Duns Skotus bis Luther* (Münster, 1963).
38 Holcot, *Lectiones super libros sapientiae*, lect. 145B 'Necessitas coactionis nullo modo cadit in deo, necessitas vero infallibilitatis cadit in deo ex promisso suo et pacto sive lege statuta, et haec non est necessitas absoluta sed necessitas consequentiae. . . Concedendo quod ex misericordia et gratia sua pro tanto, quia talem legem misericordiam statuit et observat, sed statuta lege necessario dat gratiam necessitate consequentiae.'
39 Biel, *In II Sent.* dist. xxvii q. unica a.2 concl.1 G 'Nam licet deus nullius debitor esse possit ex natura rei, potest tamen se facere debitorem nostrum ex sua libera voluntate nobis promittendo pro talibus actibus tantum praemium.' See further Heiko A. Oberman, 'Wir sint pettler. Hoc est verum. Bund und Gnade in der Theologie des Mittelalters und Reformation', *ZKG* 78 (1967), pp. 232–52; Martin Greschat, 'Der Bundesgedanke in der Theologie des späten Mittelalters', *ZKG* 81 (1970), pp. 44–63; William J. Courtenay, 'Covenant and Causality in Pierre d'Ailly', *Speculum* 46 (1971), pp. 94–119; Berndt Hamm, *Promissio, Pactum, Ordinatio: Freiheit und Selbstbindung Gottes in der scholastischen Gnadenlehre* (Tübingen, 1977), pp. 355–90.

Although there is no necessary ontological connection between man's doing *quod in se est* and justification, God has ordained that such a causal relationship shall exist *ex pacto suo*.

It is considerations such as these which suggest that the later medieval period witnessed a general transition from a concept of *ontological* to *covenantal* causality. The relationship between God and man in particular was now conceived covenantally, permitting extensive correlation with the covenant-motif of both the Old and New Testaments, rather than ontologically. This final dismantling of the ontological framework of the God–man relationship may be regarded as the necessary prelude to Luther's 'biblical realism', in that it permitted this relationship to be conceived *personally*, allowing the same realistic imagery of the Old and New Testaments to be employed in responsible theological discussion. Thus, for example, the concept of 'grace' was no longer considered primarily as a created intermediate species interposed between man and God, but rather as an aspect of God's disposition towards man.[40]

A number of points may be made in relation to this covenantal understanding of the God–man relationship.[41] First, the precondition for justification is essentially the same under both the Old and the New dispensations. There is no radical dichotomy between the Old and New Testaments in this respect: under each, the precondition for justification remains the same – that man do *quod in se est*, which Biel defines as *declinare. . . a malo et facere bonum*.[42] The 'Old Testament character' of the ethics of the *via moderna* has often been noted,[43] and reflects this point. Second, there is an evident Christological lacuna in the soteriology of the *via moderna*, in that the salvation of mankind may be discussed without reference to the incarnation and death of Christ.[44] It is thus significant that the theologians of the *via moderna*

---

40 See, e.g., the comments of Bugenhagen: '. . .insipienter errent, qui gratiam dei, de qua loquuntur scripturae per quam solam salvamur, describunt esse habitum in hominem sive qualitatem, cum sit favor potius in deo bene volente nobis ut filiis'; cited H. H. Holfelder, *Solus Christus: Die Ausbildung von Bugenhagens Rechtfertigungslehre in der Paulusauslegung (1524/25) und ihre Bedeutung* (Tübingen, 1981), p. 24.

41 See Alister E. McGrath, 'Some Observations concerning the Soteriology of the Schola Moderna', *RThAM* 52 (1985), pp. 182–93.

42 Biel, *In II Sent.* dist. xxvii q. unica a.3 dub.4 O.

43 See, e.g., Oberman, *Harvest of Medieval Theology*, pp. 108–11.

44 McGrath, 'Some Observations', p. 184; McGrath, '*Homo Assumptus*? A Study in the Christology of the *Via Moderna*, with Particular Reference to William of Ockham', *EThL* 60 (1985), pp. 283–97; pp. 285-7.

tend to refer to Christ as *Legislator* rather than *Salvator*.[45] Whatever theological shortcomings this covenantal approach to scripture may be deemed to exhibit, the fact remains that the theologians of the *via moderna* were able to exploit the *pactum* as both a soteriological and hermeneutical principle, establishing both the precondition for man's justification and a means of safeguarding the unity of Old and New Testaments.

The importance of this increasingly pervasive covenantal under-standing of the relation between God and man with regard to the intellectual origins of the Reformation will be evident. In the case of Luther, we find an understanding of the nature and function of the *pactum* which is at least continuous with, and probably also identical to, that of the *via moderna* (see below). Similarly, Zwingli's *Reply to Hubmeier* of 5 November 1525 develops a strongly covenantal theology, laying emphasis upon the soteriological demands made of man, and the hermeneutical principle of the essential unity of both Old and New Testaments, similar to that associated with the *via moderna*.[46] Significantly, the concept of a *double* covenant between God and man, so characteristic of later Reformed theology, is not to be found in the first phase of the Reformation: that phase is characterized by a covenant theology, based upon a single covenant between God and man, exhibiting remarkable parallels with the well-established theology of the *via moderna*. It is not clear whether these parallels are purely coincidental, or whether they reflect the direct or indirect influence (perhaps mediated through Luther?) of the *via moderna*. That they exist is, however, evident.[47]

The second major development of significance in relation to the later medieval period is the rise of voluntarism, which may be illus-trated with reference to the medieval discussion of merit.[48] The early

45 Oberman, *Harvest of Medieval Theology*, pp. 112–19.

46 See J. Wayne Baker, *Heinrich Bullinger and the Covenant: The Other Reformed Tradition* (Athens, Ohio, 1980), pp. xi–xxvi; 1–25, for a useful introduction, marred by a misunderstanding of late medieval thought (e.g., pp. 23–5). For a refutation of the (here, as elsewhere) alleged 'semi-Pelagianism' of the *via moderna*, see A. E. McGrath, 'The Anti-Pelagian Structure of "Nominalist" Doctrines of Justification', *EThL* 57 (1981), pp. 107–19.

47 Discussion of this question has been grossly confused through two factors: first, through a serious misunderstanding of the nature of the *pactum*-theology of the *via moderna*; second, through the misleading attempt to distinguish 'unilateral' and 'bilateral' covenants. Baker's confused analysis illustrates these failures. For a more reliable guide to the types of covenant thought then in circulation, and their relation to that of Augustine, see Hamm, *Promissio, Pactum, Ordinatio*.

48 See McGrath, *Iustitia Dei*, vol. 1, pp. 114–16.

Dominican and Franciscan schools adopted an intellectualist approach to the relation of the moral and meritorious realms, recognizing a direct correlation between the moral and the meritorious value of an act, the transition between the two being effected by grace or charity. The use of terms such as 'aequiparari', 'associatio', 'comparabilis' and 'proportionalis' in the discussion of this question indicates how initially the meritorious value of an act was understood to be directly correlated with its moral value: the divine intellect recognizes the latter, and the divine will thence effects the former. Thus Thomas Aquinas, who exemplifies this intellectualist understanding of the relationship between morality and merit, argued that merit is based upon justice.[49] The origins of the voluntarist position may be traced to Duns Scotus and William of Ockham, who emphasized the radical discontinuity between the moral and meritorious value of an act, the latter being understood to rest entirely upon an uncoerced decision of the divine will. For Scotus, every created offering is worth exactly what God accepts it for, and no more: 'dico, quod omne aliud a Deo, ideo est bonum, quia a Deo volitum, et non est converso: sic meritum illud tantum bonum erat, pro quanto acceptabatur'.[50] The meritorious value of an act need therefore bear no direct relation to its moral value, in that the *ratio meriti* is understood to lie in the divine will, in the extrinsic denomination of the *acceptatio divina*. While the possibility that God may chose to correlate the meritorious with the moral value of an act cannot be excluded on *a priori* grounds, it is no more probable than the possibility that he will not.

This voluntarism is developed by William of Ockham,[51] for whom the decision as to what may be regarded as meritorious or demeritorious lies solely within the orbit of the divine will. Inevitably, this has exposed Ockham to the serious – and apparently irrefutable – charge that the relation between the moral and meritorious realms *de potentia ordinata* is arbitrary.[52] As Gabriel Biel pointed out, however, this danger is inevitable, unless God is to be made subject to created principles of morality, so that the divine will merely *endorses*

---

49 More strictly, *iustitia secundum praesuppositionem divinae ordinationis*, rather than *iustitia secundum absolutam aequalitatem*: see *Summa Theologiae* IaIIae q.114 a.1 ad 3um; McGrath, *Iustitia Dei*, vol. 1, p. 114.
50 Scotus, *Opus Oxoniense* III dist. xix q.1 n.7.
51 Vignaux, *Justification et prédestination*, pp. 127–40.
52 Erwin Iserloh, *Gnade und Eucharistie in der philosophischen Theologie des Wilhelm von Ockham* (Wiesbaden, 1956), pp. 64–7.

rather than *effects* what is good and right. What is good, is what is accepted as such by God.[53] The divine will is thus the chief arbiter and principle of justice, establishing justice by its decisions, rather than acting according to the basis of established justice. Indeed, a study of the meaning of *iustitia Dei*, the 'righteousness of God', according to the theologians of the *via moderna*, indicates the totally arbitrary foundations of the concept: the 'righteousness of God' is nothing more and nothing less than the embodiment of the arbitrary decisions of the divine will.[54] It is, nevertheless, important to note that – whatever the ultimate basis of divine law may be – it is understood to be a permanent and reliable aspect of the *potentia ordinata*, a fact which Biel underlines by often using the phrase *de facto* or *stante lege* in place of the more usual *de potentia ordinata*. For Biel, the established moral order is to be found both in natural law and in the Old Testament law (that is, the Decalogue), as it is embodied within, and modified by, the New Testament (which Biel tends to treat as law). The voluntarism of the *via moderna* is thus linked to the Old and New Testaments. Furthermore, in that the origins of such views may be traced to Scotus, it is possible to argue that a section of the *via antiqua*, still in the ascendancy in certain Swiss and German universities in the early sixteenth centuries, adopted such a stance. The pervasiveness of such a voluntarism, both in ethics and theology, suggests an important degree of continuity between early Reformed theology and the late medieval tradition, in that the early Reformed theology appears to demonstrate such a voluntarism. This point will be illustrated later with reference to Calvin.

Our attention is next claimed by a question of great significance for Luther scholarship – the question of whether there existed a 'medieval Augustinian tradition', whether within the Augustinian Order or outside of it, and the nature and extent of its influence over the intellectual origins of the Reformation.

---

53 Biel, *Canonis Missae expositio*, 23E 'Nihil fieri dignum est nisi be tua benignitate et misericordia voluntate dignum iudiacre volueris, neque enim quia bonum aut iustum est aliquid, ipsum Deus vult, sed quia Deus vult, ideo bonum est et iustum. Voluntas nanque divina non ex nostra bonitate, sed ex divina voluntate bonitas nostra pendet, nec aliquid bonum nisi quia a Deo sic acceptum.'
54 McGrath, 'Some Observations', pp. 191–2.

SCHOLA AUGUSTINIANA MODERNA

The suggestion that there existed in the later Middle Ages a coherent school of thought, espousing a theology significantly more 'Augustinian' than that of the medieval theological schools as a whole, has exercised considerable fascination over generations of Reformation scholars. Was the young Luther familiar with such a school? Did his decisive theological insights derive from such a source? Were other Reformers also influenced in a similar manner? The unavailability of the necessary documentary sources until recently, and the concomitant absence of general agreement over precisely what was meant by the term 'Augustinian', might be thought adequate grounds for earlier generations of scholars to proceed with some caution in such a difficult area of historical research. In fact, however, two remarkably ambitious theories were put forward in the earlier part of this century. In 1912, Alphons Victor Müller suggested that Luther was a representative of an 'Augustinian' school of thought which existed in the late medieval period within the Augustinian Order.[55] In many respects, Müller's thesis was both premature and derivative, drawing heavily upon the work of Karl Werner, mediated through the writings of Carl Stange.[56] This thesis did not stand up to critical investigation, but was adopted in a significantly modified form by Eduard Stakemeier.[57] According to Stakemeier, a coherent theological tradition existed within the Augustinian Order in the later medieval period: in this respect, Müller was correct. What Müller had failed to demonstrate was a connection between such a tradition and the theology of Luther. According to Stakemeier, however, it was evident that the theologians of the Augustinian Order – particularly the general of the Order, Girolamo Seripando – present at the Council of Trent's debates on justification, were heirs to precisely this tradition.[58]

This thesis has not stood up to critical examination. First, it was

55 A. V. Müller, *Luthers theologische Quellen: Seine Verteidigung gegen Denifle und Grisar* (Giessen, 1912).

56 See Karl Werner, *Die Scholastik des späteren Mittelalters III: Der Augustinismus in der Scholastik des späteren Mittelalters* (Vienna, 1883); Carl Stange, 'Über Luthers Beziehungen zur Theologie seines Ordens', *Neue kirchliche Zeitschrift* 11 (1900), pp. 574–85; Stange, 'Luther über Gregor von Rimini', *Neue kirchliche Zeitschrift* 13 (1902), pp. 721–7.

57 Eduard Stakemeier, *Der Kampf um Augustin: Augustinus und die Augustiner auf dem Tridentinum* (Paderborn, 1937).

58 Stakemeier, *Der Kampf um Augustin*, pp. 21–2.

pointed out that Stakemeier had contented himself with the primary sources assembled earlier by Müller, rather than developing this pioneering work. Second, it was noted that Stakemeier had not demonstrated textual continuity between the Augustinian theologians he had considered – to demonstrate the influence of theologians upon their successors, extensive source-critical work was required, a task impossible at that time (1937) through the lack of reliable editions of the necessary works.[59] Finally, recent source-critical work has suggested that the evidence for an 'Augustinian school' at the Council of Trent is unconvincing, and that it is no longer possible to speak of such a 'school' at Trent in any meaningful sense of the word.[60]

The failure of these early studies of the question of the nature and characteristics of a putative 'medieval Augustinian school' does not, however, invalidate subsequent and more informed discussion of the same question. In recent years, a certain degree of clarification has been achieved with regard to this question, which has important consequences for any understanding of the intellectual origins of the Reformation.[61] In part, this clarification is due to increasing precision in vocabulary, in that the term 'Augustinian' has been recognized to be multivalent,[62] and to require strict definition if reliable conclusions are to be drawn on its basis. The term 'Augustinian', for the purposes of this section, is defined with reference to the Augustinian Order. Was there a distinctive, well-defined school of theology within the Augustinian Order in the late medieval period, irrespective of whether the theological characteristics of such a putative school correspond to the teachings of Augustine himself?[63] It is, of course, possible that such a school might have influence outside the Augustinian Order, for example, through the teaching activities of Augustinians at Paris and elsewhere. Nevertheless, the question of whether such a school existed must be investigated initially through an analysis of

---

59 See Hubert Jedin's review of Stakemeier, *Der Kampf um Augustin*, in *Theologische Revue* 37 (1938), pp. 425–30.
60 See McGrath, *Iustitia Dei*, vol. 2, pp. 66–8.
61 For a list of works relevant to this subject, see Alister E. McGrath, *Luther's Theology of the Cross: Martin Luther's Theological Breakthrough* (Oxford, 1985), p. 64 n. 122.
62 David C. Steinmetz, *Luther and Staupitz: An Essay in the Intellectual Origins of the Protestant Reformation* (Durham, NC, 1980), pp. 13–15, distinguishes five senses in which the term 'Augustinian' has been used by medieval historians, and draws attention to the confusion resulting therefrom.
63 By 'Augustine', of course, we mean 'Augustine of Hippo', and not 'Augustine of Rome' (Agostino Favaroni: a noted fifteenth century theologian of the Augustinian Order).

the writings of such Augustinian theologians themselves, and obviously
takes precedence over the question of its possible influence. Let us
therefore begin by considering the evidence for the existence of a
distinct theological school within the Augustinian Order in the fourteenth and fifteenth centuries.

In a careful study of Augustinian theologians in the fourteenth
century, Damasus Trapp was able to demonstrate a significant degree
of textual continuity within the Augustinian Order, essential to the
hypothesis of a coherent school of thought within that Order.[64] Thus
Giles of Rome, the leading thirteenth century theologian of the Order,
is cited with sufficient frequency (often being designated *doctor noster
Aegidius*) to indicate that he was regarded as a theological authority
by his followers within the Augustinian Order. Adolar Zumkeller
argued that the early Augustinian school, sometimes referred to as
the *schola Aegidiana*, was characterized by its Aristotelian–Thomist
ontological foundations, linked with certain distinctive theological
elements which were unquestionably due to the influence of Augustine.[65]
As examples of such elements, Zumkeller points to the emphasis upon
the priority of *caritas* and *gratia* in justification, both authentic elements
of Augustine's theology of justification.

Although these considerations might be thought to indicate the
existence of a reasonably coherent theological tradition within the
Augustinian Order, both Trapp and Zumkeller point to factors which
suggest the existence of *two* quite distinct traditions within the Order
in the medieval period. The polarization resulting within many university faculties of arts between the *via antiqua* and the *via moderna* in the
fourteenth and fifteenth centuries was noted earlier in this chapter.
In his study of fourteenth century Augustinian theologians, Trapp
noted the emergence of exactly the same polarization *within the
Augustinian Order*. Both *antiqui* and *moderni* may be discerned within
the Order during this period, the latter characterized by source-critical
and the latter by logico-critical techniques. Trapp thus argued that
the medieval Augustinian tradition had to be recognized as falling

64 Damasus Trapp, 'Augustinian Theology of the Fourteenth Century: Notes on Editions,
Marginalia, Opinions and Book-Lore', *Augustiniana* 6 (1956), pp. 147–265.
65 Adolar Zumkeller, 'Die Augustinerschule des Mittelalters: Vetreter und philosophisch-
theologische Lehre', *Analecta Augustiniana* 27 (1964), pp. 167–262. On Giles of Rome, see
J. Beumer, 'Augustinismus und Thomismus in der theologischen Prinzipienlehre des Aegidius
Romanus', *Scholastik* 32 (1957), pp. 542–60. Beumer argues convincingly that Giles is essentially a student of Augustine with occasional Thomist tendencies, rather than a Thomist with
a particular interest in Augustine.

into two broad periods. The earlier period of Augustinian theology may be regarded as having been initiated by Giles of Rome, including such theologians as Alexander of San Elpido, Robert Cowton and William of Ware, and ending with the fourteenth century theologian Thomas of Strasbourg. In epistemology and related matters, these theologians were realists, following the *via antiqua*. The second period, which may be regarded as having been inaugurated by Gregory of Rimini, and continuing into the sixteenth century, is characterized by the 'nominalism' of the *via moderna*. On source-critical grounds, there are excellent reasons for concluding that the 'nominalism' of the later Augustinian tradition derives directly from the *via moderna*: the way in which Gregory's crucial theory of the *complexe significabile* derives from the *modernus* Adam Wodeham was noted earlier.

Once this hypothesis was stated, evidence in its support began to accumulate. Zumkeller noted that the elements in the earlier Augustinian tradition which derived from Augustine himself were intensified in the later period, and that the Augustinians after Gregory of Rimini tended to depend more on Augustine than upon Giles of Rome. In a study of the doctrines of justification associated with the medieval Augustinian tradition,[66] it was shown that the tradition from Giles of Rome to Thomas of Strasbourg adopted a theology of justification characteristic of the early Dominican or Franciscan schools, whereas the later tradition, from Gregory onwards, tended to follow the later Franciscan school and the *via moderna*.[67] The intrinsicist and ontologically determined theology of justification associated with the earlier period is replaced with the extrinsicist and deontologized theology of the later period. In many respects, the later Augustinian tradition (exemplified by Gregory of Rimini, Hugolino of Orvieto and Dionysius of Montina) may be regarded as appropriating insights deriving from the *via moderna* – for example, an epistemological nominalism, and the speculative tool of the dialectic between the two powers of God and the results of its application, such as the critique of the role of created habits in

66 A. E. McGrath, '"Augustinianism"? A Critical Assessment of the so-called "Medieval Augustinian Tradition" on Justification', *Augustiniana* 31 (1981), pp. 247–67; McGrath, *Iustitia Dei*, vol. 1, pp. 172–9.
67 Some later theologians, such as Johannes von Retz, retained the older view through their fidelity to the teachings of Thomas of Strasbourg.

justification.[68] Thus the later Augustinian tradition followed the *via moderna* in teaching the priority of acts over habits, so that the formal cause of both justification and merit was identified as the extrinsic denomination of the *acceptatio divina*, rather than the intrinsic denomination of the created habit of grace.[69] Furthermore, it was evident that there was a significant degree of textual continuity between, for example, Gregory, Hugolino and Dionysius, indicating the development of a coherent theological tradition within the Augustinian Order. For such reasons as these, this school was designated the *schola Augustiniana moderna*. However, although there were considerable parallels between the *via moderna* and *schola Augustiniana moderna*, there were equally great divergences.

The theologians of the *schola Augustiniana moderna* developed a ferociously anti-Pelagian theology of grace, including a theology of absolute double predestination, an emphasis upon the depravity of man, and the necessity of grace for morally good acts, which is far removed from the soteriology of the *via moderna*. Indeed, it is also quite distinct from the milder theology of the earlier Augustinian tradition, from Giles of Rome to Thomas of Strasbourg. Recently, Heiko A. Oberman has clarified the manner in which this radical Augustinian theology developed in the fourteenth century.[70] Oberman demonstrated that a form of academic Augustinianism developed at both Oxford and Paris, practically simultaneously and probably independent of each other, based upon Augustine's anti-Pelagian writings. In Oxford, the movement was centred upon Thomas Bradwardine, whose *De causa Dei* appeared in 1344.[71] Although being forced to respond to theological issues current in the fourteenth century, Bradwardine seems determined to apply the anti-Pelagian insights of Augustine wherever possible. For Bradwardine, Augustine was – like Paul before him – *gratiae laudator, gratiae magnificus ac strenuus*

68 See M. Schüler, *Prädestination, Sünde und Freiheit bei Gregor von Rimini* (Stuttgart, 1934); Vignaux, *Justification et prédestination*, pp. 141–75; Adolar Zumkeller, *Dionysius de Montina: Ein neuentdeckter Augustinertheologe des Spätmittelalters* (Würzburg, 1948); Zumkeller, 'Hugolin von Orvieto über Prädestination, Rechtfertigung und Verdienst', *Augustiniana* 4 (1954), pp. 109–56; 5 (1955), pp. 5–51.

69 McGrath, *Iustitia Dei*, vol. 1, pp. 145–54, especially pp. 150–4; 172; 179.

70 Heiko A. Oberman, 'Tuus sum, salvum me fac: Augustinréveil zwischen Renaissance und Reformation', in *Scientia Augustiniana: Studien über Augustinus, den Augustinismus und den Augustinerorden*, ed. C. P. Mayer and W. Eckermann (Würzburg, 1975), pp. 349–94.

71 Heiko A. Oberman, *Archbishop Thomas Bradwardine: A Fourteenth Century Augustinian* (Utrecht, 1957); Gordon Leff, *Bradwardine and the Pelagians: A Study of His 'De Causa Dei' and Its Opponents* (Cambridge, 1957), pp. 23–124.

propugnator.[72] However, Bradwardine supports his anti-Pelagian theology with a metaphysical doctrine of divine omnipotence quite alien to Augustine, with the result that man's total soteriological dependence upon God is seen as a consequence of his creatureliness, rather than of his sinfulness.[73] The Fall is not viewed as a watershed in the economy of salvation. It is for this reason that some have questioned whether Bradwardine may be viewed as 'Augustinian' in the strict sense of the term, given the pivotal function of the Fall within Augustine's theology. It is difficult to assess the influence of Bradwardine upon the Reformation: the Hundred Years War isolated Oxford as a centre of learning from the universities of the continent, and Bradwardine, as a secular priest, had no religious order to propagate his views. It is possible to argue for some limited influence of Bradwardine upon the Reformation through Wycliffe,[74] in that Luther knew – and approved of – Wycliffe's assertion (deriving from Bradwardine), condemned at the Council of Constance, 'omnia de necessitate absoluta eveniunt'.[75] However, it is the Parisian version of this academic Augustinianism, associated with Gregory of Rimini, which has attracted most scholarly attention in the present century, and which is of particular relevance in relation to the intellectual origins of the Reformation.

The fundamental difference between Gregory and Bradwardine is that the former managed to develop a theological stance similar to that embodied in Augustine's anti-Pelagian corpus within the context of the intellectual framework of the *via moderna*. In other words, Gregory follows the *via moderna* where Bradwardine followed the *via antiqua*, constructing a remarkable synthesis between two positions which at first sight appeared incompatible. Where Bradwardine's predestinarianism is the result of his metaphysical doctrine of divine omnipotence, Gregory's arises through his Christologically concentrated concept of salvation history.[76] As a result, Gregory is able to retain Augustine's emphasis upon the Fall as the decisive anthropological element in salvation history. It is almost certain that Bradwardine

72 *De causa Dei* (London, 1618), i, 35; p. 311C.
73 See McGrath, '"Augustinianism"?', pp. 254–5.
74 See J. F. Laun, 'Thomas von Bradwardine, der Schüler Augustins und Lehrer Wiclifs', *ZKG* 47 (1928), pp. 333–56.
75 WA 7.146.5–11 (1520). Cf the earlier statement (1518), 'Liberum arbitrium post peccatum res est de solo titulo' (WA 1.359.32), which may – but need not – reflect Wycliffe's dictum.
76 Schüler, *Gregor von Rimini*, p. 31; Oberman, *Werden und Wertung*, p. 89.

is *unus modernus doctor* singled out for criticism by Gregory for his views on the Fall (see above).[77] On the basis of the evidence available, it seems that an academic Augustinianism, based upon the anti-Pelagian writings of Augustine, linked to a conceptual framework essentially that of the *via moderna*, came to be transmitted within the Augustinian Order in the fourteenth and early fifteenth centuries, corresponding with the later Augustinian tradition identified by Trapp.[78]

It will be clear that the evidence points to at least a tradition, and probably a school,[79] of thought within the Augustinian Order in the later medieval period, deriving from Gregory of Rimini, although the precise nature and extent of its influence within and outside that Order remains unclear. It will also be clear why an earlier generation of scholars found themselves so confused by the characteristics of this school, and unable to distinguish it from the *via moderna*. The *schola Augustiniana moderna* – as this Gregorian tradition is generally known – adopted not merely the epistemology (that is, 'nominalism') of the *via moderna*, but also certain characteristic aspects of the soteriology of that movement. These elements included the use of the dialectic between the two powers of God to demonstrate the secondary and contingent role of created habits in justification, and the emphasis upon the extrinsic denomination of the *acceptatio divina* in justification. Yet, despite this remarkable convergence with the *via moderna*, the radically theocentric theology of Augustine's anti-Pelagian writings dominates the soteriology of the *schola Augustiniana moderna*, and distinguishes it from that of the *via moderna*.

This complex pattern of simultaneous convergence with and divergence from the *via moderna* obviously indicates the inadequacy of the terms 'nominalist' and 'Augustinian' to designate these two rival schools of thought of the later medieval period. Not only did many 'Augustinian' theologians adopt a 'nominalist' epistemology: they also incorporated important elements of 'nominalist' theories of justification

---

77 *In II Sent.* dist. xxix q.1 a.1. The name 'Bradwardine' is found in the margins of two manuscripts: Paris Bib. Nat. lat 15891 and Mazarine 914.

78 See Manfred Schulze, '"Via Gregorii" in Forschung und Quellen', in *Gregor von Rimini: Wirk und Wirkung bis zur Reformation*, ed. H. A. Oberman (Berlin/New York, 1981), pp. 1–126, especially pp. 13–22; 25–75.

79 Trapp warns us that, when dealing with theologians of the Augustinian Order, one should speak 'cautiously of attitudes, not of schools': Trapp, 'Augustinian Theology', p. 150. Since then, the case for speaking of a 'school' has been strengthened: see Schulze, 'Via Gregorii', pp. 25–63.

into their own doctrines. It is precisely this variation between individual Augustinian theologians in respect of the extent to which they adopted elements of 'nominalism' which has caused so much of the confusion currently surrounding the characteristics of a putative 'Augustinian' school of theology at the time. Furthermore, there are reasons for supposing that some theologians of the *via moderna*, such as Pierre d'Ailly, may be dependent in matters of epistemology upon Gregory of Rimini at points,[80] thus complicating still further an already confusing picture, and reinforcing the impression of two schools which are practically identical in matters of epistemology, yet diverge so radically in matters of soteriology. Within a university faculty of arts, such differences would have been insignificant: thus at Paris, Gregory of Rimini and William of Ockham were identified as the leading doctors of the *via nominalium* within the faculty of arts.[81] Within a university faculty of theology, however, the differences between the two schools would have been considerable. A question that will concern us at several points in the later sections of this chapter is this: was the *schola Augustiniana moderna* represented at the institutions at which the various Reformers were educated? And are there any reasons for supposing that it exercised any influence over the origins of their ideas?

LATE MEDIEVAL THEOLOGY AND THE
ORIGINS OF THE REFORMED CHURCH

The relation of Zwingli to the late medieval theological schools is far from clear. It is known that he was influenced by the *via antiqua* while at the university of Basle (1502–6), and that he possessed a heavily annotated copy of the 1503 Venice edition of Scotus' *Opus Oxoniense*, as well as some minor Scotist works.[82] This suggests early affinities with Scotism. In 1510, Glarean wrote to Zwingli, indicating he wished to leave Cologne and take up a post at Basle, where he might teach according to the *via seu secta Scoti*, and clearly suggesting that Zwingli

---

80 Schulze, 'Via Gregorii', pp. 64–75.
81 Villoslada, *Universidad de Paris*, p. 118.
82 Walter Köhler, *Huldrych Zwinglis Bibliothek* (Zurich, 1921), pp. 10–11, nn. 74; 290. Cf. J. F. Gerhard Goeters, 'Zwinglis Werdegang als Erasmianer', in *Reformation und Humanismus: Robert Stupperich zum 65. Geburtstag*, ed. M. Greschat and J. F. G. Goeters (Witten, 1969), pp. 255–71; pp. 256–61.

approved of this *via*.[83] Nevertheless, evidence for a decisive influence of a late medieval school upon the development of Zwingli's thought is wanting, at two levels. First, despite the many original documents relating to Zwingli's early period, we possess no primary material from the period 1510-23 which explicitly links Zwingli with specific late medieval theologians or theological currents. Second, Zwingli's theological development over this period gives no indication of having been informed, or even catalysed, by such individuals or currents. All the evidence points to Zwingli's theological development being a direct result of humanist influence.

The influence of late medieval theological schools, such as the *via moderna* and *via antiqua*, upon John Calvin is much more difficult to assess, on account of the near-total absence of primary sources for the period 1523-34 in Calvin's career. It is clearly of crucial importance to a correct understanding of the origins of Calvin's religious thought that we know of his associations at the University of Paris in the 1520s. This information, however, is almost certainly lost to us. Antoine Marcourt's placards denouncing the mass, distributed and posted in the early morning of 18 October 1534,[84] brought to a head the simmering controversy between French catholics and *évangeliques*, and moved Francis I to implement his long-threatened campaign against 'Lutheran' teachings in France. Those with evangelical views in France at the time were not prepared to argue the distinction between 'Lutheran' and 'evangelical', and preferred not to advertise their views publicly. The dangers of doing so had been discovered the previous November by Calvin, who had fled Paris for Angoulême in the aftermath of Nicolas Cop's controversial All Saints' Day oration.[85] Within hours of his flight, the authorities had searched his rooms, and confiscated his personal papers. These papers have never been traced or recovered, even in part, with the result that we possess no documents from Calvin's own hand relating to this crucially formative period in his career. Practically all our 'knowledge' of Calvin's Paris period is

83 CR (Zwingli) 7.3. The early years of the university of Basle, from 1460-4, were marked by a confrontation between the *via moderna* and *via antiqua*: see Astrik L. Gabriel, '"Via Antiqua" and "Via Moderna" and the Migration of Paris Students and Masters to the German Universities in the Fifteenth Century', in *Antiqui und Moderni: Traditionsbewußtsein und Fortschrittbewußtsein im späten Mittelalter*, ed. A. Zimmermann (Berlin/New York, 1974), pp. 439-83; p. 474; Oberman, *Werden und Wertung der Reformation*, pp. 39-40.
84 G. Berthoud, *Antoine Marcourt, réformateur et pamphlétaire due 'Livre de Marchans' aux placards de 1534* (Geneva, 1973), pp. 157-222. For the text of these celebrated placards, see pp. 287-9.
85 As one of his early biographers emphasizes, it was a close escape: CR (Calvin) 21.56.

nothing more than an educated guess, based upon circumstantial evidence. To illustrate this point, let us consider the statement, common to most accounts of Calvin's early period, to the effect that he entered the Parisian Collège de la Marche at the age of 14.[86] Two simple points may be made.

First, we do not actually know that Calvin did, in fact, enter the Collège de la Marche prior to entering the Collège de Montaigu. In the first edition of his *Vie de Calvin*, Théodore de Bèze (Beza) omits any reference to this college from his account of Calvin's early Paris period,[87] before stating that Calvin first went to the Collège de la Barbe. This reference comes at a later point in the biography, in a reference to the celebrated pedagogue Mathurin Cordier, who Beza describes as 'son regent au college de Saincte barbe à Paris en sa premiere ieunesse'.[88] This biography was, of course, written in some haste, in order to pre-empt scurrilous accounts of Calvin's death, and prevent them from gaining any credibility: nevertheless, it remains the oldest account of Calvin's Paris period, and undoubtedly incorporates much material deriving from Calvin himself.

In the following year, Nicolas Colladon published a considerably more detailed biography of Calvin, including a more detailed account of the Reformer's Paris period. It is in this account that we encounter, for the first time, the assertion that Calvin initially studied at the Collège de la Marche.[89] Beza later harmonized his earlier biography with Colladon's, dropping his reference to St. Barbe, and mentioning La Marche in connection with Cordier.[90] In fact, of course, we possess no statement from Calvin to the effect that he studied at La Marche: the closest approximation to such a statement is a late appreciative reference to Cordier as Calvin's teacher at Paris – but no college is named.[91] We know that Cordier was engaged as a pedagogue by half a dozen Paris colleges at the time, including both

86 Most recently (1985), see Richard Stauffer, 'Calvin', in *International Calvinism 1541–1715*, ed. Menna Prestwich (Oxford, 1985), pp. 15–38; p. 16. See also the authoritative study of François Wendel, *Calvin: The Origins and Development of his Religious Thought* (London, 1974), pp. 17–18.
87 On this biography, see D. Ménager, 'Théodore de Bèze biographe de Calvin', *BHR* 45 (1983), pp. 231–55.
88 CR (Calvin) 21.36.
89 CR (Calvin) 21.54.
90 CR (Calvin) 21.121 '. . .in Gymnasio Marchiano Mathurinum Corderium'.
91 CR (Calvin) 13.525.

La Marche and St. Barbe,[92] making it impossible to disprove Beza's early statement to the effect that Calvin first studied at St. Barbe.[93]

Second, there are no compelling reasons for supposing that Calvin began his studies at Paris at the age of fourteen. The suggestion that Calvin began his studies at this age may be traced back to Doumergue,[94] who in turn bases his statement upon a somewhat tendentious paper of 1621,[95] which interprets an entry in the Noyon registers of 5 August 1523 (stating that Calvin's father had been given permission to send him away from Noyon until 1 October) as implying that Calvin went to Paris for the first time that autumn.[96] The conclusion is not demanded by the evidence. Fourteen was late by the standards of the period to begin a university education,[97] and if Calvin even approached the precocious intelligence with which his biographers credit him, he would have been capable of the university curriculum at twelve.[98] This possibility, of course, does not permit the conclusion that he *did* begin his studies at this age: the point is made merely to emphasize how little we know of Calvin's Paris period with anything even approaching certainty.

It is also unclear precisely what Calvin studied during his period at Paris. In an autobiographical reflection, Calvin indicates that his father had always intended him to study theology,[99] but this does not allow us to conclude that he ever began such studies while at Paris, and there are excellent reasons for supposing that his formal education progressed no further than attending lectures in philosophy.[100] There

92 See Charles Emile Delormeau, *Un maître de Calvin: Mathurin Cordier, l'un des créateurs de l'enseignement secondaire moderne* (Neuchatel, 1976), pp. 24–9. A list of such colleges may be found in Cordier's *Colloquia* (6 February 1564), reprinted Delormeau, pp. 122–6; p. 122.

93 Thus note the comments of J. Quicherot, *Histoire de Sainte Barbe* (3 vols: Paris, 1860–4), vol. 1, p. 206.

94 Emile Doumergue, *Jean Calvin, les hommes et les choses de son temps* (7 vols: Laussane, 1899-1917), vol. 1, p. 46.

95 Jacques Desmay, 'Remarques sur la vie de Jean Calvin, tirées des registres de Noyon, ville de sa naissance', in *Archives curieuses de l'histoire de France depuis Louis XI jusqu'a Louis XVIII*, ed. L. Cimber (= Lafait) and F. Danjou (15 vols: Paris, 1834–7), vol. 5, pp. 387–98.

96 Desmay, 'Remarques', p. 388.

97 See Charles Thurot, *De l'organisation de l'enseignement dans l'université de Paris au moyen âge* (Paris/Bresançon, 1850), p. 94; G. Dupont-Ferrier, 'La faculté des arts dans l'université de Paris et son influence civilisatrice', in *Aspects de l'université de Paris*, ed. J. Calvet *et al.* (Paris, 1949), pp. 63–80; pp. 70–1.

98 For example, Desmay, 'Remarques', p. 388; Beza, CR (Calvin) 21.121; Alexandre Ganoczy, *Le jeune Calvin: genèse et évolution de sa vocation réformatrice* (Wiesbaden, 1966), p. 34.

99 CR 31.22. Cf. Beza's statement, 'son coeur tendoit entierement à la Theologie' (CR 21.29).

100 Ganoczy, *Le jeune Calvin*, pp. 39; 186.

are also reasons for supposing that Calvin's theological education may derive largely from personal study or reading during his Paris period,[101] which, if correct, diminish considerably the relevance of the formal university theological curriculum to his development.

The identity of Calvin's teachers during his Paris period is also shrouded in obscurity. With the single exception of Cordier, Calvin does not name any individual who taught him at Paris, although it is possible to argue that several confused references to Spaniards in the early biographies[102] may rest upon Calvin's reminiscences of the celebrated Spanish dialectician Antonio Coronel, whose *Rosarium logices* was published at Paris in 1510, and who appears to have taught at the Collège de Montaigu during Calvin's time there.[103] Here, however, as with so many other aspects of the Paris period, Calvin's development must be regarded as an enigma.

The absence of sufficient reliable information pertaining to Calvin's intellectual development to permit analysis of that development forces the historian to adopt one of two courses, and explicitly acknowledge that he is doing so. Either he may be reduced to silence, in that the necessary materials for such an analysis are unavailable, or else he may proceed on the basis of an inferential analysis, drawing upon circumstantial evidence to establish conclusions of varying degrees of probability. In fact, the historian has little choice but to adopt the second course and, conceding that he knows little for certain concerning the Paris period (when did it begin? who taught Calvin? what did he study?), proceed to infer from the available evidence (including Calvin's later writings) what *might* have happened, while conceding the provisional and tentative character of any conclusions which may result. In employing the latter method, I would emphasize that I am adopting the only approach to the Paris period possible, given the absence of proper sources, and have no intention of constructing a major hypothesis upon the basis of such fragmentary evidence. First, let us consider the intellectual climate at Paris in the early sixteenth century.

101 See, e.g., W. F. Dankbaar, *Calvin: Sein Weg und Werk* (Neukirchen, 1959), p. 26.
102 Colladon refers us to two uninteresting Spaniards (CR 21.54), while Beza clearly associates Calvin's dialectical abilities with a Spanish teacher: 'Translatus deinde in Gymnasium ab Acuto Monte cognominatum Hispanum habuit doctorem non indoctum: a quo exculto ipsius ingenio, quod ei iam tum erat acerrimum, ita profecit...ad dialectices et aliarum quas vocant artium studium promoveretur.' CR 21.121.
103 P. Feret, *La faculté de théologie de Paris et ses docteurs les plus célèbres* (7 vols: Paris, 1900–10), vol. 2, p. 66.

The fourteenth century had seen the conflict between *via antiqua* and *via moderna*, so characteristic of late medieval university life, polarize the university of Paris. The Parisian faculty of arts attempted to stem the influence of the *via moderna* early in the fourteenth century: on 29 December 1340, a statute condemning the *errores Ockanicorum* took effect:[104] henceforth, any candidate wishing to supplicate for the degree of Master of Arts at Paris would have to swear to observe these statutes *contra scientia Okamicam*, and abstain from teaching such doctrines to his pupils.[105] By the end of the century, however, the ineffectiveness of the measures was evident: Pierre d'Ailly (1350–1420), a noted *modernus*, became rector of the Collège de Navarre in 1384, and chancellor of the university five years later.[106] By the second decade of the sixteenth century, the Collège de Montaigu – to which Calvin went up at some point in the following decade – had become a stronghold of the *via moderna* in a university no longer inclined to oppose the movement.[107]

Even during his brief sojourn at Montaigu during the closing years of the previous century, Erasmus had compiled a list of theological concerns at Paris which demonstrates precisely the issues that were debated within the *via moderna*.[108] Two such questions may be noted. First, can God undo the past, such as by making a prostitute into a virgin?[109] The question of whether God can undo the past was regarded as significant by the theologians of both the *via moderna* and *schola Augustiniana moderna*, raising the difficult question of future contingents and the relation between the *potentia absoluta* and *potentia ordinata*.[110] Second, could God have become a beetle or a cucumber,

---

104 Paqué, *Das Pariser Nominalistenstatut*, pp. 8–12.

105 C. E. du Boulay, *Historia Universitatis Parisiensis* (6 vols: Paris, 1665–75), vol. 4, pp. 273–4.

106 L. Salembier, *Le Cardinal Pierre d'Ailly* (Tourçoing, 1932). For his epistemology, see B. Meller, *Studien zur Erkenntnislehre des Peter von Ailly* (Freiburg, 1954).

107 Villoslada, *Universidad de Paris*, pp. 87; 106–26.

108 Erasmus, *Opera Omnia*, vol. 6, p. 962D, in which Erasmus illustrates the term 'vaniloquium' (I Timothy 1.13) with reference to some of the questions troubling the *théologastres* of the *via moderna*.

109 *Opera*, vol. 6, p. 927B 'An possit ex facto facere infectum: ac per hoc ex meretrice facere virginem.'

110 See the valuable study of William J. Courtenay, 'John of Mirecourt and Gregory of Rimini on whether God can undo the past', *RThAM* 39 (1972), pp. 244–56; 40 (1973), pp. 147–74. On the related question of future contingents, see L. Baudry, *La querelle des futurs contingents, Louvain 1465–1475* (Paris, 1950); G. Leff, *William of Ockham* (Manchester, 1977), pp. 447–54.

instead of man?[111] In its more usual form, this question was stated thus: could God have assumed the nature of an ass, or a stone, instead of man? It is in this form that Calvin encountered the question.[112] As we have shown elsewhere, the question at stake in this apparently pointless disputation related to the nature of the hypostatic union, particularly the concept of 'personification'. For Ockham, the nature of the hypostatic union was such that the assumed nature need not be rational, thus clarifying the relation of the divine and human *personae*.[113] Thus God could have assumed the nature of an ass or a stone (or, indeed, a beetle or a cucumber) without logical contradiction. The point is evident in the discussion of the question by many Parisian theologians of the *via moderna*, such as John Major.[114]

It is the figure of John Major which has attracted most attention on the part of Calvin scholars in recent decades, due to the so-called 'Reuter hypothesis'. In his important study of 1963, Karl Reuter claimed that Calvin was taught by John Major while at Paris, and that the distinguished Scottish theologian exercised a decisive influence over the formation of the young Frenchman's theology.[115] In particular, Reuter claimed that Major introduced Calvin to a 'new conception of anti-Pelagian and Scotist theology'.[116] Although earlier studies had suggested that Major taught Calvin, possibly introducing him to some form of 'Ockhamism',[117] Reuter developed this suggestion into a major working hypothesis of Calvin research. According to Reuter, it was through the influence of Major that Calvin encountered the

111 *Opera*, vol. 6, p. 927C 'An quaelibet persona divina possit quamlibet naturam assumere, quomodo Verbum humanam assumpsit...An haec propositio, Deus est scarabeus, aut cucurbita, tam possibilis sit, quam haec, Deus est homo.' Similar derisory sentiments are expressed to John Colet in a letter of 1499, with his Paris experiences fresh in his mind: *Opus Epistolarum*, ed. P. S. and H. M. Allen (Oxford, 1906–47), vol. 1, no. 108; pp. 246–9, especially lines 41–4.
112 *Institutio* II.xii.5 'Eosque erupit quorundam vesania dum praepostere acuti videri appetunt, ut quaererent an naturam asini assumeri potuerit Dei filius.' The question is raised in this form by William of Ockham, among others: *In III Sent.* q.1 G.
113 See McGrath, '*Homo Assumptus?*', for a full analysis.
114 Major, *In III Sent.* dist. ii q.2 (Paris, 1528), fol. vi[ra].
115 Karl Reuter, *Das Grundverständnis der Theologie Calvins* (Neukirchen, 1963), pp. 20–1. More recently, Reuter has defended and developed this thesis: *Vom Scholaren bis zum jungen Reformator: Studien zum Werdegang Johannes Calvins* (Neukirchen, 1981). Cf. Alister E. McGrath, 'John Calvin and Late Medieval Thought: A Study in Late Medieval Influences upon Calvin's Theological Development', *ARG* 77 (1986), pp. 58–78.
116 Reuter, *Grundverständnis der Theologie Calvins*, p. 21.
117 See, e.g., the hints of such a hypothesis in Luchesius Smits, *Saint Augustin dans l'oeuvre de Jean Calvin I: étude de critique littéraire* (Assen, 1956), p. 14; Dankbaar, *Calvin: sein Weg und sein Werk*, p. 5.

writings of Augustine, Bonaventure, Duns Scotus, Thomas Aquinas, Thomas Bradwardine and Gregory of Rimini.[118] This thesis is clearly of considerable importance in relation to the question of the origins of Calvin's reforming theology, and has been the subject of extended evaluation.

Initially, the thesis appears to have met with uncritical acceptance.[119] More careful studies suggested there was indeed an epistemological affinity between Major and Calvin,[120] although such views concerning intuitive and abstractive knowledge would not be sufficient to demonstrate the specific influence of Major upon Calvin (given their pervasive influence within the Parisian faculty of arts at the time). Nor, indeed, would it allow any conclusion concerning Major's *theological* influence on Calvin to be drawn, in that the matters in question were discussed within the faculty of arts, rather than that of theology. The hypothesis has, however, subsequently been subjected to considerable criticism, most notably by Alexandre Ganoczy. The following two points made by him against Reuter are of particular importance.[121] First, although Ganoczy concedes that Calvin may have read Major's *Commentary on the Sentences* during the period 1540–59, there is no textual evidence in the first edition of the *Institutio* (1536) to warrant the conclusion that he had read the work before 1536. Reuter had based his conclusions upon the 1559 edition of the *Institutio*, which Ganoczy felt was historically improper. Second, in the first edition of the *Institutio*, Calvin tends to identify scholastic theology with Gratian and Peter Lombard.[122] Thus there are some 35 references to the latter in this edition, and no references whatsoever to any theologian of the fourteenth or fifteenth centuries, irrespective of theological orientation. In addition, of course, it will be obvious

---

118 Reuter, *Grundverständnis der Theologie Calvins*, pp. 32–4; 154.
119 For example, Kilian McDonnell, *John Calvin, the Church and the Eucharist* (Princeton, NJ, 1967), pp. 7–22.
120 Thomas F. Torrance, 'La philosophie et la théologie de Jean Mair ou Major (1469–1550)', *Archives de philosophie* 32 (1969), pp. 531–47; 33 (1970), pp. 261–94; Torrance, 'Intuitive and Abstractive Knowledge from Duns Scotus to John Calvin', in *De doctrina Ioannis Duns Scoti: Acta tertii Congressus Scotistici Internationalis* (Rome, 1972), pp. 291–305.
121 Ganoczy, *Le jeune Calvin*, pp. 189–92.
122 Ganoczy, *Le jeune Calvin*, pp. 179–85. For a detailed breakdown of Calvin's use of Peter Lombard and Gratian in the 1536, 1539, 1543 and 1559 editions, see Smits, *Saint Augustin dans l'oeuvre de Jean Calvin I*, p. 210. Of the 40 references to Peter Lombard and Gratian, only one relates to the theology of grace. Note in particular the virtual elimination of all sacramental references in the 1539 edition, with a new interest in the theology of grace: of the ten references to these two theologians, eight now relate to the theology of grace.

that, if Calvin's entry to Paris is to be dated as early as 1521, the possibility of his being taught by Major requires re-evaluation, in that the latter was absent from Paris until 1525.

Although Reuter's hypothesis, in its original form, is probably untenable, it would seem that the criticism of Ganoczy and others[123] requires the modification, rather than the rejection, of the underlying suggestion that Calvin has been influenced by currents of thought prevalent in the late medieval period – exemplified by, but by no means restricted to, Major. For example, Reuter points to six aspects of Calvin's religious thought which may reasonably be held to be due to late medieval influence:[124] while they need not point directly to Major, they certainly point to the thought-world of the *via moderna* or *schola Augustiniana moderna* in general. Similar comments apply to the observation that Calvin is familiar with the *modus loquendi theologicus* of the late medieval period.[125] The Parisian faculty of arts recognized three *viae* in the late medieval period, *via sancti Thomae, via Scoti et via nominalium,*[126] and identified two recognized representatives of this last *via* – William of Ockham and Gregory of Rimini.[127] This immediately suggests that the epistemological 'nominalism' or 'terminism' so characteristic of both the *via moderna* and *schola Augustiniana moderna* was current in the Paris faculty of arts at the time. Even if his studies progressed no further than the *trivium*, Calvin could scarcely have avoided such logical and epistemological questions. The favourable reference to a dialectically minded Spaniard in Beza's biography is significant, whether he is to be identified with Antonio Coronel or not,[128] in that it points to Calvin's encounter with dialectics, and hence almost certainly to the 'nominalism' so pervasive a feature of the period at Montaigu. The distinctively terminist foundations and dialectical structure of Calvin's thought have frequently been noted.[129] It is therefore necessary to point out that Calvin may have absorbed much of the dialectical outlook of either the *via moderna* or

---

123 I have been unable to examine the thesis of A. A. LaVallee, referred to by H. Schützeichel, *Die Glaubenslehre Calvins* (Munich, 1972), p. 68.

124 Reuter, *Vom Scholaren bis zum jungen Reformator*, pp. 6–12.

125 Louis Goumaz, *Le doctrine de la salut d'après les commentaires de Jean Calvin sur le Noveau Testament* (Noyon, 1917), p. 92.

126 Villoslada, *Universidad de Paris*, p. 76.

127 Villoslada, *Universidad de Paris*, p. 118.

128 For the text, see n. 112 above.

129 See, e.g., Ganoczy, *Le jeune Calvin*, pp. 196–200; Reuter, *Vom Scholaren bis zum jungen Reformator*, pp. 6–7.

schola Augustiniana moderna during his Paris period, without specificially attaching this influence to any one named individual.

A more serious objection to Ganoczy's dismissal of Reuter's hypothesis concerns the nature of the 1536 *Institutio* itself, and may best be appreciated by considering the very different situations faced by Luther and Calvin. Luther, writing some 20 years earlier than Calvin, was obliged to deal directly with what he regarded to be the most significant threat to the gospel as he perceived it – and Luther identified this threat, whether rightly or wrongly, as deriving from the theology of the *via moderna*. Luther is therefore obliged to engage directly with the leading representatives of this theology,[130] and mount a point-by-point refutation of their views. The Lutheran Reformation originated as a *university* reforming movement in an academic context, initially fighting an essentially academic battle until the intervention of the humanist movement turned a minor local academic debate into a major cosmopolitan ecclesiastical confrontation. Thus Karlstadt's 151 Augustinian theses of 1517 or Luther's *Disputatio contra scholasticam theologiam* of the same year were aimed, not at the church, but at an academic theological movement, initiating an essentially academic debate which was conducted in academic terms in an academic context. As this chapter will emphasize, the origins of the Reformed church appear to owe little, if anything, to such a university dispute: the early polemical literature of the Lutheran church, particularly in the period 1517–20, cannot therefore be permitted to serve as a model for that of the later Reformed church, in the period 1536–9.

I would address the following question to Ganoczy: why should Calvin wish to, or need to, make any sort of reference to *any* late medieval theologian, let alone one as obscure as Major, in the 1536 edition of the *Institutio*? The work was intended as a religious primer, not as an attack on the theology of the later medieval period. If any Lutheran work serves as a model for the *Institutio*, it is the Catechisms, rather than the academic disputations. Furthermore, scholastic theology posed no serious threat to the emerging Swiss Reformed church – the most serious difficulty appears to have been posed by religious ignorance and indifference, requiring a pedagogical, rather

---

130 Thus the 1517 *Disputatio contra scholasticam theologiam* is now recognized to be aimed directly at Gabriel Biel: see Leif Grane, *Contra Gabrielem: Luthers Auseinandersetzung mit Gabriel Biel in der Disputatio contra scholasticam theologiam 1517* (Gyldendal, 1962).

than a polemical, response. A systematic and attractive presentation of doctrine, rather than a sustained debate with certain named and extensively cited late medieval theologians was required. Where Luther's primary concern was the radical critique of the (allegedly) Pelagian soteriologies of the *via moderna*, Calvin's primary concern appears to have been the radical critique of the ecclesiology underlying the late medieval church.[131] Rather than engage in extensive debate with late medieval writers, Calvin employs the standard Melanchthonian device of discrediting the medieval era as a whole by a direct attack upon the *fons et origo* of its ecclesiology – Gratian and Peter Lombard. Thus Calvin's references to Peter Lombard in the 1536 *Institutio* are, without exception, drawn from the fourth book of the *Libri quattuor sententiarum*, dealing with the doctrines of the church and sacraments.[132] Calvin, by attacking a stream of tradition at its source, relieves himself of the necessity of dealing with subsequent developments, and opens the way to a pre-medieval ecclesiology more conducive to his reforming activities. At no point is it necessary, or even useful, for Calvin to engage in debate with any representatives of late medieval religious thought – and to suggest that this silence reflects an absence of familiarity with such sources, or that it indicates that Calvin has not been influenced by them to any significant extent, is simply a *non sequitur*. The question of the significance of Calvin's *use* of theological sources is secondary to a discussion of Calvin's religious concerns, literary and polemical techniques and potential audiences.

I would therefore wish to emphasize that the absence of specific references in the writings of Calvin to named late medieval theologians – such as Gregory of Rimini or John Major – cannot be taken as implying an ignorance of their views, or an absence of continuity with them. The possibility that Calvin may have defensively minimized his continuity with certain late medieval writers for polemical reasons

---

131 Jaques Courvoisier, *De la Réforme au Protestantisme: Essai d'ecclesiologie réformée* (Paris, 1977), pp. 65–100.

132 Ganoczy, *Le jeune Calvin*, p. 179. See further M. Reulos, 'Le Décret de Gratian chez les humanistes, les Gallicans et les réformés français du XVIe siècle', *Studia Gratiana* 2 (1954), pp. 692–6.

An interesting observation, of obvious relevance here, is the reluctance of many sixteenth century writers to identify contemporary sources in the first place: see G. Mattingly, 'International Diplomacy and International Law', in *New Cambridge Modern History III: The Counter Reformation and the Price Revolution 1558–1610*, ed. R. B. Wernham (Cambridge, 1968), pp. 168–9.

133 Reuter, *Grundverständnis der Theologie Calvins*, p. 21.

cannot be excluded. Perhaps, then, Reuter's thesis – that Calvin learned a 'new conception of anti-Pelagian and Scotist theology, and a renewed Augustinianism'[133] at Paris – may be restated in terms of the influence of a general late medieval theological current, rather than of a *specific individual* (i.e., John Major). Le us remind ourselves of the leading characteristics of the epistemology and theology of the *schola Augustiniana moderna*, exemplified by Gregory of Rimini.

1 A strict epistemological 'nominalism' or 'terminism'.
2 A voluntarist, as opposed to intellectualist, understanding of the *ratio meriti*.
3 The extensive use of the writings of Augustine, particularly his anti-Pelagian works.
4 A strongly pessimistic view of original sin, with the Fall being identified as a watershed in the economy of salvation.
5 A strong emphasis upon the priority of God in justification, linked to a doctrine of special grace.
6 A radical doctrine of absolute double predestination.

The second of these points may be singled out for further discussion.

Earlier in the present chapter, we noted how the later medieval tradition as a whole (including the later Franciscan school, the *via moderna* and *schola Augustiniana moderna*) adopted a strongly voluntarist approach to the basis of merit. This observation applies equally to the merits of Christ as to human merit. Scotus' maxim, that the value of an offering is determined solely by the divine will, was generally accepted: 'dico, quod omne aliud a Deo, ideo est bonum, quia a Deo volitum, en non est converso: sic meritum illud tantum bonum erat, pro quanto acceptabatur'.[134] In the *Institutio*, Calvin adopts an identical position in relation to the merit of Christ. Although this is implicit in earlier editions of the work, it is only made explicit in the 1559 edition, in the aftermath of Calvin's correspondence with Laelius Socinus.[135] In 1555, Calvin responded to questions raised by Socinus concerning the merit of Christ and the assurance of faith,[136] and

---

133 Reuter, *Grundverständnis der Theologie Calvins*, p. 21.
134 Scotus, *Opus Oxoniense* III dist. xix q.1 n.7. See the discussion earlier in the present chapter.
135 *Responsio ad aliquot Laelii Socini Senensis quaestiones*; CR (Calvin) 10a.160–5. The 1554 edition of the *Institutio* gives a purely cursory analysis of the question (vii, 18: CR 1.523–4).
136 The replies are incorporated into the 1559 *Institutio* at the following points: II.xvii.1–5; III.ii.11–12.

appears to have incorporated these replies into the 1559 edition of the *Institutio* without significantly modifying them. In the course of this correspondence, the strongly voluntarist approach which Calvin adopts to the *ratio meriti Christi* becomes obvious. Calvin makes clear that the basis of Christ's merit is not located in Christ's offering of himself (which would correspond to an intellectualist approach to the *ratio meriti Christi*), but in the divine decision to accept such an offering as of sufficient merit for the redemption of mankind (which corresponds to the voluntarist approach). For Calvin, 'apart from God's good pleasure, Christ could not merit anything (*nam Christus nonnisi ex Dei beneplacito quidquam mereri potuit*).[137] The continuity between Calvin and the late medieval voluntarist tradition will be evident.

In the past, this similarity between Calvin and Scotus has been taken to imply the direct influence of Scotus on Calvin, or perhaps an indirect influenced mediated via Socinus: thus Alexander Gordon argued that Calvin adopted a Scotist approach to the *ratio meriti Christi*, and on the basis of his presupposition that Scotism constituted the basis of Socinianism, traced the continuous development of that movement from Scotus through Calvin.[138] In fact, however, Calvin's continuity appears to be with the late medieval voluntarist tradition, deriving from William of Ockham and Gregory of Rimini, in relation to which Scotus marks a point of transition. No reason may be given for the meritorious nature of Christ's sacrifice, save that God benevolently ordained to accept it as such. The continuity of Calvin with this later tradition is evident, whatever its explanation may be.

These six features of the *schola Augustiniana moderna* noted above clearly include those of Calvin's thought identified by Reuter, and attributed to the influence of John Major.[139] It is perhaps significant that, in the preface to his *Commentary on the Sentences*, Major explicitly acknowledges his debt to three theologians: Scotus, William of Ockham and Gregory of Rimini.[140] It is certainly true that all the above six features are also leading aspects of the thought of John Calvin (not to mention others, such as the rejection of the implication of created habits of grace in justification or merit). It is certainly therefore a remarkable coincidence, to say the least, that Calvin should reproduce

---

137 *Institutio* II.xvii.1.
138 See, e.g., Alexander Gordon, 'The Sozzini and their School', *Theological Review* 16 (1879), pp. 293–322.
139 Reuter, *Grundverständnis der Theologie Calvins*, p. 21.
140 Major, *In I Sent.*, praefatio (Paris, 1530).

the leading features of an academic Augustinianism which developed at the same university as that which he himself attended, if he had not himself been familiar with such theological currents. Nor need he have encountered these views in lectures: Gregory's *Commentary* went through three editions at Paris (1482, 1487, 1520), the last appearing shortly before Calvin's arrival.[141] If Calvin read as widely as we are led to believe by his contemporaries, it is not improbable that this work – a standard of both logic and theology by one of the two recognized doctors of the *via nominalium* at Paris – would have attracted his attention. Reuter, of course, put forward his thesis before the *schola Augustiniana moderna* had been identified and characterized, and his theory is considerably weakened through unnecessary subsidiary hypotheses (such as personal contact with Major). I would therefore suggest that the relation of the young Calvin to the *schola Augustiniana moderna* at Paris is potentially a fruitful area of Reformation scholarship.

This point may be developed by considering the origins of the religious thought of Peter Martyr Vermigli. Probably in 1516, Vermigli entered the Augustinian Order at Fiesole, moving to Padua in 1519.[142] It seems that a well-established academic school, based upon the writings of Gregory of Rimini, existed in northern Italy in the first two decades of the sixteenth century, particularly associated with Paolo da Soncino and his pupil Gaspare Mansueti da Perugia,[143] and that this school was encountered by Vermigli. Furthermore, the Augustinian house at Padua was described by a contemporary of Vermigli as a 'roccaforte dell'agostinismo',[144] and there are good reasons for relying upon this judgement. Vermigli's biographer records his preference for 'the school divines, speciallie *Thomas* [Aquinas], and *Ariminensis* [Gregory of Rimini]'.[145] Four editions of Gregory's *Commentary* were published in northern Italy (Milan, 1494; Venice, 1503, 1518 and 1522), suggesting considerable interest in the views of the great Augustinian theologian at Padua and elsewhere.

---

141 A copy of this work (though not necessarily Calvin's personal copy) was included in the library of the Genevan Academy in 1572: see Alexandre Ganoczy, *La bibliothèque de l'Académie de Calvin*, (Geneva, 1969), pp. 102–5.

142 The chronology is disputed: see Philip McNair, *Peter Martyr in Italy: An Anatomy of Apostasy* (Oxford, 1967), pp. 78–82.

143 McNair, *Peter Martyr*, pp. 100–6, especially p. 106 n.3.

144 McNair, *Peter Martyr*, p. 94.

145 Cited McNair, *Peter Martyr*, p. 106.

The obvious question arising from these observations is the following: was Vermigli influenced by the *schola Augustiniana moderna*? Vermigli was a member of the Augustinian Order, and appears to have both encountered and responded positively to the views of Gregory of Rimini. Furthermore, it is evident that Vermigli adopted all the leading features of the theology of the *schola Augustiniana moderna* noted above in the course of our discussion of Calvin's possible relation to this school.[146] Once more, a remarkable degree of coincidence must be conceded if this is not the case. It is difficult to argue for the influence of Calvin, for example, at this point.[147] Although much work remains to be done on Vermigli's relation to late medieval thought, the clarification of the relationship between his soteriology and that of Gregory of Rimini is clearly of considerable interest and importance. Where Stakemeier argued for a medieval Augustinian school in Italy which influenced Seripando, perhaps there is a stronger case for such a school in Italy influencing Vermigli. This question, however, awaits clarification.

This discussion has considered the possible influence of late medieval theology upon the intellectual origins of Reformed theology. Although the further investigation of the relation between Gregory of Rimini and the origins of the distinctive ideas of Calvin and Vermigli is clearly important in this respect, the evidence to date is suggestive, rather than conclusive. It is nevertheless clear that both Calvin and Vermigli independently exhibit remarkable continuity with the leading features of an academic Augustinianism characteristic of the late medieval period, no matter what the explanation of this continuity may eventually prove to be. The previous chapter drew attention to the considerable influence of humanism in relation to the intellectual origins of the Reformed church, and it seems that this conclusion must, at present, stand. The intellectual origins of the Reformed church are not, it would seem, to be sought primarily in the context of tensions within late medieval theology, but in the context of the emergence of the new methods and presuppositions of the Renaissance. This point is reinforced by a consideration of the hermeneutics of the early Lutheran and Reformed theologians, to be considered later. This also highlights the quite distinct origins of the ideas of the Lutheran Reformation, as will become clear in the following section.

146 It is not, however, clear whether Vermigli was a 'nominalist' in his logic and epistemology.
147 See John Patrick Donnelly, *Calvinism and Scholasticism in Vermigli's Doctrine of Man and Grace* (Leiden, 1976), pp. 125–9.

LATE MEDIEVAL THEOLOGY AND THE
ORIGINS OF THE LUTHERAN CHURCH

In turning to deal with the origins of the Lutheran Reformation, the primary consideration must be the question of the relationship of Martin Luther to late medieval thought. It is, however, important to appreciate from the outset that neither the intellectual origins of the Reformation as a whole, nor even those of the reforming theology within the Wittenberg theological faculty in the period 1515–19, can be discussed with exclusive reference to the question of the origins of Luther's theological insights. Assumptions of this sort are frequently implicit in the earlier literature, but the complexity of the situation at the time precludes such simplistic generalisations.[148] Nevertheless, the question of the origins of Luther's distinctive theology over the period 1513–19 is clearly of enormous interest, whatever the relation of this theology to the emergence of the Wittenberg Reformation must ultimately be acknowledged to be. The first consideration in this discussion is therefore the academic currents which Luther encountered during his theological education.

In 1505, Luther entered the Augustinian house at Erfurt, where he began the study of theology under the direction of his superiors in the Augustinian Order. Although Stange argued that the taking of such monastic orders would imply the recognition of the theological authority of Giles of Rome and Gregory of Rimini,[149] it is now recognized that this rests upon a simple misunderstanding.[150] However, in view of the fact that the *schola Augustiniana moderna* has now been identified and characterized as a significant theological current in the late medieval Augustinian Order, it might be thought that an excellent case may be made for Luther encountering such

---

148 Heiko A. Oberman, 'Headwaters of the Reformation: *Initia Lutheri – Initia Reformationis*', in *Luther and the Dawn of the Modern Era*, ed. H. A. Oberman (Leiden, 1974), pp. 40–88.

149 Stange, 'Über Luthers Beziehung zur Theologie seines Ordens', p. 578, where it is argued that Jerome Dungersheim's statement 'Egydius Rhomanus ordinis heremitarum s. Augustini, quem et Luther professus est', implies that Luther vowed canonical obedience to the teachings of Giles of Rome.

150 Heinrich Hermelink, *Die theologische Fakultät in Tübingen vor der Reformation 1477–1534* (Tübingen, 1906), p. 95 n.1, where it is pointed out that Dungersheim was merely noting that Giles of Rome and Luther both belonged to the same monastic Order (in other words, the antecedent to *quem* is *ordo*, rather than *Egydius Rhomanus*).

currents, either at Erfurt or Wittenberg, and appropriating and shaping them for his own purposes. As Oberman states this suggestion:

> We can point to the *schola Augustiniana moderna*, initiated by Gregory of Rimini, reflected by Hugolino of Orvieto, apparently spiritually alive in the Erfurt Augustinian monastery, and transformed into a pastoral reform-theology by Staupitz, as the *occasio proxima* – not the *causa!* – for the inception of the *vera theologia* at Wittenberg.[151]

This suggestion is clearly of considerable importance, and requires careful evaluation. In what follows, I shall suggest that no case of any substance may be made for Luther having encountered such an Augustinian school at any point prior to 1519.

Although it is clear that Luther began his theological studies under the guidance of Erfurt Augustinian masters, there is no evidence to connect these masters with the *schola Augustiniana moderna*. As Hermelink pointed out in a seminal essay, there is evidence that the theologians of religious orders tended to be influenced by theological currents prevalent in their local university. Thus at Cologne, where the university was dominated by the *via antiqua* in the early sixteenth century, the local Dominican theologians appear to have regarded Thomas Aquinas as their master, whereas in Vienna and Erfurt, where the *via moderna* was dominant, they recognized the rival authority of William of Ockham.[152] A similar observation may be made concerning the Augustinian house at Erfurt, in which the influence of the *via moderna* is evident.[153] Thus Luther's teachers Johannes Nathin and Bartholomaus Arnoldi of Usingen were both noted exponents of the *via moderna*. Arnoldi's doctrine of justification in particular is practically indistinguishable from that of Gabriel Biel.[154]

Luther had studied within the faculty of arts at Erfurt prior to entering the local Augustinian priory, and would thus almost certainly have encountered both Arnoldi and Jodocus Trutvetter at this earlier

151 Oberman, 'Headwaters of the Reformation', p. 82.

152 Hermelink, *Die theologische Fakultät*, pp. 95–6. Cf. Gabriel, '"Via antiqua" and "via moderna"', p. 443.

153 Wolfgang Urban, 'Die 'via moderna' an der Universität Erfurt am Vorabend der Reformation', in *Gregor von Rimini: Werk und Wirkung bis zur Reformation*, ed. H. A. Oberman (Berlin/New York, 1981), pp. 311–30.

154 Oberman, *Harvest of Medieval Theology*, pp. 178–81.

stage.[155] The influence of both these representatives of the *via moderna* upon the Erfurt faculty of arts was considerable, particularly after the celebrated 'quodlibetal disputation' of 1497, generally regarded as marking a point of transition in the history of that faculty.[156] The influence of the *via moderna* upon Luther while at Erfurt is further indicated by the fact that Luther later frequently demonstrated first-hand familiarity with Gabriel Biel's *Lectura super canonem missae* and *Collectorium circa quattuor sententiarum libros*, both of which he would have encountered while studying theology at the Erfurt priory. In marked contrast, Luther does notappear to have encountered the writings of Gregory of Rimini until 1519[157] – a serious difficulty for those who suggest that he encountered a school of thought based upon Gregory's writings at this early stage.

In the autumn of 1508, Luther arrived at Wittenberg to take up the chair of moral philosophy within the university faculty of arts. A major alteration to the statutes of that faculty had taken place earlier that year, under the supervision of Christoph Scheurl. From its foundation, Wittenberg demonstrated a marked bias towards the *via antiqua*. Thus in the *Rotulus* of May 1507, lectures within the faculty of arts were carefully distinguished on the basis of whether they were *in via sancti Thomae* or *in via Scoti*.[158] Thus in the important contemporary dialogue of Andreas Meinhardi, we find reference to both major schools of the *via antiqua*, but no reference is made to any factions associated with the *via moderna*.[159] The tension between *via antiqua* and *via moderna*, so characteristic of many German universities in the late fifteenth century, does not appear to have surfaced at Wittenberg in the first five years of its existence. This situation, however, appears to have altered in 1508 – the year of Luther's arrival.

In the autumn of 1507, Christoph Scheurl was succeeded as rector

---

155 For background material, see Nicolaus Paulus, *Der Augustiner Bartholomäus von Usingen, Luthers Lehrer und Gegner* (Freiburg, 1893); Nikolaus Härung, *Die Theologie des Erfurter Augustiner-Eremiten Bartholomäus von Usingen* (Limburg, 1939); Gustav Plitt, *Jodocus Trutfetter von Eisenach der Lehrer Luthers in seinem Wirken geschildert* (Erlangen, 1876).

156 Urban, '"Via moderna" an der Universität Erfurt', pp. 315–19.

157 See the careful study of Leif Grane, 'Gregor von Rimini und Luthers Leipziger Disputation', *Studia Theologica* 22 (1968), pp. 29–49.

158 For example, those of Karlstadt and Amsdorf: Friedensburg, *Urkundenbuch der Universität Wittenberg I*, p. 15.

159 Andreas Meinhardi, *Dialogues illustrate ac augustissime urbis Albiorenae vulgo Wittenberg dicte* (Leipzig), 1508), chapter 15 'Reinhard: Cuius opinio verior, Divi Thome an subtilissime domini Scoti? Meinhard: Uterque fundatas habe rationes.' I owe this reference to Dr Martin Treu (Halle).

of the University of Wittenberg by Jodocus Trutvetter, who had recently left Erfurt. The arrival of so noted a *modernus* – who regarded Jean Buridan and Gabriel Biel as his mentors[160] – at Wittenberg, along with his elevation to the prestigious position of rector, suggests that the scene was set for a challenge to be posed to the prevailing ascendancy of the *via antiqua*. This challenge appears to have been laid down in the revised statutes for the faculty of arts of 1508. The new *statuta collegii artistarum* defined three *viae* whose methods and doctrines members of the faculty of arts were permitted to teach. In addition to the two main *viae* of the *via antiqua* (that is, *via Thomae* and *via Scoti*), a third *via* is specified: the *via Gregorii*.[161] It is clear that the reference is to Gregory of Rimini – but are we to understand this as a reference to the *via moderna*, or the *schola Augustiniana moderna*?

In an important essay, Oberman argued that the statutes of 1508 established the presence of the *schola Augustiniana moderna* within the Wittenberg faculty of arts.[162] The implications of this suggestion are considerable, in that the origins of Luther's reforming theology could be investigated with reference to an academic Augustinianism newly established at Wittenberg. In my opinion Oberman's suggestion cannot be sustained, and the older view – that *via Gregorii* is simply a synonym for the *via moderna*[163] – is essentially correct. The following points seem to be conclusive.

First, the *via moderna* was known by various synonyms at the time. Thus at Heidelberg, it was referred to as the *via Marsiliana*, after Marsilius of Inghen.[164] It is interesting to note that Marsilius refers to Gregory as *magister noster*,[165] indicating the affinity between the two thinkers, and their claims to represent the *via moderna*. The growing recognition of the points of contact between Gregory and Gabriel Biel should also be noted in this connection.[166]

160 F. W. Kampschulte, *Die Universität Erfurt in ihrem Verhältnis zu dem Humanismus und der Reformation I: Der Humanismus* (Trier, 1858), pp. 43–5.

161 *Statuta* cap. 3, 5; Friedensburg, *Urkundenbuch* pp. 53, 56. An earlier version of these statutes is based upon a single source, in which references to *Gregorius* were replaced with *Guilelmus*: Theodor Muther, *Die Wittenberger Universität- und Fakultätsstatuten von Jahre MDVIII* (Halle, 1867), pp. 41, 45.

162 Oberman, 'Headwaters of the Reformation'. But see note 170 below.

163 See, e.g., Karl Bauer, *Die Wittenberger Universitätstheologie und die Anfänge der Deutschen Reformation* (Tübingen, 1928), p. 9, n.4; Franz Ehrle, *Der Sentenzenkommentar Peters von Candia, des Pisaner Papstes Alexanders V* (Münster, 1925), p. 233.

164 Ritter, *Studien zur Spätscholastik I*, p. 46.

165 Ritter, *Studien zur Spätscholastik I*, p. 11 n.4; p. 38, n.3.

166 Urban, "Via Gregorii' in Forschung und Quellen', pp. 84–100.

Second, there are well-established precedents for universities adopting the practice of defining three *viae*, of which two represent the *via antiqua*, and the third the *via moderna*. An excellent example is provided by Paris, which stipulated that members of the university faculty of arts could teach according to *via sancti Thomae, via Scoti et via nominalium*.[167] Significantly, two doctors are noted in connection with the *via nominalium*: William of Ockham and Gregory of Rimini.[168] A reference to the *via Gregorii*, in addition to the *via Thomae* and *via Scoti*, would appear to suggest that the *via moderna* is intended.

Third, Christoph Scheurl himself appears to have been aware of one major academic school, in addition to the *via Thomae* and *via Scoti*, and to have regarded Jodocus Trutvetter as its representative at Wittenberg. Thus in a letter of 12 August 1513, he refers to Trutvetter as *modernorum princeps*,[169] clearly implying his affinity with – and, indeed, local pre-eminence within – the *via moderna*. In view of the fact that Trutvetter was rector of the university at the time the revisions were being drawn up, and a close personal friend of Scheurl (evident from their correspondence), the possibility that Scheurl intended the *via* associated with Trutvetter to be permitted within the faculty of arts can hardly be overlooked.

Fourth, it must be remembered that these statutes pertain to the faculty of *arts*, not *theology*. It has been emphasized in the present chapter that, viewed from the standpoint of the subject-matter of the faculty of arts, the methods and views of the *via moderna* and *schola Augustiniana* are practically indistinguishable (so that Gregory may legitimately be referred to as *antesignanus nominalistarum*). A reference to Gregory within the context of the curriculum of the faculty of *arts* concerns his *epistemology*, not his *soteriology*. The soteriological differences which are so evident between Gregory of Rimini and Pierre d'Ailly or Gabriel Biel would not have been encountered in this context.

It would therefore appear reasonable to suggest that Luther went to Wittenberg, possibly as a representative of the *via moderna*, to a university faculty of arts which had recently (and belatedly, by the

---

167 Villoslada, *Universidad de Paris*, p. 76.
168 Villoslada, *Universidad de Paris*, p. 118.
169 *Christoph Scheurl's Briefbuch: Ein Beitrag zur Geschichte der Reformation und ihre Zeit*, ed. F. von Soden and J. K. F. Knaake (2 vols: Potsdam, 1867–72), vol. 1, no. 80; pp. 123–5. The term *modernus* was not, it should be noted, generally used in the sense of 'a *temporally recent* writer' (the term *recencior* generally being used for this purpose), but was a technical term for the 'post-realist' or 'non-realist' school.

standards of the day) recognized this *via*. The suggestion that *via Gregorii* is a synonym for *schola Augustiniana moderna* does not appear to be justified by the evidence.[170] This does not, however, permit us to conclude that Luther did not encounter the *schola Augustiniana moderna* at Wittenberg: as Oberman reminds us, we have to contend with the possibility that Luther encountered precisely this movement in the person of Johannes von Staupitz.

Three major difficulties attend this suggestion. First, it is impossible to establish the precise nature of Staupitz' influence upon Luther with any degree of certainty.[171] A number of factors conspire to cause this difficulty. Staupitz' influence over Luther appears to have been at its greatest in the period 1510–12, for which we have practically no literary evidence relating to either individual. There is no surviving literary evidence to indicate that Luther ever heard Staupitz preach or lecture, let alone to indicate the influence which the latter might thence have exercised over the former. This influence appears to have been exercised through private pastoral conversations, to which no third party was privy. The absence of such minor Boswells is amply rectified with the *Table-Talk*: however, in that much of this material is fragmentary and unreliable, it would be unwise to base any judgement upon its tantalizing *dicta*, many of which are clearly confused. Thus, for example, Luther seems to minimize in a defensive manner his debts to the literary researches of humanism, and particularly Erasmus, by emphasizing his obligation to Staupitz.[172] There is also every possibility that this evidence is seriously distorted, either through the inaccuracies of those who jotted down (and subsequently occasionally embellished!) Luther's comments, or though the effects of the passage of time on Luther's memory of events, or perception of their significance. The *Table-Talk*, it must be remembered, dates from a quarter of a century after the period when Staupitz exercised pastoral oversight over Luther.

Second, no significant dependence of Luther upon Staupitz may be demonstrated on the basis of a point-by-point comparison of their

170 Recently, Oberman appears to have withdrawn this suggestion: *Werden und Wertung der Reformation*, p. 434 contains a reference to the *via Gregorii*, not noted in his index, which concedes the identity of *via Gregorii* and *via moderna*: 'Die in Heidelberg vertretene Lehrrichtung der *via moderna* wird als *via Marsilii* bezeichnet, wie 1508 in Wittenberg, wo im Anschluß an Gregor von Rimini die *via moderna* als *via Gregorii* Eingang in die Statuten findet.' This revision is not reflected in his discussion of the *via Gregorii* earlier in the work: pp. 91; 131 n.172.

171 For a careful study, see Steinmetz, *Luther and Staupitz*, pp. 3–34.

172 For example, WATr 1.173 'Ex Erasmo nihil habeo. Ich hab al mein ding von Doctor Staupitz.'

writings for the period 1512–19. Oberman's suggestion that Staupitz mediated a late medieval Augustinian tradition to Luther; Bauer's suggestion that what was mediated was a hermeneutical programme; Bizer's thesis concerning a doctrine of justification – all must be deemed to rest upon quite insufficient evidence.[173] Luther appears to have exhibited a remarkable degree of independence in all these matters from Staupitz, if he was influenced by him at all. It is certainly true that Luther developed certain themes which may have originated from Staupitz – such as the recognition of the pastoral significance of the wounds of Christ, and the insight that penance begins with the love of God – but these were commonplaces in much late medieval thought, and are perhaps more appropriately designated as 'spirituality', rather than 'theology', and not as specific insights of the *schola Augustiniana moderna*. These themes in themselves cannot be regarded as establishing the intellectual origins of Luther's reforming theology.

Finally, the question must be asked whether Staupitz can in any sense be regarded as a representative of the *schola Augustiniana moderna*. Although this assumption is implicit in Oberman's thesis, it cannot be sustained on the basis of the evidence available. In his writings, Staupitz does not refer to any theologians usually held to be associated with this school – such as Gregory of Rimini. Indeed, where he does refer to Augustinian theologians, he seems to demonstrate a distinct preference for the earlier Augustinian tradition, associated with Giles of Rome, suggesting that he is, if anything, a representative of the *schola Aegidiana*, rather than the *schola Augustiniana moderna*.[174]

On the basis of considerations such as those which we have outlined above, Luther's relationship to the 'medieval Augustinian tradition' may be summarized as follows. Although there are excellent reasons for suggesting that a distinctive school of thought – which is now generally designated the *schola Augustiniana moderna* – developed within the Augustinian Order in the late medieval period, the evidence suggests that Luther did not encounter such a school in either his Erfurt or Wittenberg periods. Thus there is no literary evidence of a direct connection between Luther and any representative of this school prior to 1519: although it is possible to place Luther and certain late medieval

173 See Steinmetz, *Luther and Staupitz*, p. 141.
174 Ernst Wolf, *Staupitz und Luther: Ein Beitrag zur Theologie des Johannes von Staupitz und deren Bedeutung für Luthers theologischen Werdegang* (Leipzig, 1927), pp. 23–5; David C. Steinmetz, *Misericordia Dei: The Theology of Johannes von Staupitz in its Late Medieval Setting* (Leiden, 1968), pp. 22–8; Steinmetz, *Luther and Staupitz*, pp. 27–31.

Augustinians in parallel columns at points, the necessary evidence for the *direct textual* influence of the latter upon the former is wanting.[175] Furthermore, the suggestion that the *schola Augustiniana moderna* was well established within the Augustinian Order by the sixteenth century does not permit us to conclude that it was represented at every Augustinian priory in Europe, such as that at Erfurt. Those Augustinian theologians who exercised the most influence over Luther in his formative years – such as Nathin, Arnoldi and Staupitz – may not have been typical of the currents of thought which some have suggested were prevalent within the late medieval Augustinian Order, but the fact remains that it was these theologians who exercised the greatest influence over the development of Luther's theology. There can be little doubt that Luther was influenced, at least to some extent, by theological currents and methods associated with his Order – but he appears to have encountered these in the form of specific personalities at Erfurt and Wittenberg, who simply were not typical of this school of thought which some have identified within the Augustinian Order at the time. Finally, certain points at which the influence of the *schola Augustiniana moderna* upon Luther's early theology might be detected may more plausibly be explained in terms of the direct influence of the *via moderna*. An excellent example of this difficulty is provided by Luther's critique of the implication of created habits of grace in justification.

The concept of a created habit of grace had its origins in the twelfth century,[176] and was understood as an ontologically necessary intermediate in the process of justification. In other words, the theologians of High Scholasticism, working on the basis of an ontological or *ex natura rei* concept of causality, argued that such a habit was a necessary intermediate in justification. As noted earlier, the later medieval period was characterised by a covenantal or *ex pacto divino* concept of causality, which rendered such habits unnecessary in justification. As a result, the theologians of both the *via moderna* and *schola Augustiniana moderna* treated created habits as unnecessary hypotheses in the theology of justification, so that their existence was deemed to be irrelevant, if they existed at all. Within the *schola Augustiniana moderna*, a tendency to shift the emphasis away from the work of created grace to that of

---

175 See the comments of Hubert Jedin on Stakemeier's attempt to relate Seripando to such theologians: *Theologische Revue* 37 (1938), pp. 425–30.
176 McGrath, *Iustitia Dei*, vol. 1, pp. 145–54.

uncreated grace (in other words, to the Holy Spirit) is particularly
evident, although not sufficiently marked to to distinguish this school
decisively from the *via moderna*.

Luther's marginal comments on the *Sentences* of Peter Lombard,
dating from 1509–10, demonstrate precisely this critique of the role
of created habits in justification.[177] For Luther, the concept of a
created habit of grace is both unhelpful and unnecessary: if the concept
is to be retained in any form, it should be understood to refer to the
bond of love which unites God to man – in other words, the uncreated
grace of the Holy Spirit: habitus autem est spiritus sanctus.[178]
Although this radical critique of the role of created habits in justification
was once thought to mark a complete break with the theology of the
medieval period, it is clear that Luther merely reproduced the common
late medieval attitude to such habits, characteristic of both the *via
moderna* and *schola Augustiniana moderna* alike. Far from marking a break
with the late medieval tradition, Luther demonstrates his continuity
with it at this point. It is not clear, however, whether Luther's critique
parallels that of the *via moderna* or *schola Augustiniana moderna*: his
comments are too compressed and concise to permit this potentially
important distinction to be made at this point. It is on the basis of
other considerations that the young Luther is to be identified as an
exponent of the soteriology of the *via moderna*.

The *pactum*-theology noted above (pp. 81–3) is a leading feature
of the soteriology of the *via moderna*, but not of the *schola Augustiniana
moderna*.[179] Two leading features of this theology may be noted. First,
a minimum precondition is specified for justification. Man must do
'his best (*quod in se est*)', and once this precondition has been met, God
is under a self-imposed obligation to reward him with the gift of justifying grace: facienti quod in se est, Deus non denegat gratiam.[180]
Second, the relation between man doing *quod in se est* and his subsequent justification is not a consequence of the necessary relationship
of these two entities, but is solely a consequence of the divine ordination
that they should be causally related in this way – in other words, this

---

177 See McGrath, *Luther's Theology of the Cross*, pp. 84–5. The older study of Paul Vignaux,
Luther Commentateur des Sentences (Livre I, Distinction XVII) (Paris, 1935), is still useful.
178 WA 9.44.1–4. Cf. 9.42.35–43.6.
179 McGrath, *Iustitia Dei*, vol. 1, pp. 65–7; 126–8.
180 For the origins and development of this axiom, see McGrath, *Iustitia Dei*, vol. 1,
pp. 83–91.

relationship is based upon an *ex pacto divino*, rather than *ex natura rei* causality.

Both these aspects of this *pactum*-theology are developed with characteristic brilliance in Luther's *Dictata super Psalterium* of 1513–15.[181] For example, five significant points of contact between Luther's soteriology and that of the *via moderna* may be demonstrated, including both those noted above.[182] Luther endorses the soteriological axiom of the *via moderna* – *facienti quod in se est, Deus non denegat gratiam* – on the basis of its covenantal foundations.[183] The only reason why grace and faith are implicated in justification is on account of the divine covenant (*pactum*) with man.[184] Indeed, at times Luther seems to draw directly upon the statements of Gabriel Biel concerning the *pactum* between God and man.[185]

A further point of importance here concerns Luther's theological breakthrough, which was centred upon the question of the meaning of the phrase 'the righteousness of God'.[186] In his celebrated auto-biographical statement of 1545, Luther explains how he could not conceive how the concept of the 'righteousness of God (*iustitia Dei*)' could be thought of as gospel, in that it appeared to promise nothing but condemnation for the sinner.[187] Underlying Luther's statements is the concept of *iustitia Dei* associated with the *pactum*-theology of the *via moderna*:[188] the 'righteousness of God' is that (ultimately unknowable) divine quality which rewards the man who does *quod in se est* with justification, and punishes the man who does not. Luther's early difficulties with this concept were only resolved in 1515, when he abandoned the soteriological framework of the *via moderna*: his earlier wrestlings with the concept represent nothing more than attempts to

181 McGrath, *Luther's Theology of the Cross*, pp. 85–92.

182 McGrath, *Luther's Theology of the Cross*, p. 88, based on WA 4.261.32–9.

183 WA 4.262.4–7 'Hinc recte dicunt doctores, quod homini facienti quod in se est deus infallibiliter dat gratiam et licet non de condigno sese possit ad gratiam praeparare, quia est incomparabilis, tamen bene de congruo propter promissionem istam dei et pactum misericordia'.

184 WA 3.289.1–5.

185 As noted, with documentation, by Oswald Bayer, *Promissio: Geschichte der reformatorischen Wende in Luthers Theologie* (Göttingen, 1971), pp. 129–32.

186 McGrath, *Luther's Theology of the Cross*, pp. 95–147, for a full critical discussion of this central question of Luther scholarship.

187 WA 54.185.12–186.21; English translation in McGrath, *Luther's Theology of the Cross*, pp. 95–8.

188 McGrath, *Luther's Theology of the Cross*, pp. 100–19; McGrath, *Iustitia Dei*, vol. 1, pp. 65–7; vol. 2, pp. 3–10.

clarify it within the context of that framework.[189] Luther's reference
to the views of the 'doctors who taught him' in the autobiographical
fragment is clearly a direct reference to the Erfurt *moderni*.

The evidence available concerning the continuity between Luther
and the *via moderna* can be summarized as follows. First, there is
unequivocal literary evidence to the effect that Luther was directly
dependent upon theologians of the *via moderna*, supremely Gabriel Biel.
Second, the soteriological framework which Luther employed in the
period 1513–15 is unquestionably that of the *via moderna*. This is
particularly clear from his use of the *pactum*-theology and the associated
concepts of *facere quod in se est* and *ex pacto divino* causality, and the
crucial concept of the 'righteousness of God'. Third, there are points in
Luther's later writings where he denounces the soteriological views of
the *via moderna*, occasionally adding that he once held such views himself,[190] where the views condemned are those he himself expounded
in the *Dictata super Psalterium*. Finally, there are more ambiguous
considerations – for example, the fact that his early teachers at Erfurt
were *moderni*, the possibility that Luther may to have gone to Wittenberg
as a representative of the *via moderna*, and the fact that his critique
of the role of created grace in justification may (but need not) parallel
that of the *via moderna*. The overall picture is that of a theologian
initially committed to the soteriology of the *via moderna*, who finally
broke free from it over a period of time. As such, the intellectual origins
of Luther's reforming theology may be stated with some confidence
to be linked with the theology of the *via moderna*.

This conclusion, if correct, is of considerable importance, in that
it suggests that Luther's theological breakthrough did not arise through
any fundamental *methodological* innovation, which could be ascribed
to the influence of humanism. As we shall indicate later, Luther's early
biblical hermeneutics are thoroughly medieval, and his theological
breakthrough cannot be correlated directly with any prior shift in his
hermeneutical presuppositions. There are reasons for suggesting that
Luther's theological breakthrough may parallel those of Augustine and
Thomas Aquinas before him – both of whom came to develop more
theocentric soteriologies for reasons which reflect an increased

189 A point which needs to be borne in mind when assessing the thesis that a breakthrough
took place during the exposition of Psalm 70 or 71, which is clearly not the case: McGrath,
Luther's Theology of the Cross, pp. 119–28.
190 The most important being WA 56.502.32–503.5. Cf. 56.382.26–7.

awareness of the priority of divine grace over human actions, rather than any fundamental methodological shift.[191] Thus it is significant that Luther occasionally refers to Augustine's account of his own theological breakthrough (contained in the eighth book of the *Confessions*) in the *Dictata super Psalterium*, apparently treating it as a paradigm for divine illumination.[192] Although the theological developments associated with Luther's early period are notoriously difficult to analyse, there are reasons for suggesting that Luther may have read the seminal anti-Pelagian writing of Augustine, *de spiritu de litera*, by late 1515,[193] and that this treatise probably at least catalysed Luther's soteriological deliberations, and may possibly even have informed them. It is certainly significant that Karlstadt, in turning (1516–17) to consider substantially the same soteriological questions as those which appear to have confronted Luther in the period 1513–15, chose to discuss them with reference to precisely this anti-Pelagian writing.[194] There are thus grounds for suggesting that the origins of the Wittenberg Reformation are linked to a rediscovery of Augustine, and an ensuing criticism *initially* of the soteriology of the *via moderna*, and *subsequently* of aspects of Augustine's theology of grace (particularly his views on the nature of justifying righteousness).[195] Luther appears to have taken several years to work fully through his initial theological insights, with the result that his theology over the period 1513–19 consists essentially of a programme of reworking (ultimately to reject) the soteriology of the *via moderna* in the light of his new insights.[196]

The intellectual origins of the Wittenberg Reformation are thus quite distinct from those of the Reformed church, as will become

191 On the background to these two figures, see T. Salguiero, *La doctrine de Saint Augustin sur la grâce d'après le traité à Simplicien* (Porto, 1925); Henri Bouillard, *Conversion et grâce chez Saint Thomas d'Aquin* (Paris, 1944); Gustaf Nygren, *Das Prädestinationsproblem in der Theologie Augustins* (Göttingen, 1956), pp. 41–8; McGrath, *Iustitia Dei*, vol. 1, pp. 24–5; 80–2; 85–6; 104–8.
192 See, e.g., WA 3.169.28–34; 3.535.20–2; 3.549.26–32. See A. Hamel, *Der junge Luther und Augustin* (2 vols: Gütersloh, 1934–5), vol. 1, pp. 157–62.
193 See C. Boyer, 'Luther et le "De spiritu et litera" de Saint Augustin', *Doctor Communis* 21 (1968), pp. 167–87; Leif Grane, *Modus loquendi theologicus: Luthers Kampf um die Erneuerung der Theologie (1515–1518)* (Leiden, 1975), pp. 65–6.
194 See E. Kähler, *Karlstadt und Augustin: Der Kommentar des Andreas Bodenstein von Karlstadt zu Augustins Schrift De spiritu et litera* (Halle, 1952); Ronald J. Sider, *Andreas Bodenstein von Karlstadt: The Development of His Thought 1517–1525* (Leiden, 1974), pp. 17–44. Sider fails to note the full extent of the continuity between Augustine and Karlstadt on justification: see McGrath, *Iustitia Dei*, vol. 2, pp. 20–2.
195 See McGrath, *Iustitia Dei*, vol. 2, pp. 1–25.
196 For a study of this process, see McGrath, *Luther's Theology of the Cross*, pp. 95–161.

increasingly clear when their hermeneutical methods are considered.
The leading members of the Wittenberg theological faculty over the
period 1513–18 were university theologians with well-established
affinities with the theological schools of the later medieval period.[197]
The origins of that Reformation concerned aspects of Augustine's
theology of grace, initially in relation to Luther's difficulties concerning
the 'righteousness of God', and subsequently in relation to Karlstadt's
critical study of the Augustinian provenance of late medieval soteriology, culminating in the 151 theses of April 1517. The origins of the
Lutheran Reformation thus differ from those of the Reformed church
in two central areas.

First, the Wittenberg theologians were primarily concerned with
soteriology, expressed in the doctrine of justification. Luther's personal
difficulties in this area may well have led to others, such as Karlstadt,
developing this concern. This interest in the doctrine of justification
is conspicuously absent from the first phase of the development of
Reformed theology:[198] indeed, as was noted in the previous chapter,
there are grounds for suggesting that the first Reformed theologians
may have developed a moralist doctrine of justification which was
potentially opposed to the theocentric soteriology being forged at
Wittenberg.

Second, the first period of the Wittenberg Reformation was characterized by a growing realization of the incompatibility of the *vera
theologia* and the soteriology of the *via moderna*. As a result, the emerging
vera theologia was increasingly articulated in conscious opposition to
that soteriology, as in Karlstadt's 151 theses of April 1517, or Luther's
Disputatio contra scholasticam theologiam of September of that year.
Whereas the early theologians of the Reformed church were equally
dismissive of scholastic theology, they felt under no obligation to
enter into a sustained debate with its representatives: as Zwingli's
Commentarius of 1525 indicates, it was deemed adequate to dismiss

---

197 Thus Amsdorf was a Scotist, and Karlstadt initially a neo-Thomist (before becoming a
Scotist): see R. Kolb, *Nikolaus von Amsdorf: Popular Polemics in the Preservation of Luther's Legacy*
(Nieuwkoop, 1978), p. 28; Kähler, *Karlstadt und Augustin*, 3.19–21 'quia sectam Capreolinam
et Scotisticam manifesta interpretatione successive profitebar'. On Capreolus and neo-Thomism,
to which Karlstadt here refers, see Martin Grabmann, 'Johannes Capreolus O.P., der 'Princeps
Thomistarum', und seine Stellung in der Geschichte der Thomistenschule', in idem, *Mittelalterliches
Geistesleben III*, ed. L. Ott (Munich, 1956), pp. 370–410.
198 See A. E. McGrath, 'Humanist Elements in the Reformed Doctrine of Justification', *ARG*
73 (1982), pp. 5–20.

the *theologastri* on Erasmian grounds. The direct and sustained engagement with the theology of the *via moderna* is a leading feature of the
early reforming theology of the Wittenberg faculty. The fact that the
Wittenberg reforming theology demonstrated both intellectual continuity and discontinuity with that of the later medieval period made
it imperative at the time that these discontinuities be identified and
defended. There are thus excellent reasons for suggesting that, in
regard to their motivation, methods and substance, the Lutheran and
Reformed theologies were quite distinct – a theme that will be returned
to later.

The last two chapters have been concerned with the identification
and evaluation of the influence of humanism and late medieval
theology upon the intellectual origins of the Reformation. It will be
clear that this influence extends to include theological sources and
methods. In the following chapters the changing attitudes towards
theological sources and methods in the late medieval period will be
considered, in order to establish the extent of the continuity between
this period and that of the Reformation.

4

Sources and Methods:
The Text of Scripture

The importance of Holy Scripture as a source of Christian theology
was universally recognized in the medieval period. Thomas Aquinas
spoke for the medieval tradition as a whole when he emphasized that
Christian theology was based upon revelation beyond the discoveries
of the natural sciences.[1] It is interesting to note that Thomas does
not deduce the necessity of revelation from man's sin or corruption,
but from the fact that this knowledge transcends man's natural capacities. Had this knowledge not been revealed to man through divine
intervention, it would have remained beyond his reach. Revelation
establishes the axiomatic points of departure for theological speculation, in much the same way as self-evident principles (*principia per se
nota*) do in the philosophical disciplines.[2] The source of this revelation is scripture, and Christian theology may thus be defined as 'Holy
Scripture received in a human intellect'.[3] For Thomas, *sacra doctrina*
and *sacra scriptura* are virtually synonymous, in that theology is essentially the clarification, vindication and transmission of the truth
revealed in scripture, through the *ratio* of the theologian. While
non-biblical terms and concepts may be used in this process of the
interpretation and explanation of scripture, these terms and concepts
must be chosen in such a manner that they fully express the 'sense' of

1 *Summa Theologiae* Ia q.1 a.1 'Necessarium igitur fuit, praeter philosophicas doctrinas, quae
per rationem investigantur, sacram doctrinam per revelationem haberi'. Cf. J.-F. Bonnefoy,
'La théologie comme science et l'explication de la foi selon saint Thomas d'Aquin', *EThL* 14
(1937), pp. 421–46; 15 (1938), pp. 491–516.
2 *Summa Theologiae* Ia q.1 a.8 'Haec doctrina non argumentatur ad sua principia probanda,
quae sunt articuli fidei, sed ex eis procedit ad aliquid aliud ostendendum'. On the developing
role of axioms in theological method, see Gillian R. Evans, 'Boethian and Euclidian Axiomatic
Method in the Theology of the Later Twelfth Century', *Archives Internationales d'Histoire des Sciences*
103 (1980), pp. 13–29.
3 E. Gilson, *Le Thomisme: Introduction au système de saint Thomas d'Aquin* (Paris, 2nd edn, 1922),
pp. 21–2. Cf. *Summa Theologiae* Ia q.1 a.2 'Revelatio divina...super quam fundatur sacra
scriptura seu doctrina'.

scripture.[4] The principle of confining theological argument to scripture as the source and norm of revealed truth thus functions as a formal methodological principle: for Thomas, theology is *doctrina quaedam secundum revelationem divinam*.[5] Despite the evident differences between Thomas and his contemporaries over many matters, they are united in their belief that Christian theology is ultimately nothing more and nothing less than the exposition of scripture.

On the basis of his understanding of the relationship of *scriptura* and *doctrina*, outlined above, Thomas is able to assert that scripture is the ground of faith, *fidei fundamentum*.[6] The certitude of faith is based upon the authority of scripture,[7] and this authority ultimately derives from the fact that it is God himself who is the author of scripture.[8] The canonical scriptures transmit the truth which men need to know if they are to be saved.[9] But although scripture is both normative, and in itself clear and sufficient as a basis of theology, it does not follow from this that the truth revealed within it is in any sense readily accessible: indeed, quite the reverse is the case.[10] Scripture requires reliable interpretation if it is to function as the foundation of Christian theology, in the manner suggested by Thomas. It is therefore evident that the medieval debate over the interpretation of scripture, considered in chapter 6, is of central importance to our study of the intellectual origins of the Reformation.

It will therefore be evident that the *content* of that theology will be determined by the prior understanding of the correct text of scripture, and the correct interpretation of that text. In other words, doctrine depends upon textual criticism, philology and biblical hermeneutics. Disagreement upon any of these matters, or developments relating to any of them over a period of time, is pregnant with a potential doctrinal pluralism. In the present and following chapters, we propose

4 A principle embodied in the famous statement of the *Prima Pars*: *Summa Theologiae* Ia q. 36 a.2 ad 2um 'De Deo dicere non debemus quod in sacra scriptura non invenitur vel per verba, vel per sensum'.

5 *Summa Theologiae* Ia q.1 a.1. Cf. Per Erik Persson, 'Le plan de la Somme théologique et le rapport 'ratio-revelatio', *Revue philosophique de Louvain* 56 (1958), pp. 545–72.

6 *Summa Theologiae* IIIa q.55 a.5 '...per auctoritatem sacrae scripturae, quae est fidei fundamentum'.

7 *Summa Theologiae* IIaIIae q.110 a.3 ad 1um.

8 *Summa Theologiae* Ia q.1 a.10 'auctor sacrae scripturae est Deus'. Cf. Gillian R. Evans, *The Language and Logic of the Bible: The Road to Reformation* (Cambridge, 1985), pp. 7–14.

9 *Quaestiones quodlibetales*, q.7 a.14. Cf. *Summa Theologiae* Ia q.1 a.8 ad 2um 'Innititur enim fides nostra revelationi Apostolis et Prophetis factae, qui canonicos libros scripserunt'.

10 See, e.g., *Summa Theologiae* Ia q.9 a.9 ad 2um; IIaIIae q.1 a.9 ad 1um.

to consider the nature and extent of diversity of opinion on such matters in the later medieval period. The discussion opens with the question of the text of scripture.

The medieval period based its scriptural exegesis upon the Vulgate version of the bible.[11] Despite a number of moves in the thirteenth century to revise this translation against the Hebrew and Greek originals,[12] the Vulgate text continued to be the basis of medieval theological speculation. In part, this reluctance to revise the Vulgate arose from the inability of most medieval theologians to deal with the Hebrew language: Andrew of St Victor is perhaps the most important biblical commentator of the twelfth century on account of his use of the Hebrew original of the Old Testament, although he was obliged to seek the assistance of Hebrew scholars among the Jews in dealing with more puzzling phrases.[13] Despite this flirtation with the Old Testament in its original language, there does not appear to have been any attempt to go behind the Vulgate to the original Hebrew and Greek texts.

Such was the importance attached to the Vulgate text that by the middle of the fourteenth century Latin had practically come to have the status of a sacred language, along with Hebrew and Greek. A number of factors appear to have converged to bring about the medieval reluctance to study scripture in the vernacular. (The use of the term 'reluctance' is considered: no universal or absolute prohibition of the translation of the scriptures into the vernacular was ever issued by a medieval pope or council, nor was any similar prohibition directed against the use of such translations by clergy or laity.) We have already noted Thomas Aquinas' insistence that the interpretation of scripture was complex, beyond the competence of the masses. It was believed that the translation of scripture into the vernacular would open the way to serious misinterpretation of the text. The medieval

11 Occasionally, however, medieval commentators abandoned the Vulgate version of the Psalter in favour of Jerome's later *Psalterium iuxta Hebraicam veritatem*. An example of this is provided by Herbert of Bosham's commentary on the Psalter, discovered by N. R. Ker in the library of St Paul's Cathedral, London: see Beryl Smalley, 'A Commentary by Herbert of Bosham on the Hebraica', *RThAM* 18 (1951), pp. 29–65.

12 Evans, *The Language and Logic of the Bible: The Road to Reformation*, pp. 70–3.

13 See Beryl Smalley, 'Andrew of St Victor, Abbot of Wigmore', *RThAM* 10 (1938), pp. 358–73; Smalley., 'The School of Andrew of St Victor', *RThAM* 11 (1939), pp. 145–67. Peter the Chanter should also be noted in this context: see Gilbert Dahan, 'Les interpretations juives dans les commentaires du pentateuqe de Pierre le Chantre', in *The Bible in the Medieval World*, ed. Katherine Walsh and Diana Wood (Studies in Church History: Subsidia 4: Oxford, 1985), pp. 131–55.

hostility towards the reading of the bible in the vernacular may possibly be traced to a situation which arose in the diocese of Metz, probably in June 1199. The bishop of Metz, in a letter to Innocent III, reported that a large group of laymen and women were gathering regularly in secret to study the gospels and letters of Paul in their native language, and requested guidance on how to proceed.[14] It is clear from Innocent's reply to the bishop that he regards the real threat posed by this activity as the usurpation of the office of preaching, a matter in which they should be taken to task (*in eo tamen apparent merito arguendi*). The real objection to the practice lies in its potential implications for the doctrine and order of the church, through the usurpation of a clerical role, rather than in a deeper knolwedge of the text of the scripture.

The influence of the bible upon western European society – such as in the concept of established government, in which the Old Testament concept of kingship appears to have been regarded as paradigmatic – from the ninth to the late eleventh centuries is well established, as is the fact that its *direct* influence diminished considerably from the twelfth to the fourteenth centuries.[15] Nevertheless, the *indirect* influence of the bible over this later period was considerable, in that this influence was mediated through canon law and scholastic theology.[16] One reason for the diminution of the direct influence of the bible in matters of theology and canon law appears to have been the tendency to approach the biblical text itself indirectly, through a filter of glosses – the *Glossa Ordinaria*.

Although this gloss had traditionally been regarded as the work of the ninth century monk Walafrid Strabo,[17] it is now known that the compilation of the work represented an important milestone in the development of later twelfth century theological method. In effect,

---

14 See Leonard E. Boyle, 'Innocent III and Vernacular Versions of Scripture', in *The Bible in the Medieval World*, ed. Katherine Walsh and Diana Wood, pp. 97–107, with valuable criticism of the earlier study of Margaret Deanesley, *The Lollard Bible and Other Medieval Biblical Versions* (Cambridge, 1920). For the correspondence between the bishop and Innocent III over this matter, see *Die Register Innocenz III: Pontifikatsjahr 1199/1200*, ed. O. Hagenreder *et al.* (Rome, 1979), pp. 271–6.
15 The best study of this phenomenon remains Beryl M. Smalley, *The Study of the Bible in the Middle Ages* (Oxford, 3rd edn, 1983).
16 The virtual absence of any influence of exegetical considerations upon this later period is well illustrated from the role of the lawyers in the Becket dispute: see Beryl M. Smalley, *The Becket Conflict and the Schools: A Study of Intellectuals in Politics in the Twelfth Century* (Oxford, 1973).
17 On whom see J. Blic, 'L'oeuvre exègètique de Walafrid Strabon et la *Glossa Ordinaria*', *RThAM* 16 (1949), pp. 5–28.

the *Glossa Ordinaria* may be regarded as a composite running commentary upon the text of the bible, characterized by its brevity, clarity and authoritativeness, drawing upon the chief sources of the patristic period. The *Glossa* seems to have been largely the work of Anselm of Laon, although other major contributors included Berengar of Tours, Manegold of Lautenbach, Lambert of Utrecht and Gilbert the Universal.[18] So influential did this commentary become that, by the end of the twelfth century, much biblical commentary and exegesis was reduced to restating the comments of the gloss. It is this feature of the biblical commentaries of Stephen Langton – the mere restating of 'extracts from the gloss' – which eventually led to the unravelling of the mystery of the origins of the *Glossa Ordinaria*.[19] But it will be obvious that the contemporary reader of scripture tended to approach the text of scripture indirectly, through the interpretative gloss, encountering directly the accumulated wisdom of previous interpreters, rather than the text itself.

Although the translation of the bible into the vernacular – such as the Wycliffite versions of the fourteenth century[20] – is often regarded as a turning point in the medieval interpretation of the bible, there are reasons for questioning this judgement. Although the struggle to make such translations available to a wider audience was a significant element in pre-Reformation religious polemic – as in early fifteenth century England – their theological significance should not be exaggerated. Such translations would ultimately depend upon philological techniques such as those that would be developed in the Italian Renaissance. Without direct access to the original Hebrew and Greek texts of the Old and New Testament, and without the philological techniques necessary to translate them, vernacular versions of scripture

18 See Beryl Smalley, 'Gilbertus Universalis, Bishop of London (1128–34) and the Problem of the *Glossa Ordinaria*', *RThAM* 7 (1935), pp. 235–62; 8 (1936), pp. 24–46; Smalley, 'La *Glossa Ordinaria*, quelques prédécesseurs d'Anselme de Laon', *RThAM* 9 (1937), pp. 365–400; Smalley, 'Les commentaires bibliques de l'époque romane: glose ordinaire et gloses périmées', *Cahiers de Civilisation Médiévale* 4 (1961), pp. 23–46'; E. Bertola, 'La *Glossa Ordinaria* biblica ed i suoi problemi', *RThAM* 45 (1978), pp. 34–78.

19 See the seminal study of Beryl Smalley and Georges Lacombe, 'Studies on the Commentaries of Cardinal Stephen Langton', *Archives d'histoire doctrinale et littéraire du moyen âge* 5 (1931), pp. 1–220.

20 See Henry Hargreaves, 'The Wycliffite Versions', in *Cambridge History of the Bible* (3 vols: Cambridge, 1963–70), vol. 2, pp. 387–415. The continued use of glosses is significant, in that it points to a reluctance to allow a *direct* engagement with the text: see Hargreaves., 'Popularising Biblical Scholarship: The Role of the Wycliffite *Glossed Gospels*', in *The Bible and Medieval Culture*, ed. W. Lourdaux and D. Verhelst (Louvain, 1979), pp. 171–89.

could not hope to achieve any authoritative status, despite their evident use in popularizing anti-establishment views. These techniques would be developed and increasingly refined in the Italian Renaissance of the later fifteenth century, and be put to uses of considerable theological significance in the sixteenth century. Yet, perhaps curiously, those who then developed these techniques appear to have done so for reasons that had little direct bearing upon matters of theology: the humanists seem to have regarded these methods as an essential aspect of their broad educational and cultural programme, and, with perhaps occasional exceptions, not to have noticed (or chosen to overlook) their potential theological significance, when applied to the New Testament text. It is to a consideration of the humanist movement of the fifteenth century that we must now turn.

It is clear that the humanists of the Renaissance, in their search for written and spoken eloquence, considered in an earlier chapter, turned to the acknowledged masters of antiquity in order to learn from them. The high regard in which Cicero's *Orationes* were held led to intense study of his works – to which Bartolommeo della Fonte's orations bear eloquent witness.[21] This interest in the literature of classical antiquity was not regarded as an end in itself, but as a means to the end of *eloquentia*. Thus Jerome, Augustine, Arnobius and Cyprian – and especially Lactantius – were regarded as models of Christian *eloquentia*,[22] whilst scripture itself was nothing less than *eloquentia vera theologiae*.[23] For the humanist, it was therefore imperative to turn (or *re*turn) to the sources of antiquity, whether they were pagan or Christian, in order to learn from them. The renewed interest in classical philology was particularly associated with the need to engage directly with the classics of antiquity, both Greek and Latin. The slogan *ad fontes* came to embody the cultural and educational programme of the Renaissance: the direct return to the writings of the classical period – whether secular or sacred – in order to benefit from their eloquence.

---

21 On the influence of Cicero upon the Latin usage of the early sixteenth century, see Angiola Gambaro, 'Il Ciceronianismus di Erasmo da Rotterdam', *Scritti Vari I* (Turin, 1950), pp. 129–84; Giorgio Petrocci, *La dottrina linguistica del Bembo* (Messina, 1959). On Renaissance Ciceronianism in general, see Giuseppe Toffanin, *Storia letteraria d'Italia: Il Cinquecento* (Milan, 6th edn, 1960), pp. 34–81.
22 See, e.g., Erasmus' *Antibarbari: Opera Omnia*, ed. J. Leclerc (Leiden, 1703), vol. 10, cols. 1691–1743.
23 Erasmus, *Opera*, vol. 6, col. 335C.

The immediate results of this new interest in *eloquentia vera theologiae* will be obvious. First, there was a new interest in studying both scripture and the fathers directly, rather than through a 'filter' of glosses and commentaries. Second, there was a growing recognition of the need to engage directly with both scripture and the fathers in their original languages, rather than in Latin translation. The new interest in philology thus came to be linked with a concern for the accurate original text of scripture, and its subsequent translation. In both these areas, the influence of Florentine humanism was decisive. This point was acknowledged by the more humanist among the Reformers. Thus Philip Melanchthon argued that Florence attracted Greek scholars, exiled after the fall of Constantinople, and by doing so, rescued the Greek language from oblivion. Furthermore, the new interest in the study of the Greek language at Florence led to a more informed use of the Latin language – which had threatened to degenerate into some form of barbarism – as well as providing a key to the study of the bible in its original language.[24] In his *Oratio de studiis linguae graecae* (1549), Melanchthon emphasized that it was impossible to return *ad fontes* without a knowledge of Greek: it is, according to Melanchthon, the language most capable of expressing the highest truths, and both the New Testament and the earliest patristic works (Melanchthon's theological source-texts) were written in it.[25] In order to engage directly with scripture, and to hear the living voices of Paul and the apostles, it was essential to study Greek.[26] In this, Melanchthon spoke as much as a representative of the humanist tradition as a Reformer, in that the two schools – if, indeed, they could be distinguished at all – converged in their programme of returning directly to the original texts of the New Testament in its original language. In fact, however, the Florentine Renaissance of the *Quattrocento* was somewhat slow to realize the importance of the Greek language, perhaps through the influence of men such as Lorenzo da Monaci.[27]

---

24 Melanchthon, *In laudem novae scholae*; *Werke*, ed. H. Engelland and R. Nürnberger (3 vols: Tübingen, 1952–61), vol. 3, p. 67. Melanchthon suggests that a barbaric language inevitably leads to barbaric modes of thought: p. 146.
25 Melanchthon, *Werke*, vol. 3, pp. 135–46. For the relation between scripture and the patristic testimony in Melanchthon's theological method, see Peter Fraenkel, *Testimonia Patrum: The Function of the Patristic Argument in the Theology of Philip Melanchthon* (Geneva, 1961), pp. 162–252; 338–62.
26 Melanchthon, *Werke*, vol. 3, p. 140.
27 See Deno Geanokoplos, 'The Discourse of Demetrius Chalcondyles on the Inauguration of Greek Studies at the University of Padua in 1463', *Studies in the Renaissance* 21 (1974), pp. 119–44.

Valla's contribution to the serious study of Greek lay chiefly in his argument, justified by appeal to classical Latin writers, that a knowledge of Greek was necessary if the Latin language itself was to be properly understood and exploited.[28]

The study of Hebrew, although undertaken sporadically in the twelfth century, became a more serious proposition through the researches of Giovanni Pico della Mirandola in the final quarter of the *Quattrocento*, although it does not seem to have been regarded as of equal value as the study of Greek. Pico della Mirandola is reported to have found an unacceptably high number of translation errors in the Vulgate version of the Old Testament, and thus to have demonstrated the need for its revision.

It is at this point that consideration of the impact of printing upon the intellectual origins of the Reformation may most conveniently be introduced. That the introduction of printing was at least a catalyst, and probably also an agent, of intellectual and social change is beyond dispute.[29] The role of the printing presses of Europe in the dissemination of the ideas of the Reformation is too well known to require further discussion at this point: it is merely necessary to draw attention to the role of the medium in relation to the origins, rather than merely the propagation, of the Reformation.[30] Thus the establishment of presses capable of handling Hebrew characters paved the way for a general familiarity among humanists with that language, and hence more accurate editions and translations of the Old Testament itself. Initially, these presses were located solely in the Iberian peninsula and Italy.[31] Although the production of Hebrew printed works was under way in Italy by 1475, and quite extensive a decade later,[32] the rise of anti-Jewish feeling led to the suspension of production

28 Sarah S. Gravalle, 'Lorenzo Valla's Comparison of Latin and Greek and the Humanist Background', *BHR* 44 (1982), pp. 269–89.

29 The most extensive documentation may be found in Elizabeth L. Eisenstein, *The Printing Press as an Agent of Change* (2 vols: Cambridge, 1979). On the role of printing in the propagation of the Reformation, see Louise W. Holborn, 'Printing and the Growth of a Protestant Movement in Germany from 1517 to 1524', *Church History* 11 (1942), pp. 123–37.

30 The impact of printing upon New Testament scholarship, of considerable importance in this respect, is discussed by Eisenstein, *The Printing Press*, vol. 1, pp. 329–67.

31 Of those works printed prior to 1501, only one is presently known to have been printed elsewhere (at Constantinople, in 1493): see A. K. Offenberg, 'The First Printed Book Produced at Constantinople', *Studia Rosenthalia: Tijdschrift voor joodse wetenschap et geschiedenis in Nederland* 3 (1969), pp. 96–112. A recent estimate places the number of such works at 175: *Encyclopaedia Judaica* (16 vols: Jerusalem, 1971), vol. 8, cols. 1319–44.

32 See Adriaan K. Offenberg, 'Untersuchungen zum hebräischen Buchdruck in Neapel um

of such works, except in the kingdom of Naples. Here the establishment of a sizeable Jewish community led to the issuing of licences *ad stampandum libros to magister Jacob hebreo* and *magister Josep hebreo* on 18 March 1487,[33] leading to considerable expansion and development of such printing techniques. It was merely a matter of time before the necessary technology found its way to northern Europe.

Although the earliest published guide to the Hebrew language aimed primarily at Gentiles appears to have been Konrad Pellikan's *De modo legendi et intelligendi Hebraeum* (1504),[34] the most celebrated such introduction to the language remains Reuchlin's *De rudimentis Hebraicis* (1506). For Reuchlin, the task of sacred philology was to enable the reader to encounter the Old Testament text in the very words with which God himself had spoken it (*quale os dei locutum est*). Having mastered the Hebrew language – apparently through studying the medieval Jewish grammarians – during a period spent in late Renaissance Italy, Reuchlin returned to northern Europe to write an introduction to the language which would permit direct access to the original of the Old Testament text.[35] An edition of the seven penitential psalms followed in 1512, allowing the reader without access to manuscripts to master some Hebrew texts of the Old Testament. Among those grateful readers was Martin Luther, who purchased a copy of *De rudimentis* before leaving Erfurt for Wittenberg in 1508. The increasing skill with which Luther applied his knowledge of Hebrew to his biblical exegesis over the period 1513–18 is an adequate testimony to the significance of this development,[36] even if it is possible to argue that Luther's theological breakthrough was not a direct result of this facility. The impact of Reuchlin's *De rudimentis* at Wittenberg was, however, by no means restricted to Luther. Attention has recently been drawn to the influence of this work upon Karlstadt's *Distinctiones Thomistarum*, published on 30 December 1507, a year after

---

1490', in *Buch und Text im 15. Jahrhundert*, ed. Lotte Hellinga and Helmar Härtel (Hamburg 1978), pp. 129–41.

33 Offenberg, 'Untersuchungen', p. 132.

34 For Pellikan's work on the rabbinical biblical commentaries, see Christoph Zürcher, *Konrad Pellikans Wirken in Zürich 1526–1556* (Zurich, 1975), pp. 153–236.

35 See, e.g., M. Brod, *Johannes Reuchlin und sein Kampf: Eine historische Monographie* (Stuttgart, 1965), for further details.

36 See the three seminal studies of Siegfried Raeder, *Das Hebräische bei Luther untersucht bis zum Ende der ersten Psalmenvorlesung* (Tübingen, 1961); *Die Benutzung des masoretischen Textes bei Luther in der Zeit zwischen der ersten und zweiten Psalmenvorlesung* (Tübingen, 1967); *Grammatica Theologica: Studien zu Luthers Operationes in Psalmos* (Tübingen, 1977).

Reuchlin's work made its appearance.[37] The continued interest on the part of Karlstadt in the language went some considerable way towards facilitating its introduction into the theological curriculum at Wittenberg in 1518.[38]

This programme of direct engagement with the bible in its original languages was to have considerable theological significance. The theologians of the Latin west were largely dependent upon the Vulgate for their theological deliberations, and the accuracy of both the text and the translation would be called increasingly into question in the later *Quattrocento*, with important theological implications. The textual and philological researches of Lorenzo Valla (c. 1406–57) may be noted here. Valla's textual skill was more than adequately demonstrated through his exposure of the spurious character of the so-called 'Donation of Constantine'.[39] His work on the Greek text of the New Testament convinced him of the serious inaccuracy of the Vulgate translation, and hence of the theology of those who relied upon it.[40] The editing and publication of this work by Erasmus in 1505 as *Adnotationes in Novum Testamentum* brought these researches to the attention of a wider public, and served as a basis for Erasmus' own Latin translation of the New Testament a decade later.[41] Valla frequently castigates theologians who base their conclusions upon a Latin translation of the Greek text of the New Testament: 'Has ineptias effutiunt qui, graecae linguae ignari, exponunt e graeco traducta'.[42] Thus he criticizes Thomas Aquinas' doctrine of cooperative grace as relying upon faulty Latin translations of Pauline texts – for example, 1 Corinthians 15.10. The Vulgate translated the Greek as *non autem ego, sed gratia Dei mecum*, where Valla had *non autem ego, sed gratia Dei quae est mecum*. Valla comments thus upon the Vulgate version: 'Nihil dicant qui hanc

37 Hans Peter Rüger, 'Karlstadt als Hebraist an der Universität Wittenberg, *ARG* 75 (1984), pp. 297–309; pp. 299–302.

38 G. Bauch, 'Die Einführung des Hebräischen in Wittenberg mit Berücksichtigung der Vorgeschichte des Studiums der Sprache in Deutschland', *Monatschrift für Geschichte und Wissenschaft des Judentums* 48 (1904), pp. 22–32; 77–86; 145–60; 214–23; 283–99; 328–40; 461–90.

39 For the importance of this document, see D. Maffei, *La Donazione di Constantino nei giuristi medievali* (Milan, 1964).

40 His *Collatio Novi Testamenti* was written about 1444, and has been published in an original form by Alessandro Perosa (Florence, 1970).

41 See Salvatore I. Camporeale, *Lorenzo Valla: umanesimo e teologia* (Florence, 1972), pp. 277–403.

42 For what follows, see Camporeale, *Lorenzo Valla*, p. 309. The reflections of Guillaume Budé on Valla's philological work are interesting: *Annotationes in Pandectas*, in *Opera Omnia* (4 vols: Basle, 1557), vol. 3, pp. 56C–7A.

vocant gratiam Dei *cooperanter*: Paulus enim sibi hoc non tribuit, sed totum a Deo refert acceptum'. This programme of reverting to the direct study of the original Greek text of the New Testament necessitated the production of editions of the Greek New Testament, leading to the production of the Complutensian Polyglot edition of the Greek New Testament (1514),[43] and Erasmus' *Novum Instrumentum omne* (1516).[44]

By the end of the second decade of the sixteenth century, therefore, the exegesis of the New Testament, whether in monastery or university, could not be realistically undertaken without an appeal to the Greek text of the New Testament. (Although there was also increasing recognition of the need to study the Old Testament in the original Hebrew, the humanist preference for Greek as the language of *eloquentia* inevitably led to the concentration of their attention upon the New Testament documents.) As a consequence of this new interest in the New Testament the accuracy – and eventually thence the *authority* – of the Vulgate was increasingly called into question.

It will, of course, be obvious that the new interest in the Greek text of the New Testament, evident in the later *Quattrocento*, leading to increasing unease concerning the accuracy of the Vulgate translation, had potential theological significance only within the Latin-speaking (that is, the western) church. The Greek-speaking (that is, the eastern) church had always relied directly upon the Greek text of the New Testament, rather than upon an intervening translation. In that the early western church tended to depend upon the eastern for its theology

43 This was not published until 22 March 1520. For details, see M. Bataillon, *Erasmus y España* (Mexico City, 2nd edn, 1966), pp. 10–43; Basil Hall, 'The Trilingual College of San Ildefonso and the Making of the Complutensian Polyglot Bible', in *Studies in Church History 5*, ed. G. J. Cuming (Leiden, 1969), pp. 114–46; José López Rueda, *Hellenistas españoles del siglo XVI* (Madrid, 1973), pp. 340–8; Jerry H. Bentley, 'New Light on the Editing of the Complutensian Polyglot', *BHR* 42 (1980), pp. 145–56.

44 See Roland H. Bainton, *Erasmus of Rotterdam* (London, 1970), pp. 164–84. For the issues raised, see Jacques Chomorat, 'Les *Annotations* de Valla, celles d'Erasme et la grammaire', in *Histoire de l'exégèse au XVIe siècle*, ed. Olivier Fatio and Pierre Fraenkel (Geneva, 1978), pp. 202–28. On the importance of the *Annotationes* in relation to the *Novum Instrumentum*, see Jerry H. Bentley, 'Erasmus' *Annotationes in Novum Testamentum* and the Textual Criticism of the Gospels', *ARG* 67 (1976), pp. 33–53. The word 'Instrumentum' was chosen by Erasmus in preference to 'Testamentum' but was abandoned in favour of the original term in later editions.

The first edition of Erasmus' Greek New Testament was seriously inaccurate at points, particularly in relation to printer's errors. There also remain a number of puzzling matters concerning Erasmus' editorial methods. For example, at several points, Erasmus' textual readings do not correspond to the printed text: see K. W. Clark, 'Observations on the Erasmian Notes in Codex 2', *Texte und Untersuchungen* 73 (1959), pp. 755–6.

(such as its Christology and Trinitarianism), but developed essentially independently in the aftermath of the theological renaissance of the twelfth century,[45] one would expect that the most serious difficulties would arise in relation to doctrines which developed within the Latin-speaking church during the period 1150–1450. It is this period which coincides with the period of theological decline or doctrinal corruption identified by the Reformers, such as Melanchthon. It will therefore be clear that the new concern with the Greek text of the New Testament was of potential significance in relation to areas of doctrine in which development took place within the western church during the scholastic period – areas such as Mariology and the theology of the sacraments.

In their translations of the original Greek of Luke 1.28 (*ave gratia plena Dominus tecum*), both Valla and Erasmus pointed out that the Latin *gratia plena* was an inaccurate translation of the Greek participle, which actually meant 'accepted into grace', or 'favoured'.[46] Thus Erasmus comments somewhat caustically on the tendency of 'certain theologians, such as Bernard, who philosophize marvellously about these words *gratia plena*', diverting their readers from the true meaning of the gospel text. The Greek participle should be translated as *gratificata*, or perhaps as *gratiosa*.[47] There had been a tendency, perhaps more marked in popular than in academic Mariology, to treat the phrase as implying that Mary was essentially a vessel of grace: this interpretation was excluded, or at least robbed of its initial plausibility, through the new philology.

Perhaps more significant, however, was the severing of the semantic link between the mental attitude of repentance and the sacrament of penance, which had become accepted through the Vulgate translation of Matthew 4.17: Exinde coepit Jesus praedicare et dicere *paenitentiam agite* adpropinquavit enim regnum caelorum. This had been taken to imply the need to 'do penance', in preparation for the coming of

45 C. Haskins, *The Renaissance of the Twelfth Century* (Cambridge, Mass., 1927); G. Paré, A. Brunet and P. Tremblay, *La renaissance du XIIe siècle* (Paris, 1933); W. A. Nitze, 'The so-called Twelfth Century Renaissance', *Speculum* 23 (1948), pp. 464–71; E. M. Sandford, 'The Twelfth-Century: Renaissance or Proto-Renaissance?', *Speculum* 26 (1951), pp. 635–42.

46 Valla, *Collatio*, ed. Perosa, 95.2–28, especially 13–20 'Sciant ergo apud Grecos non dici "gratia plena" sed, ut sic dicam, "gratiata" vel "gratificata", hoc est "que donata est gratia". . . Maria in gratia Dei esse dicitur'; Erasmus, *Opera Omnia*, vol. 6, p. 223 D-F.

47 Erasmus, *Opera Omnia*, vol. 6, p. 223 D-F. Erasmus' translation of certain Vulgate passages caused considerable misgivings, particularly his translation of John 1.1 as 'In principium erat sermo'. See C. A. L. Jarrott, 'Erasmus' *In principio erat sermo*: A Controversial Translation', *Studies in Philology* 61 (1964), pp. 35–40.

the Kingdom of God.[48] (The ambiguity of the Latin word *poenitentia*, which could be translated as the mental state of 'repentance', or the sacrament of 'penance', should be noted.) This link was initially weakened, and subsequently eliminated, through the rise of the new philology. Thus Erasmus initially translated the Greek verb as *poeniteat vos* ('be penitent'), and subsequently as *resipiscite* ('come to your senses').

Perhaps the most debated point to arise from the new approach to the Vulgate text was the proper translation of Hebrews 2.7, the subject of a heated controversy between Lefèvre d'Etaples and Erasmus in the years 1515–17.[48] Lefèvre had noted the discrepancy between the Septuagint and the Hebrew versions of Psalm 8.6 in his *Quincuplex Psalterium* of 1509, and that the Letter to the Hebrews, in citing this verse, used the Septuagint, rather than the Hebrew. Hebrews 2.7 thus declared that Christ was 'made a little lower than the angels', whereas Lefèvre argued that the text should be corrected to read 'made a little lower *than God (minuisti eum paulominus a Deo)*'. In his *Annotationes* of 1516, Erasmus responded unsympathetically to this suggestion, arguing that the original text of Hebrews must be allowed to remain unaltered, despite the fact that it contained what seemed to be an error.[49] In the second edition of his *Epistolae Pauli* of the same year, Lefèvre took issue with Erasmus' response to the difficulty.[50] Such was the interest the debate aroused that contemporary exegetes were obliged to make reference to the controversy, as may be seen from the comments of Wendelin Steinbach and Martin Luther, both writing towards the end of the second decade of the century. For Steinbach – a convinced adherent of the *via moderna*, and hence inclined to emphasize the importance of the *determinationes ecclesiae* – the authority of the church, and the long-standing use of the Vulgate text in theological debates, was adequate to justify its continued use in its present form: 'sufficit nobis auctoritatis ecclesiae et usus multorum temporum in ecclesia Dei legencium, ut nostra habet translacio'.[51] Luther, discussing the question at some length,[52] demonstrates that the

---

48 See Alister E. McGrath, *Iustitia Dei: A History of the Christian Doctrine of Justification* (2 vols: Cambridge, 1986), vol. 1, pp. 91–100, for a full discussion.
48 See Helmut Feld, *Martin Luthers und Wendelin Steinbachs Vorlesungen über den Hebräerbrief* (Wiesbaden, 1971), pp. 43–52.
49 Erasmus, *Opera Omnia*, vol. 6, pp. 985–6.
50 Feld, *Vorlesungen über den Hebräerbrief*, pp. 47–51.
51 Feld, *Vorlesungen über den Hebräerbrief*, p. 56 n.165.
52 WA 57 III.116–20.

intricacies of the technical philological debate (not to mention the details of the personal rancour which developed between Lefèvre d'Etaples and Erasmus) were fully appreciated at Wittenberg.[53]

The importance of this debate lies in its relevance to the new understanding of the nature of exegesis in the early sixteenth century. Whereas earlier generations of exegetes had tended to confine themselves to the repetition of the views of the *Glossa Ordinaria* or other established authorities, the humanist exegetes concerned themselves directly with the original text, in the original language. The growing awareness of the inaccuracy and inadequacy of the Vulgate inevitably raised questions in the minds of exegetes concerning its theological reliability and authority. Unless theology and exegesis were to become divorced, as disciplines of no relevance to each other, it was clear that some accommodation to the new humanist exegetical methods was necessary. But it must not be thought that theologians alone were confronted with a dilemma through the philological and textual work of the humanists. Precisely the same difficulties were being raised through the work of French humanist jurists.

The early sixteenth century saw a major controversy develop within legal circles concerning the nature of law. The older Italian school (*mos italicus*) was based upon the glosses and commentaries of the medieval jurists, whereas the rival French school, developing at Bourges in the early sixteenth century (*mos gallicus*) appealed directly to the original legal sources of antiquity.[54] This may be illustrated from Guillaume Budé's *Annotationes in quattuor et vigintii Pandectarum libros* (1508), in which the glosses of Accursius and Bartholus on the text were by-passed, in order to engage directly with the Justinian *Pandects* themselves. Critical source studies were substituted for glossing or commenting.[55] The theological significance of this technique was not overlooked by Budé: in 1526, he re-edited his *Annotationes*, and applied the same techniques to the Vulgate text. In many respects, the *mos gallicus* parallels the new humanist approach to scripture, in

---

53 Feld, *Vorlesungen über den Hebräerbrief*, pp. 58–65.
54 See the classic study of Guido Kisch, *Humanismus und Jurisprudenz: Der Kampf zwischen mos italicus und mos gallicus an der Universität Basel* (Basle, 1955), pp. 9–76. The older study of Roderich Stinzing, *Geschichte der deutschen Rechtswissenschaft I* (Munich, 1880), pp. 106–45, is still useful.
55 Kisch, *Humanismus und Jurisprudenz*, p. 20 'An die Stelle der glossierenden oder kommentierenden Methode sollte die kritische Quellenforschung treten, und aus ihrer Ergebnissen sich das Streben nach umfassender und dauerend gültiger Rechtserkenntnis entwickeln'. Cf. p. 18 'Rückkehr zur reinen Rechtsquelle statt bloßer Anerkennung der Tradition, Erkenntnis der Rechtsidee statt des Autoritätenkults, System statt Exegese nach der "Legalordnung".'

which the original text is addressed directly, and interpreted on the basis of scientific philological and historical methods, whereas the *mos italicus* parallels the older scholastic approach to scripture, in which the original text is approached through a 'filter' of glosses (such as the *Glossa Ordinaria*) or commentaries, which are invested with the accumulated authority of tradition.)

The tension between the *mos gallicus* and *mos italicus* also points to another factor relevant to the present study. Although the new philological and exegetical techniques which were destined to exercise so powerful an influence over early sixteenth century humanism were developed in Italy, they were not applied there, neither in matters of theology nor jurisprudence. Valla's *Collatio* of 1444, it may be recalled, was not published until 1505, when Erasmus discovered a manuscript of the work in the library of the Praetermonstratensians near Louvain.[56] The rapid development of 'sacred philology' – in relation to which the publication (by Erasmus) of Valla's *Adnotationes* (1505), Reuchlin's *De rudimentis Hebraicis* (1506) and *Psalterium Quincuplex* (1512), and Erasmus' *Novum Instrumentum omne* (1516), are milestones – although originally based upon Italian ideas and methods, received its fullest development in northern Europe. The ideas of the Renaissance appear to have made their way north of the Alps through the interchange of persons, the exchange of letters and through manuscripts and printed works,[57] and to have exercised a greater influence upon jurisprudence and theology in England, France, the Lowlands and Germany than in their native Italy. The influence of John Colet at Oxford,[58] Lefèvre d'Etaples at Paris,[59] Johannes Reuchlin at Württemberg,[60] and the *philosophia Christi* of Erasmus throughout much of Europe,[61] is an adequate testimony to the vitality

56 Bainton, *Erasmus of Rotterdam*, p. 85

57 P. O. Kristeller, 'The European Diffusion of Italian Humanism', in *Renaissance Thought II: Papers on Humanism and the Arts* (New York, 1965), pp. 69–88.

58 S. Jayne, *John Colet and Marsilio Ficino* (Oxford, 1963); J. K. McConica, *English Humanists and Reformation Politics* (Oxford, 1965).

59 A. Renaudet, 'Un problème historique: la pensée religieuse de J. Lefèvre d'Etaples', in *Medioevo e Rinascimento: Studi in onore di Bruno Nardi II* (Florence, 1955), pp. 621–50; E. F. Rice, 'The Humanist Idea of Christian Antiquity: Lefèvre d'Etaples and His Circle', *Studies in the Renaissance* 9 (1962), pp. 126–60; R. M. Cameron, 'The Charges of Lutheranism Brought Against Jacques Lefèvre d'Etaples', *HThR* 63 (1970), pp. 119–49.

60 Brod, *Johannes Reuchlin und sein Kampf*; L. W. Spitz, *The Religious Renaissance of the German Humanists* (Cambridge, Mass., 1963), pp. 61–80.

61 McConica, *English Humanists*, pp. 13–43; Robert Stupperich, 'Das Enchiridion Militis

and creativity of humanism in Northern Europe, and indicative of the potential influence of the new historical and philological techniques upon biblical exegesis – and hence theological speculation.

The rapid developments in 'sacred philology' in northern Europe in the first and second decades of the sixteenth centuries thus called into question the scriptural basis of a number of doctrines, even if it did not necessarily totally undermine them. For the humanists, whatever authority scripture might possess derived from the original texts in their original languages, rather than from the Vulgate, which was increasingly recognised as unreliable and inaccurate. In that the catholic church continued to insist that the Vulgate was a doctrinally normative translation, a tension inevitably developed between humanist biblical scholarship and catholic theology. It is therefore significant that the first generation of Reformers, in both Germany and Switzerland, were men deeply influenced by the 'new philology': Luther in particular regarded the rise of 'sacred philology' (*die Sprachen*) as nothing less than providential, in that God had, in his wisdom and providence, provided the means by which purification and reform of doctrine might come about.[62] Through immediate access to the original text in the original language, the theologian could wrestle directly with the 'Word of God',[63] unhindered by 'filters' of glosses and commentaries which placed the views of previous interpreters between the exegete and his text. For the Reformers, 'sacred philology' provided the key by means of which the theologian could break free from the confines of medieval exegesis, and return *ad fontes*, to the title deeds of the Christian faith rather than their medieval expressions, to forge once more the authentic theology of the early church.

The rise of the view that it was scripture, and scripture alone, which could function as the foundation and criterion of such an authentic theology (*vera theologia*),[64] gave added weight to the importance of the new exegetical methods for Christian theology. The great humanist

---

Militis Christiani des Erasmus von Rotterdam nach seiner Entstehung, seinem Sinn und Charakter', *ARG* 69 (1978), pp. 5–23.

62 Luther's views on the role of language serve to emphasize the importance of this point: see Bengt Hägglund, 'Martin Luther über die Sprache', *Neue Zeitschrift für systematische Theologie und Religionsphilosophie* 26 (1984), pp. 1–12.

63 It is important to appreciate a tension which existed between humanist and Reformer at this point: the humanist regarded the authority of scripture to lie in its antiquity, whereas the Reformers (especially Luther) regarded it as grounded in its nature as the 'Word of God': see Alister E. McGrath, *Luther's Theology of the Cross: Martin Luther's Theological Breakthrough* (Oxford, 1985), p. 51.

64 See, e.g., Egli, 'Zur Einführung des Schriftprinzips in der Schweiz'.

vision of *Christianismus renascens*, shared by so many of the early Reformers, was linked with the recreation of the world of early Christianity through a direct appeal to its sources. As Zwingli remarked, 'today the rejected Christ rises again everywhere'[65] – and instrumental in this resurrection was the direct engagement with the title-deeds of Christendom. The essential unity of the formal and material principles of the Reformation lies in the fact that *solus Christus* was perceived by the Reformers ultimately to depend upon *sola scriptura*.

The new emphasis on the part of the Reformers upon the importance of 'sacred philology' as a pre-requisite for biblical hermeneutics, and hence theology, was not without its ironies. It is perhaps one of the more intriguing paradoxes of the Reformation that a movement which was initially dedicated to making the 'word of God' available to *Herr Omnes* (to use Luther's phrase for 'everyman') should actually have *inhibited* this very possibility through an insistence upon the necessity of approaching the biblical text in its original language. Thus Zwingli, in his debate against the anabaptist radicals, insisted that the bible had to be read in its original language if it was to be properly understood, and that such understanding could not come about through a direct appeal to the Holy Spirit.[66] Similar views were expressed by Luther in the 1524 tract *An die Ratsherren*, in which he argued that Christian schools should be established, in which the classical languages, particularly Greek and Hebrew, would be taught. For Luther, the medium through which the Holy Spirit operated was *die Sprachen*,[67] and an ignorance of Greek and Hebrew was thus effectively an obstacle to the gospel itself.[68] Although Luther initially appears to have favoured the view that every individual could and should read the bible in the vernacular, and base his theology directly upon that reading, he subsequently became somewhat sceptical concerning the ability of *Herr Omnes* to interpret scripture.

A study of the school curricula in Lutheran towns makes this point clear. The *Schulordnungen* of the Duchy of Württemberg (1559) make provision for the New Testament to be studied only by able students in their final years – and even then, only in the original Greek, or

---

65 CR (Zwingli) 3.445.6.
66 CR (Zwingli) 4.417.23–419.6.
67 WA 15.37.4–16; 38.8–12.
68 WA 15.28.30–1; 42.23–43.1.

Latin translation.[69] Less able students are required to study Luther's *Smaller Catechism* of 1529 instead. A similar pattern is evident throughout Lutheran Germany.[70] As a result, direct engagement with the scriptural text is reserved for scholars; others must approach scripture through the 'filter' of the catechism, which provided a framework within which scripture could be interpreted. There is thus a curious twist to the Reformation *sola scriptura* principle, in that the interpretation of scripture was effectively restricted to a limited group of people. The direct engagement with the original text was reserved for those with the necessary linguistic abilities – and in this respect, the Reformation followed both Erasmus and medieval scholasticism in declining to allow the masses to interpret scripture for themselves.

The perceived importance of the establishment of an accurate text and translation of scripture is, of course, directly proportional to the perceived theological significance of scripture. The following chapter will show that scripture was widely regarded as the sole materially sufficient theological source in the later medieval period – a factor which goes some considerable way towards explaining the crisis occasioned within early sixteenth century theology as humanist textual and philological investigations increasingly challenged the prevailing view that 'scripture' could be identified with 'the Vulgate text'.

---

69 *Die evangelischen Schulordnungen des 16. Jahrhunderts*, ed. R. Vormbaum (Gütersloh, 1860), vol. 1, pp. 68–73.
70 Gerald Strauss, 'Lutheranism and Literacy: A Reassessment', in *Religion and Society in Early Modern Europe 1500–1800*, ed. Kasper von Greyerz (London, 1984), pp. 109–23; pp. 114–15.

5

Sources and Methods:
Scripture and Tradition

One of the most enduring, if not endearing, stereotypes of the relation between the Reformation and the late medieval period is that the latter is characterized by an appeal to *both* scripture *and* tradition as theological sources, whereas the former appealed to scripture alone (*sola scriptura*). The Council of Trent, in its decree on scripture and tradition, has generally been regarded as endorsing the medieval view in recognizing these two distinct theological sources. The Reformation, therefore, may be regarded as marking a break with the medieval period in this important respect, and Wycliffe and Huss may thus be regarded as 'Forerunners of the Reformation'.[1] In fact, however, it is becoming increasingly clear that the medieval period in general was characterized by its conviction that scripture was the sole material base of Christian theology, thus forcing us to reconsider what, if anything, was distinctive concerning the Reformation principle of *sola scriptura*.[2]

Recent studies have indicated a general medieval consensus on the material sufficiency of scripture – in other words, that scripture contained all that is necessary for salvation.[3] Thus Duns Scotus affirms that 'theology does not concern anything except what is contained in scripture, and what may be drawn (*elici*) from this', the latter being 'contained there *virtualiter*'.[4] Indeed, it is evident from

---

1 e.g., G. Lechler, *Johann von Wiclif und die Vorgeschichte der Reformation* (Leipzig, 1873), p. 469.

2 This recognition dates from earlier in the present century: see Friedrich Kropatschek, *Das Schriftprinzip der lutherischen Kirche I: Die Vorgeschichte: Das Erbe des Mittelalters* (Leipzig, 1904), pp. 438–41.

3 See the seminal study of Paul de Vooght, *Les sources de la doctrine chrétienne d'après les théologiens du XIVᵉ siècle et du début du XVᵉ* (Paris, 1954), which may be compared with the older study of Johannes Beumer, 'Das katholische Schriftprinzip in der theologischen Literatur der Scholastik bis zur Reformation', *Scholastik* 16 (1941), pp. 24–52.

4 Scotus, *Ordinatio*, praefatio, 123; 204. Cf. Eligius Buytaert, 'Circa doctrinam Duns Scoti de traditione et de scriptura adnotationes', *Antonianum* 40 (1965), pp. 346–62.

even the most superficial reading of late medieval sources that scripture, and scripture *alone*, was regarded as the materially sufficient source and norm of Christian theology.[5] No other theological source could be regarded as having this status. Is not this what is expressed by the Reformation principle of *sola scriptura*? In fact, however, the situation is considerably more complex, both in relation to the later medieval period and the Reformation itself, and the question demands discussion in more detail.

THE CONCEPT OF TRADITION

An important attempt to clarify the question of the relation between scripture and tradition in late medieval theological method was made by Heiko A. Oberman,[6] with potentially significant consequences for our understanding of the intellectual origins of the Reformation. Oberman draws attention to two main understandings of this relation in the period, while noting the difficulties attending this division. The first view, which Oberman designates 'Tradition I', treats scripture and tradition as coinherent or coterminous, so that the *kerygma*, scripture and tradition essentially coinhere. The second view, which Oberman designates 'Tradition II', recognizes an extra-scriptural oral tradition as a theological source, in addition to scripture itself, and not necessarily coinherent or coterminous with it. It is in connection with this second view of the relation of scripture and tradition that several influential studies have located the seeds of the disintegration of the medieval synthesis.[7] To clarify the situation, we shall consider the 'single source' and 'two sources' theories – which Oberman

5 See the important study of Hermann Schüssler, *Der Primät der Heiligen Schrift als theologisches und kanonistisches Problem im Spätmittelalter* (Wiesbaden, 1977), p. 73 'Daß die Hl. Schrift die maßgebende Quelle und Norm der Theologie wie der Kirchenlehre sei, ist der gesamten Spätscholastik selbstverständliche Voraussetzung gewesen.' Cf. de Vooght, *Les sources de la doctrine chrétienne*, p. 255 'Lorsque les théologiens du XIVe siècle affirmaient ainsi que l'Écriture *seule* est la source de la doctrine chrétienne, ils entendaient par là qu'elle était, seule, purement et simplement la parole de Dieu, infaillible et immuable, dictée par le Saint-Esprit, complète et sans rivale.'

6 Heiko A. Oberman, *The Harvest of Medieval Theology: Gabriel Biel and Late Medieval Nominalism* (Cambridge, Mass., 1963), pp. 361–412; Oberman, *Forerunners of the Reformation: The Shape of Late Medieval Thought* (Philadelphia, 1981), pp. 53–66.

7 For example, George H. Tavard, *Holy Writ or Holy Church: The Crisis of the Protestant Reformation* (London, 1959).

designates as 'Tradition I' and 'Tradition II' respectively – as they developed in the medieval period.

The anti-Gnostic polemic of the early church led to the development of a *regula fidei*, by which scripture as received by the church was regarded as embodying in a materially sufficient manner the Christian *kerygma*.[8] In other words, all truths which were in any sense necessary to salvation were those given directly in, or which could be directly inferred from, scripture. Christian theology was thus essentially the exegesis of scripture within the context of the church.[9] Thus Gerald of Bologna, writing in the early fourteenth century, draws attention to the organic relation of scripture and church, indicating their mutual dependency.[10] Oberman, however, argues that this early medieval consensus disintegrated through the adoption of the 'two source' theory of the canonists. In the twelfth and thirteenth centuries, when theologians appear to have adopted a 'single source' theory, the canonists (such as Ivo of Chartres and Gratian of Bologna) began to develop a 'two source' theory, based upon scripture and tradition. According to Oberman, when the influence of the canonists was at its greatest in the fourteenth century, 'the canon-law tradition started' to feed into the theological tradition'.[11] In other words, at a time when the theories of the canon lawyer were held in high esteem, theologians began to adopt their methods.

Oberman points to Basil of Caesarea as the ultimate source of this development. Basil traced certain liturgical developments back to an unwritten tradition, and argued that ecclesiastical traditions, whether written or oral, were to be treated with respect by the faithful.[12] In taking up this text and its associated concept of oral tradition, the canonists were, according to Oberman, recognizing two sources of divine revelation, and thus foreshadowing later medieval theology in

---

8 J. N. Bakhuizen van den Brink, 'Tradition und Heilige Schrift am Anfang des dritten Jahrhunderts', *Catholica* 9 (1953), pp. 105–14; Bengt Hägglund, 'Die Bedeutung der 'regula fidei' als Grundlage theologischer Aussagen', *Studia Theologica* 12 (1958), pp. 1–44.

9 See the important early study of Gerhard Ebeling, *Kirchengeschichte als Geschichte der Auslegung der Heiligen Schrift* (Tübingen, 1947), where this theme is fruitfully developed.

10 *Summa* q.5 a.1; edn in de Vooght, *Sources de la doctrine chrétienne*, 356.32–4 'Si congregacio alica uellet scripturam istam mutare et oppositum tenere, iam non esset congregacio et ecclesia Dei. Et sic isti scripture esset credendum, et non tam tali ecclesiae.' See further de Vooght, pp. 33–59. Cf. Thomas Aquinas, *Summa Theologiae* Ia q.1 a.8 ad 2um.

11 Oberman, *Harvest of Medieval Theology*, pp. 369–75; p. 372. Cf. Oberman, *Forerunners of the Reformation*, p. 58.

12 Basil, *De spiritu sancto*, 66. This passage is incorporated into Gratian's *Decretum*: dist. xi cap. 5.

this respect. It would seem, however, that Oberman has seriously misunderstood the nature and function of canon law in making this assertion. It is certainly true that Gratian frequently refers to canon law as *divina lex* – but this does not mean that he regarded it as having the status of divine revelation. For Gratian, canon law drew upon two sources: scripture and *mores*, this latter meaning 'customary practice' or 'human law'. 'Humanum genus duobus regitur, naturali videlicet iure et moribus. Ius naturale est quod in lege et evangelio continetur.'[13] In other words, canon law is concerned with the natural law (that is, immutable, divinely revealed law) and with human law. This latter – and this latter alone – was subject to revision and amendment by the pope, who had no authority to deny or modify divinely revealed truth. The canonists therefore attempted to distinguish what was divine (and hence permanent) from what was human (and hence transitory) in the field of canon law.

It will be clear that a clear distinction between *theology* and *law*, between doctrine and discipline, is presupposed by this approach. Thus in distinction 19 of the *Decretum*, Gratian insists upon the doctrinal authority of scripture, while in the following distinction, he insists upon the judicial authority of the pope – without being guilty of inconsistency. Nevertheless, there are points at which the doctrinal and judicial spheres overlap – for example, in the question of identifying heresy. At this point, the pope's authority as the interpreter of scripture was conceded. Thus Tierney draws our attention to a text which insists upon the priority of scripture in matters of doctrine (*primum locum et principale obtineat lex naturalis, vetus testamentum et novum*), while conceding that at points the authority of the pope as the interpreter of scripture must be acknowledged (*in obscuris scripturis et maxime circa articulos fidei maioris auctoritatis esset interpretatio papae*).[14] This authority, however, relates to the pope as the *interpreter* of scripture, and not as the *source* of an extra-scriptural tradition. Oberman interprets Ambrosius of Speier's remarks, restating precisely this position, as 'a very sharp and most succinct formulation of Tradition II'[15] (in other words, the 'two source' theory), whereas it is evident that Ambrosius is merely restating the common view of the pope's role as arbiter in disputed matters of doctrine.

13 *Decretum* dist. i, cap. 1.
14 Brian Tierney, 'Pope and Council: Some New Decretist Texts', *Medieval Studies* 19 (1957), pp. 197–218; p. 201 n.20.
15 Oberman, *Harvest of Medieval Theology*, p. 373.

A further point of relevance to this matter concerns the weighting to be given to various sources of ecclesiastical authority, a point frequently discussed by the canonists.[16] At no stage are papal decretals treated as having anything even approaching the status of scripture. Theological authority is understood to be primarily invested in scripture itself, and only in a derivative and restricted manner in the decisions of the pope.[17]

There are, however, passages in the fourteenth century decretalist writings suggesting that the pope was at liberty to 'dispense from scripture' – in other words, to go against the obvious sense of scripture.[18] This suggestion has been treated by some scholars as implying that the pope was regarded as embodying a second source of divine revelation, in addition to scripture. A closer examination of the decretalist sources, however, indicates that the pope was regarded only as having such liberty only in the limited sphere of ecclesiastical discipline, not doctrine. The question at stake was not one of the eternal truths of doctrine (in which the pope, like everyone else, was regarded as absolutely bound by scriptural revelation), but of determining whether a given scriptural text was intended to establish an absolute and permanently binding law, valid for all time, or simply to define a provisional code of conduct for the early church (or the Israelites, if the Old Testament is involved), which served as a nothing more than a point of departure for contemporary reflection on the same issue.[19] The power to 'dispense from scripture' was not regarded as enabling the pope to act as a second source of divine revelation in matters of doctrine, but simply as conceding that an absolute biblical literalism in matters of church discipline was an impossibility at the time – hence raising the question of who might function as the interpreter of scripture at such points. As with other disputed matters of

---

16 See, e.g., C. Munier, *Les sources patristiques du droit de l'église* (Mulhouse, 1957), p. 200.
17 The following list, from Guido de Baysio, *Rosarium*, dist. xx cap. 3, is instructive. 'Primo recurrendum est ad rescripti novi et veteris testamenti. Secundo ad canones apostolorum et conciliorum. Tertio ad decreta vel decretalia romanorum pontificum. Quarto ad scripta graeca. Postea ad scripta sanctorum patrum latinorum.' Cf. Schüssler, *Der Primät der Heiligen Schrift*, pp. 78–80.
18 As pointed out, with documentation, by Tavard, *Holy Writ or Holy Church*, pp. 38–9.
19 This question was generally discussed in relation to whether the scriptural prescriptions concerning candidates for ordination might be relaxed (which is not a matter of doctrine!): see the careful and well-documented study of Stephan Kuttner, 'Pope Lucius III and the Bigamous Archbishop of Palermo', in *Medieval Studies presented to Aubrey Gwynn*, ed. J. Watt *et al.* (Dublin, 1961), pp. 409–53.

biblical interpretation, the recognition of the need for a final court of appeal was regarded as an endorsement of, rather than as a challenge to, the primacy of scripture.

The debate between John XXII and the Franciscans served to clarify the relation between pope and scripture, and to eliminate a possible misunderstanding which had gained some credence in the previous century. John insisted that scripture was the sole essential foundation upon which articles of faith might be based, and argued that the Franciscans, by their irresponsible appeal to scripture, called into question both the source of doctrine and the articles of faith based upon it.[20] In making this assertion, John further clarified the position of Alexander III's decretal *Cum Christo* (1170), directed against the Christological nihilianism of Peter Lombard (the view *quod Christus secundum quod est homo non est aliud*). Although Alexander in fact did nothing other than reaffirm the Chalcedonian principle, that Christ was *verus deus et verus homo*, some canonists appear to have interpreted him as introducing a *new* article of faith. Thus Guido de Baysio reports an earlier canonist ('Alanus') as drawing the conclusion 'et ita papa potest facere novos articulos fidei'.[21] This interpretation of the significance of *Cum Christo*, which is clearly incorrect, was emphatically excluded by early fourteenth century canonists, at the insistence of John XXII. Thus Zenzellinus de Cassanis insisted that the pope had not, and never could have, powers to innovate in matters of doctrine: 'Non credas papam posse facere articulum per quem nova fides inducatur aut veritatis fidei detrahatur aliquid vel accrescat quo ad substantiam.'[22] As Zenzellinus made clear, the only basis of Christian theology was scripture: 'Fides nisi per scripturam sacram probari penes homines non possit'. There is simply no trace of a 'two sources' theory to be found in these ideas: indeed, it may be argued that it was those who were opposed to John XXII (such as William of Ockham) who were obliged to develop a 'two source' theory, in

---

20 *Extravagantes Johannis XXII* (Antwerp, 1572), tit. xiv, cap. 5 'Profecto hoc ad fidem non pertinet, cum de hoc articulus non sit aliquis, nec sub quo valeat comprehendi, ut patet in symbolis in quibis articuli fidei continentur, nec etiam reducte, ne quasi hoc sacra scriptura contineat, quo negato tota scriptura sacra redditur dubia, et per consequens articuli fidei, qui habent per scripturam sacram probari, redduntur dubii et incerti.' See further Malcolm David Lambert, *Franciscan Poverty: The Doctrine of the Absolute Poverty of Christ and the Apostles in the Franciscan Order 1210-1323* (London, 1961).
21 Guido de Baysio, *Rosarium*, dist. xv, cap. 1.
22 *Extravagantes Johannis XXII*, tit. xiv, cap. 4.

that the 'single source' theory so evidently failed to give an adequate basis to their views.

This discussion calls into question Oberman's analysis of the precise relation between scripture and tradition in the fourteenth century. Oberman clearly assumes that the 'two source' theory derives from the canon law tradition – whereas the decretals and decretalists do not appear to endorse the concept of an extra-scriptural *doctrinal* source. Oberman's confusion over this important point appears to arise from a failure to discriminate between the permanent truths of doctrine and the provisional rulings of church discipline. In fairness to Oberman, we may point out that there were many in the fourteenth century who shared the same confusion. Thus John Wycliffe appears to have assumed that papal decretals were regarded by his opponents as having the same authority as Holy Scripture: as any decretal could be revoked at any time, this position seemed to him to be absurd, in that allegedly permanent theological truths could be altered at will.[23] And absurd it would have been – but this is not what the canonists were suggesting.

Oberman's thesis concerning 'Tradition II' (the 'two source' theory), however, is not invalidated through the demonstration of the inaccuracy of his opinions concerning its origins. Whatever the origins of the 'two source' theory may have been, the late medieval tradition unquestionably included representatives of a school which insisted that 'there are many truths which are necessary for salvation which are neither contained in scripture, nor which are necessary consequences of its contents'.[24] But what, it may reasonably be asked, are these truths? In his analysis of this question, Breviscoxa gives seven main lines of argumentation for this 'more probable' view of the relation between scripture and tradition. He includes three examples of truths which are neither included in scripture, nor can be necessarily deduced from it: 'The Apostles' Creed was drawn up by the apostles'; 'The See of Peter was translated from Antioch to Rome'; 'The Roman popes succeed Peter'.[25] If these are illustrative of the truths that may be derived from this theological source, it will be evident that they contain

---

23 See de Vooght, *Sources de la doctrine chrétienne*, p. 186 n.4.

24 For example, Johannes Breviscoxa (= Courtcuisse), *De fide et ecclesia*, in Jean Gerson, *Opera*, ed. L. E. duPin (5 vols: Antwerp, 1706), vol. 1, pp. 805–903; p. 830A. See Oberman, *Harvest of Medieval Theology*, pp. 387–8; Oberman, *Forerunners of the Reformation*, pp. 60–2. A partial English translation of this work may be found in this latter work, at pp. 67–92.

25 Breviscoxa here draws his examples from Ockham's *Dialogus*, ed. Melchior Goldast (Graz, 1960), p. 413.

little of significance for our purposes. Breviscoxa also adduces the
following argument for the 'two source' theory:

> Catholics are obliged to believe the doctrinal pronouncements
> of the pope so long as they assert nothing which is contrary to
> the will of God. We know that catholics are obliged to obey these
> laws through canon law. Therefore, we know that they are also
> bound to believe doctrinal pronouncements.

In that we have discussed the points raised by this argument above,
its weakness is at once apparent, in that the practice referred to was
regarded by the canonists as the *canonical enforcement of papal doctrinal
pronouncements made within the context of a 'single source' theory of theological
sources*. A similar point emerges from Gabriel Biel's discussion of the
same thesis. Biel notes that the time and place of the institution of
the sacraments of baptism and confirmation are unknown, yet it must
be believed that they *were* instituted. An appeal to an unwritten
tradition relieves this difficulty.[26]

But is this really tantamount to a 'two source' theory? If the truths
of Christian theology were to be arranged hierarchically, such 'truths'
(which often appear to be nothing more than 'truisms') would not be
expected to feature prominently. To use Biel's categories, they would
appear to belong to *fides implicita*, rather than *fides explicita*. This point
appears to be recognized by the proponents of this theory (such as
Breviscoxa), who graded the truths of Christian theology hierarchically,
with those truths found in scripture, or deducible from it, constituting
the first rank. Thus, as de Vooght points out, the idea of 'unwritten
tradition' tended to be employed in subsidiary areas of Christian
theology – for example, in relation to the practice of extreme unction,
the consecration of the chalice and the validity of indulgences.[27] This
'source' was not used, for example, to establish the Mariological
doctrines which represent one of the areas of genuine theological
innovation or development within the medieval period. As Schüssler
points out, a critical analysis of the discussion of the concept of an
'extra-biblical tradition' in the later Middle Ages indicates that the
concept actually had considerably less theological weight than might

---

26 See Oberman, *Harvest of Medieval Theology*, pp. 398–401.
27 de Vooght, *Sources de la doctrine chrétienne*, pp. 159–50.

have been expected,[28] relating primarily to matters of liturgical custom and church discipline, rather than doctrine.

THE PRINCIPLE *SOLA SCRIPTURA*

'Ipsa [theologia] est solum de his quae in sacra scriptura revelantur et de his quae possunt elici ex ipsis illatione necessaria et evidenti.'[29] For many theologians of the later medieval period, the material sufficiency of scripture as a theological source was tantamount to the assertion that theology was essentially nothing other than the exposition of scripture within the sphere of the church.[30] This is not to say that the later medieval period was characterized by homogeneity or general consensus concerning this point. Three broad schools of thought on the matter may be discerned within the later medieval period.[31] The later Franciscan school and *via moderna* tended to develop a ecclesiastical positivism, which laid considerable emphasis upon the *determinationes ecclesiae*. In this, they may be regarded as developing Bonaventure's principle concerning the *consensus ecclesiae*, enunciated in connection with the verbal formula employed in baptism.[32] The Thomists laid considerable emphasis upon the coinherence, if not identity, of scripture and theology, with due recognition being given to the role of the pope as an arbiter in disputed or obscure matters of theology. Perhaps most interesting is the tendency of the medieval Augustinian tradition, initially with Giles of Rome and subsequently with Gregory of Rimini and the *schola Augustiniana moderna*, to emphasize that the basis of Christian theology

---

28 Schüssler, *Primät der Heiligen Schrift*, p. 91 'Der Befund bei den wichtigsten spätmittelalterlichen Zeugen für die "mündliche Tradition" zeigt also, daß diese für die Diskussion um die Schriftauthorität eine geringere Bedeutung besessen hat als heute gelegentlich angenommen wird. Wir haben schon oben darauf hingewiesen, daß die Theologie des 14. und 15. Jahrhunderts sich auch weiterhin grundsätzlich als Schrifttheologie verstanden und die Hl. Schrift als *die* Grundlage der theologischen Arbeit wie des Glaubens überhaupt betrachtet wird.'

29 Johannes Hiltalingen of Basle, *In IV Sent.* prol. q.4 a.3; cited de Vooght, *Sources de la doctrine chrétienne*, p. 121.

30 de Vooght, *Sources de la doctrine chrétienne*, p. 149 'Les textes ne manquent pas – ils sont au contraire fréquents – où la désignation de l'Ecriture comme la source de la doctrine chrétienne est accompagnée du mot *sola*.'

31 Schüssler, *Primät der Heiligen Schrift*, p. 72 and references therein.

32 Bonaventure, *In IV Sent.* dist. iii pars 1 a.2 q.2 'Si Christus non instituit, instituit Ecclesia instinctu Spiritus sancti, et hoc tantum est ac si proprio ore dixisset.'

was *scriptura sola*, with a corresponding tendency to minimize other elements in theology, such as the *determinationes ecclesiae* or metaphysical concepts.[33] The question of the relation of the Reformers to the *schola Augustiniana moderna*, discussed at some length in chapter 3, thus assumes an additional significance: can the scriptural positivism of the early Reformation be ascribed to the influence of this, or a comparable, element of late medieval thought?

There are certainly reasons for supposing that one element of the scriptural positivism of the *schola Augustiniana moderna* – the radical critique of the role of Aristotle in theological speculation – was known to the young Luther.[34] In his marginal comments on the *Sentences* (1509–10), Luther appears to parallel Hugolino of Orvieto's critique of Aristotle.[35] What is particularly significant is the observation that, although Luther criticized Aristotle frequently from 1509 onwards, his reasons for doing so underwent a radical alteration in the period 1516–17.[36] Although Luther criticized Aristotle for reasons similar to those given by Hugolino initially, his subsequent criticism was made on the basis of his new soteriological insights, arising from his discovery of the 'righteousness of God'. On the basis of the marginal comments on the *Sentences*, Luther's attitude towards scripture, however, is unclear, and difficult to correlate with the later medieval period. In the *Dictata super Psalterum*, however, these attitudes are clarified, and allow us to relate Luther to his late medieval context.

Luther's early views on scriptural exegesis are those which Oberman designates as 'Tradition I' (the 'single source' theory). Luther upholds the material sufficiency of Holy Scripture, as understood by the fathers and doctors of the church; in the case of disagreement between these interpreters, the final authority must be regarded as resting in scripture.[37] Nevertheless, it is the *regula fidei* of the church which determines the limits within which the interpretation of scripture may proceed:[38] 'Extra enim ecclesiam non est cognitio vera

---

33 For the views of Bradwardine (usually regarded either as a precursor or early representative of the *schola Augustiniana moderna*) on the sufficiency of scripture, see Heiko A. Oberman, *Archbishop Thomas Bradwardine: A Fourteenth Century Augustinian* (Utrecht, 1957), pp. 22–7.
34 See Adolar Zumkeller, 'Die Augustinertheologen Simon Fidati von Cascia und Hugolin von Orvieto und Martin Luthers Kritik an Aristoteles', *ARG* 54 (1963), pp. 13–37.
35 WA 9.23.7; 43.5.
36 As I demonstrated elsewhere: Alister E. McGrath, *Luther's Theology of the Cross: Martin Luther's Theological Breakthrough* (Oxford, 1985), pp. 136–41.
37 For example, WA 3.318.3–6; 516.40–517.4.
38 For example, WA 3.517.33-40; 4.25.12–17.

Dei.'[39] The mutual coinherence of scripture and tradition is clearly affirmed, in terms indicating that Luther stands in the 'Tradition I' line associated with Bradwardine, Wycliffe,[40] Huss, Wessel Gansfort and theologians of the *schola Augustiniana moderna*. Luther appears to demonstrate continuity in this important respect with a well-established line of interpretation of the nature and identity of the sources of theology associated with the later medieval period.

If the sixteenth century saw the continuation of the fourteenth and fifteenth century debate over the relation between scripture and tradition, it becomes increasingly important to identify what, if any, novel elements were introduced into the discussion by the Reformers.

One obvious difference concerns the extent to which the 'scripture principle' was applied. It is certainly true that the *sola scriptura* principle was employed more radically by the early Reformed theologians than had ever been previously envisaged. The importance of the 'scripture principle' in the Swiss Reformation, following the Zurich disputation of 29 January 1523, has already been noted (see pp. 43–4). The 'Zurich disputation decision' – the mandate to preach on the basis of scripture alone, which rapidly became the basis of similar decisions elsewhere in Switzerland and southern Germany[41] – represents an important milestone in the political development of the Reformation, but it does not primarily concern the intellectual origins of the Reformation.

Nevertheless, it is significant that the origins of the early Reformed church may be explained, at least in part, through the intensification of an element of late medieval theology (Tradition I), whereas the Tridentine decree on scripture and tradition may equally be regarded as the intensification of a different element (Tradition II).[42] For the early Reformed theologians, scripture was now the touchstone of matters of church order and morality, as well as of theology (and in this, as is indicated below, there may well be some considerable degree

---

39 WA 3.268.37–8.
40 The suggestion that Wycliffe *denies* tradition (e.g., Michael Hurley, '*Scriptura sola*: Wyclif and His Critics', *Traditio* 16 (1960), pp. 275–352, following Thomas Netter Waldensis, *Doctrinale antiquitatum fidei catholicae ecclesiae*) is misleading, apparently arising from a failure to distinguish 'Tradition I' and 'Tradition II', and restricting the sense of 'tradition' to the latter. As de Vooght so perceptively points out (*Sources de la doctrine chrétienne*, p. 197 n.1): 'Prétendre que Wiclif n'admettait pas la tradition...c'est lui attribuer gratuitment une opinion dont il n'avait pas l'idée.'
41 See Emil Egli, 'Zur Einführung des Schriftprinzips in der Schweiz', *Zwingliana* 1 (1903), pp. 332–9.
42 Oberman, *Harvest of Medieval Theology*, pp. 406–12.

of continuity between the early Reformed theologians and late medieval thinkers such as Wycliffe and Huss). The expansion of the areas in which scripture was recognized to be competent is one of the most significant features of the early Reformed church: even the authority and interpretation of scripture were held to be based upon scripture itself, and not upon the church – scriptura sui ipsius interpres.

This does not, however, account for the intellectual origins of the *Lutheran* Reformation. In his remarkably perceptive account of the relation between the *sola scriptura* principle and the Lutheran Reformation, Kropatschek observed that the principle – a commonplace in the medieval period – was rendered sterile and useless through the absence of a proper hermeneutical scheme by which it might be interpreted.[43] Scripture is interpreted as nothing more and nothing less than *lex divina*.[44] Noting that Wycliffe is rightly regarded as an exponent of the 'scripture principle', he pointed out that Wycliffe's theology is thoroughly moralist, with no distinction being recognized between *lex* and *evangelium*.[45] A similar point might be made with regard to Huss, who treated scripture as *lex Dei*, which might be opposed to *leges humanas* deriving from the pope.[46] Scripture is thus treated as a source of law, of morals, of rules for the regulation of human behaviour. In many respects, the early radical proponents of the *sola scriptura* principle (such as Wycliffe and Huss) may be regarded as extending the scope of scripture to discipline, as well as doctrine, thus calling into question the methods of the decretalists and canon lawyers. In this respect, they may be regarded as forerunners of the Swiss Reformation (and how often the moralism of that Reformation in its early phase has been noted!) – but *not* of the Lutheran Reformation. The equation of *lex, scriptura* and *evangelium*, implicit (and often explicitly stated) in the writings of such late medieval theologians was, if anything, a hindrance (rather than a catalyst) to the emergence of the reforming theology at Wittenberg. The crucial question at Wittenberg was not so much that of the status of scripture, as how it might be interpreted – a question that is all too frequently neglected, and one to which we now turn.

---

43 Kropatschek, *Schriftprinzip der lutherischen Kirche*, pp. 438–41.
44 Kropatschek, *Schriftprinzip der lutherischen Kirche*, pp. 348–59.
45 Kropatschek, *Schriftprinzip der lutherischen Kirche*, pp. 357–9.
46 Huss, *Tractatus de ecclesia*, cap. 18 N; ed. S. Harrison Thomson (Cambridge, 1956), p. 167 'Signum autem defectus pape est si postposita lege dei et devotis ewangelii professoribus tradicionibus attendit humanis. . . permitteret garrire leges humanas in palacio et silere legem Christi, que est lex immaculata convertens animas.'

6

Sources and Methods:
The Interpretation of Scripture

It will be obvious that neither establishing and translating the text
of scripture, nor recognizing its material sufficiency as a theological
source, exhausts the problems associated with that theological source.
How is scripture to be *interpreted*? The Reformation principle of *sola
scriptura* is rendered either meaningless or unusable without a reliable
hermeneutical programme. Scripture might indeed contain (or even
be identical with) the Word of God – but an inability to interpret
scripture inevitably precludes access to that Word. In that scripture
was regarded as the primary foundation of theology throughout the
medieval period, including the foundational era of the Reformation,
it will be clear that an examination of biblical hermeneutics in the
late medieval and Reformation periods is an integral part of this
present study. A theologian's hermeneutical presuppositions inevitably
exercise considerable influence over his theological conclusions. In
this chapter, I propose to consider both the traditional medieval
hermeneutical techniques and the new literary methods introduced
by the humanists, with a view to establishing the relation of the
hermeneutical methods of the Reformers to those of the late medieval
period. A starting point will be consideration of the standard medieval
hermeneutical tool: the *Quadriga*.

THE FOUR-FOLD SENSE OF SCRIPTURE

The difficulty of interpreting the different literary styles within both
Old and New Testaments was recognized from the time of Clement
of Alexandria and Origen onwards.[1] The distinction between the

---

1 Henri de Lubac, *Histoire et ésprit: l'intelligence de l'écriture d'après Origène* (Paris, 1950). For an excellent general guide to recent literature on the exposition of scripture in the Reformation period, see Beate Stierle, 'Schriftauslegung der Reformationszeit', *Verkündigung und Forschung* 16 (1971), pp. 55–88.

'literal' and 'allegorical' (which initially appears to have meant little more than 'non-literal') sense of scripture originates from this period, and would surface as an issue of some importance in the Arian controversy of the fourth century.[2] It was, however, Augustine who transmitted to the medieval period the idea that there were a number of higher (that is, non-literal) senses of scripture, an idea that eventually became formalized in the hermeneutical device of the 'four-fold sense of scripture', or *Quadriga*.[3] In addition to the literal sense, three spiritual senses were to be distinguished: the *allegorical*, which concerns what is believed; the *anagogical*, which concerns what is hoped for; and the *tropological*, which concerns moral conduct.[4] The relation between these four senses was often summarized in the lines of the thirteenth century Dominican, Augustine of Denmark:

> Littera gesta docet; quid credas allegoria,
> Moralis quid agas; quo tendis, anagogia.[5]

In order to prevent such a hermeneutical scheme degenerating into the arbitrary personal interpretation of scripture, the theologians of the period insisted upon the priority of the literal sense of scripture: nothing could be believed on the basis of any of the three spiritual senses of scripture unless it had first been established on the basis of the literal sense.[6] In effect, this hermeneutical scheme was primarily intended to allow otherwise obscure, or apparently irrelevant, portions of scripture to be harmonized with those whose meaning was clearer:

---

2 See the debate over the putative influence of Lucian of Antioch and Peter of Alexandria upon Origen: T. E. Pollard, 'The Origins of Arianism', *Journal of Theological Studies* 9 (1958), pp. 103-11; Pollard, 'The Exegesis of Scripture and the Arian Controversy', *Bulletin of the John Rylands Library* 42 (1958-9), pp. 414-29.

3 Gillian R. Evans, *The Language and Logic of the Bible: The Earlier Middle Ages* (Cambridge, 1984), pp. 114-22.

4 See, e.g., Bonaventure, *Breviloquium*, prol. 4, 1; *Collationes in Hexameron* xiii, 11. See further George H. Tavard, *Transiency and Permanence: The Nature of Theology according to St Bonaventure* (New York/Louvain, 1954), pp. 31–55.

5 S. A. Walz, 'Des Aage von Dänemark 'Rotulus Pugillaris' im Lichte der dominikanischen Kontroverstheologie', *Classica et Medievalia* (Copenhagen) 15 (1954), pp. 198–252; 16 (1955), pp. 136–94.

6 See, e.g., Thomas Aquinas, *In I Sent.* prol. q.1 aa.5, 7; A. Haufnagel, 'Wort Gottes: Sinn und Bedeutung nach Thomas von Aquin', in *Wort Gottes in der Zeit*, ed. Helmut Feld and J. Nolte (Düsseldorf, 1973), pp. 236–56; Fritz Hahn, 'Zur Hermeneutik Gersons', *ZThK* 51 (1954), pp. 34–50; Helmut Feld, *Die Anfänge der modernen biblischen Hermeneutik in der spätmittelalterlichen Theologie* (Wiesbaden, 1977), pp. 70–83.

of scripture to be harmonized with those whose meaning was clearer: a failure to permit such harmonization would be tantamount to conceding that theology was concerned merely with certain biblical texts, rather than the entire canon of scripture.

This four-fold hermeneutical scheme is employed by the young Luther in his exposition of the Psalter in the period 1513–15.[7] Here the *Quadriga* is employed in keeping with the medieval tradition: thus, for example, Luther insists that the three spiritual senses are subordinate to the literal (historical) sense.[8] Indeed, even as late as 1519, Luther was prepared to defend the value of the *Quadriga* as an exegetical aid, provided that it was not abused.[9] Luther's use of this standard medieval hermeneutical device is of importance in relation to his deliberations concerning the meaning of the phrase 'the righteousness of God (*iustitia Dei*)', in that some scholars have argued that Luther's theological breakthrough is a consequence of his recognition of the priority of the *tropological* sense of the phrase, which is interpreted as 'faith in Christ (*fides Christi*)'.[10] Although this suggestion is questionable, it nevertheless indicates the importance of Luther's hermeneutical continuity with the medieval period to the study of his theological development.

In fact, it seems that Luther's early hermeneutics were considerably influenced by developments in the period 1503–15, which identified a crucial problem relating to the first of the four senses of scripture – the literal sense. In that the remaining three senses were ultimately dependent upon this first sense, its importance in relation to the use of the *Quadriga* was considerable. The key development of the period was the emergence of a clear distinction between the 'letter' and the 'spirit' of scripture.

THE LETTER AND THE SPIRIT

The rise of the new humanist philological and textual techniques in the first two decades of the sixteenth century resulted in a new interest

7 Karl Holl, 'Luthers Bedeutung für den Fortschritt der Auslegungskunst', in *Gesammelte Aufsätze zur Kirchengeschichte* (3 vols: Tübingen, 7th edn, 1948), vol. 1, pp. 544–82, especially pp. 545–50.
8 WA 3.11.33–5 'In Scripturis. . . nulla valet allegoria, tropologia, anagoge, nisi alibi hystorice idem expresse dicatur. Alioquin ludibrium fieret Scriptura.' Cf. WA 4.305.6–8.
9 WA 2.550.34–552.19.
10 For example, E. Vogelsang, *Die Anfänge von Luthers Christologie* (Berlin/Leipzig, 1929), based particularly upon WA 3.466.26–8. For a criticism of this view, and the suggestion that Luther merely clarifies (rather than alters) his existing views at this point, see Alister E. McGrath, *Luther's Theology of the Cross: Martin Luther's Theological Breakthrough* (Oxford, 1985), pp. 119–28.

in the literal sense of scripture. Thus whereas in his *Enchiridion* of 1503 Erasmus had shown a marked predilection for the spiritual sense of scripture,[11] he subsequently came to lay increasing emphasis upon its grammatical sense. The literal sense, he now believed, could be uncovered through the application of the methods of literary and textual criticism.[12] For this reason, the exegete had to be competent in the sacred languages. Thus Erasmus developed a hermeneutical programme in which the literal sense of scripture was first established on the basis of the new scientific literary, textual and philological techniques, before its spiritual senses were further developed.[13] Of those spiritual senses, it is clear that the tropological or moral was regarded as primary by Erasmus. Thus he observes that, while any passage can be interpreted tropologically, not all may be interpreted allegorically.[14] An illustration of this tropological exegesis may be found in his interpretation of the *fides Abraam*: Abraham's faith serves as an example of virtue, which may be contrasted with a sterile reliance upon circumcision and other such Old Testament ceremonies.[15]

This emphasis upon the literal sense of scripture, however, raised a serious difficulty: the literal exegesis of the Old Testament would thence seem destined to be nothing more than *Judaica expositio*. In an important letter to Wolfgang Capito of 26 February 1517, Erasmus drew attention to precisely this danger: the literal exegesis of the Old Testament was potentially the seedbed of a revived Judaism, which

11 Erasmus, *Opera Omnia*, vol. 5, p. 9 A–B. Note also the tendency to treat the allegorizing Origen as equal to Paul: p. 29 F. Critics have noted his tendency to revert to Origenistic spiritualism (e.g., Gerhard Ebeling, *Evangelische Evangelienauslegung: Eine Untersuchung zu Luthers Hermeneutik* (Munich, 1942), p. 139). For an excellent study of the later (1516) use made of Origen, see André Godin, 'Fonction d'Origène dans la pratique exégétique d'Erasme: les annotations sur l'épître aux Romains', in *Histoire de l'exégèse au XVIᵉ siècle*, ed. Olivier Fatio and Pierre Fraenkel (Geneva, 1978), pp. 17–44.

12 See *Ratio verae theologiae* (1518), ed. Hajo and Annemarie Holborn (Munich, 1933), pp. 284–92. Note the critical reference to Origen at 284.26–7: 'Immodicus est ac plerumque iniquior historico sensui quam par est.' With his predilection for Jerome's philological achievements, Erasmus could hardly overlook the latter's criticism of Origen (287.27–9), 'quod aliquoties vim faciat Scripturae, opinor, ut nos prorsus abducat a littera, plerumque sterili.'

13 John B. Payne, 'Towards the Hermeneutics of Erasmus', in *Scrinium Erasmianum II*, ed. J. Coppens (Leiden, 1970), pp. 13–49, especially pp. 45–8.

14 *Opera Omnia*, vol. 5, p. 1050 A–B. Tropological exegesis also possesses the virtue of simplicity – Erasmus frequently criticizes Origen for his elaborate allegorical exegesis: *Opera Omnia* vol. 6, pp. 554 A; 560 B; 564 C.

15 *Opera Omnia* vol. 7, pp. 787–9.

could pose a serious threat to the Christian faith.[16] Although this point had been appreciated for some considerable time, the return *ad fontes* associated with the late Renaissance and early Reformation made it an acutely sensitive area. How could the literal exegesis of the Old Testament be undertaken without reverting to Judaism? The problem was compounded still further through the need to gain the necessary philological techniques to handle the Hebrew text of the Old Testament: the philological works most frequently consulted by Christian Hebraists (such as Reuchlin's *De rudimentibus*) were actually written by Jews. In addition, several important exegetical works of the early Reformation period – such as Bucer's commentary on the Psalter (1529) – drew heavily upon medieval rabbinical sources, such as David Kimhi and Abraham Ibn Ezra (of the medieval Hispano-Provençal *peshat* school) and Solomon ben Isaac (Rashi) of Troyes.[17]

Despite these evident difficulties, Bucer indicates that his commentary on the Psalter represents an attempt to interpret an Old Testament text strictly upon the basis of the historical (or literal) sense. Three reasons are given for this procedure: first, it is this form of exegesis alone which will command respect from Jews;[18] second, it alone can withstand the assault of academic disputation; third, doctrine is ultimately based upon this sense of scripture.[19] It will thus be clear that the new emphasis upon the historical sense of the Old Testament text, linked with the need for reliable philological insights into the Hebrew text, inevitably meant that sixteenth century Christian Hebraists and Jews found themselves engaged in (an ultimately indecisive) battle on this terrain. The need to distinguish the Jewish and Christian historical understandings of the historical sense was

16 *Opus epistolarum Erasmi*, ed. P. S. Allen (12 vols: Oxford, 1906–58), vol. 2, no. 541, pp. 487–92; 491.133–9 'Unus adhuc scrupulus habet animum meum, ne sub obtextu priscae litteraturae renascentis caput erigere conetur paganismus . . . aut ne renascentibus Hebraeorum literis, Judaismus meditetur per occasionem reviviscere: qua peste nihil adversius nihilque infensius inveniri potest doctrinae Christi.' For the earlier letter of Capito, dated 2 September 1516, see no. 459, pp. 333–8. See further Gerald Hobbs, 'Monitio amica: Pellican à Capito sur le danger des lectures rabbiniques', in *Horizons européens de la Réforme en Alsace*, ed. Marijn de Kroon and Marc Lienhard (Strasbourg, 1980), pp. 81–93. On Capito, see James M. Kittelson, *Wolfgang Capito: From Humanist to Reformer* (Leiden, 1975).
17 Gerald Hobbs, 'Martin Bucer on Psalm 22: A Study in the Application of Rabbinical Exegesis by a Christian Hebraist', in *Histoire de l'exégèse au XVIᵉ siècle*, ed. Olivier Fatio and Pierre Fraenkel (Geneva, 1978), pp. 144–63.
18 For the apologetic importance of this consideration, see Erwin Rosenthal, 'Anti-Christian Polemic in Medieval Biblical Commentaries', *Journal of Jewish Studies* 11 (1960), pp. 115–35.
19 Hobbs, 'Bucer on Psalm 22', p. 151.

thus urgent. A partial solution to this difficulty appears to have emerged during the first decade of the sixteenth century, and is associated with Jacques Lefèvre d'Étaples.

For Lefèvre, the only literal sense of any importance is the Christological, 'qui scilicet est intentionis prophetae et Spiritus sancti in eo loquimus'.[20] *Two* literal senses may be recognized: the false, carnal literal sense of the rabbinical exegesis, which applies the words of the Psalmist or prophet only to the specific historical situation pertaining at the time of writing, and the true literal sense ('as the Holy Spirit intends') which interprets such words as applying to Christ. The true sense of scripture is thus not the tropological, the anagogical or allegorical, but the literal sense – a literal sense, that is, which discloses its hidden Christological spiritual sense through the illumination of the Holy Spirit.[21] In making this assertion, Lefèvre draws upon a tradition that can be traced back to Nicolas of Lyra. Lyra argues that there are points – such as Isaiah 1.11 – where it is clear that the Old Testament writer refers to Christ, and not to Israel, hence necessitating the recognition of a double literal sense, one applying to the time of the prophet, or the Old Testament, the second applying to Christ, or the New Testament. A similar theory is developed by Paul of Burgos.[22]

Lefèvre designates these two literal senses as the *sensus literalis historicus* and the *sensus literalis propheticus*, corresponding to the 'literal–carnal' and 'literal–spiritual' senses respectively.[23] To read the Old Testament as a series of narratives dealing with the history of ancient Near Eastern semitic tribes is to miss the deeper meaning to the text, brought out by the Holy Spirit. Drawing on Augustine's distinction, based upon 2 Corinthians 3.6, between the killing *litera* and life-giving *spiritus*,[24]

---

20 *Quincuplex Psalterium* (Paris, 1509), praefatio. Cf. Fritz Hahn, 'Faber Stapulensis und Luther', *ZKG* 57 (1938), pp. 356–432.

21 Lefèvre elsewhere makes it clear that he is prepared to recognize subsidiary senses of scripture, such as the tropological or allegorical: *Quincuplex Psalterium*, fol. 159 A. However, the *primary* sense of scripture is the 'literal–spiritual' sense noted above, and contrasted with the 'literal–carnal' sense of rabbinical exegesis.

22 Heiko A. Oberman, *Forerunners of the Reformation: The Shape of Late Medieval Thought* (Philadelphia, 1981), p. 286.

23 The former is also occasionally designated the *sensus literalis improprius* or *sensus literalis humano sensu fictus*; the latter the *sensus literalis proprius* or *sensus literalis divino spiritu infusus*.

24 Augustine, *De spiritu et litera* iv, 6–v, 8. For a detailed analysis of Lefèvre's methods, see Guy Bedouelle, 'La lecture christologique du Psautier dans le *Quincuplex Psalterium* de Lefèvre d'Étaples', in *Histoire de l'exégèse au XVIe siècle*, ed. Olivier Fatio and Pierre Fraenkel (Geneva, 1978), pp. 133–43.

Lefèvre identifies the former with the historical sense of the Old Testament, and the latter with its prophetic sense. In that Lefèvre's *Quincuplex Psalterium* was widely used by early sixteenth century commentators anxious to deal with the Hebrew text of the Psalter at first hand, its considerable influence upon Old Testament exegesis in the second decade of the sixteenth century comes as no surprise. Thus the noted Tübingen exegete Wendelin Steinbach insisted that, in its literal sense, the Old Testament must be taken as referring to Christ and his church.[25] For our purposes, however, the most important application of Lefèvre's *litera–spiritus* dialectic is Martin Luther's *Dictata super Psalterium* (1513–15).

HERMENEUTICS AND THE ORIGINS OF

THE LUTHERAN CHURCH

For Luther, as for the medieval tradition in general, the literal sense of scripture is fundamental.[26] However, Luther recognizes the necessity of distinguishing *two* literal senses of scripture, and develops a hermeneutical scheme which is best regarded as a combination of the traditional four-fold sense of scripture with Lefèvre's distinction between the *sensus literalis historicus* and *sensus literalis propheticus*, thus yielding eight senses of scripture.[27] Luther develops this point – playfully, it would seem – by considering the eight senses which the phrase 'Mount Zion' might bear, on the basis of this scheme.[28] Taking the term in its literal–historical sense – 'the killing letter (*litera occidens*)', as Luther terms it, following Lefèvre – the following four senses may be deduced. In its literal sense, it refers to the land of Canaan; in its allegorical sense, to the synagogue; in its tropological sense, to the righteousness of the law; in its anagogical sense, to the future glory of the flesh. Taking the term in its literal–prophetic sense – 'the life-giving spirit (*spiritus vivificans*)', as Luther terms it – four very different senses may be deduced. In its literal sense, it refers to the people of Zion; in its allegorical sense, to the church; in its

25 Helmut Feld, *Martin Luthers und Wendelin Steinbachs Vorlesungen über den Hebräerbrief* (Wiesbaden, 1971), pp. 145–52, especially pp. 146–7.
26 For example, WA 3.11.33–5.
27 See the masterly essay of Gerhard Ebeling, 'Die Anfänge von Luthers Hermeneutik', in *Lutherstudien I* (Tübingen, 1971), pp. 1–68, especially pp. 51–61.
28 WA 3.11.17–31.

tropological sense, to the righteousness of faith; in its anagogical sense, to the eternal glory of the heavens. This eight-fold distinction allows Luther to develop two important points. First, he argues that Christ is the *sensus principalis* of scripture.[29] In other words, the literal–prophetic sense of scripture gives rise to a Christological concentration. Second, he argues that the entire distinction between law and gospel is contained in the correlative distinction between *litera* and *spiritus*: the former merely makes (impossible) demands of man, whereas the latter enables him to meet them. We shall consider these two points further, beginning with Luther's 'Christological concentration'.

Luther follows in the tradition of Augustine by treating the Psalter as a Christological text. Christ is the key to the text which he proposes to expound.[30] Thus Luther opens his exposition with the affirmation 'PRAEFATIO IHESV CHRISTI filii dei et domini nostri in Psalterium DAVID'.[31] David was a prophet, and the substance of his prophecy is none other than Christ himself.[32] For this reason, Luther criticizes Lyra for his failure to bring out the full significance of the prophetical sense of the text, arguing that to interpret the text *historice*, rather than *prophetice*, is to use a rabbinical tool to develop a Judaized interpretation of the text. For Luther, as we have seen, the *sensus literalis* is the *sensus propheticus*. The danger which Luther emphasizes is that of mistaking the shadow for the substance, or the sign for the thing which is signified.[33] For Luther, the substance which is foreshadowed in the Old Testament is Christ;[34] the thing signified by the law is the life, death and resurrection of Jesus Christ.[35] Thus the New Testament, and supremely its Christological elements, is essentially the law of Moses understood according to the spirit – in other words, *litera* become *spiritus*.[36] In a remarkable turn of phrase, which clearly foreshadows (or may even already express) the *theologia crucis*, Luther argues that the literal–historical sense is *sensus in dorso*, whereas the literal–prophetic sense is *sensus in*

29 WA 3.46.28–9; 369.6 'Hec omnia Christus simul.'
30 WA 3.12.14–19. For what follows, see Ebeling, 'Anfänge von Luthers Hermeneutik', pp. 54–61.
31 WA 3.12.11–13.
32 WA 3.13.6–13.
33 WA 3.318.24–8.
34 WA 55 II.67.16–19.
35 WA 3.318.18–24.
36 WA 4.134.20 'lex spiritualis et evangelium idem sunt'; WA 55 I.92.16–20 'lex spiritualiter intellecta est idem cum evangelio'.

facie.[37] This Christological exposition of the Psalter, although traditional in its results, nevertheless draws upon the more recent exegetical
methods associated with Lefèvre d'Étaples, also taken up by catholic
exegetes (such as Steinbach) at the same time. It is therefore important
to notice that Luther's hermeneutics at this point are characteristic of
the period. If any genuine theological breakthrough took place during
Luther's exposition of the Psalter, it would seem that that breakthrough
did not occur on account of any radical new hermeneutical insights.

The dialectic between *lex* and *evangelium* is the second major aspect
of Luther's hermeneutics. The law of Moses, according to Luther,
may be understood according to the letter as a visible external
righteousness, valid *coram hominibus* but not *coram Deo*.[38] It may alternatively be understood according to the spirit as the gospel of grace
(hence Luther's occasional reference to the gospel as *lex spiritualis*,[39]
meaning 'the law understood according to the spirit'). Luther emphasizes that the gospel may also be misunderstood as *litera*, and thus
reduced to law: the crucial distinction between *litera* and *spiritus* is not
confined to the period of the Old Testament. In this assertion may
be detected the dialectic between law and gospel which is so
characteristic a feature of his thought in the period 1519–25. The
essential unity of the Old and New Testaments is grounded in a correct
understanding of the dialectic between *litera* and *spiritus*. Life according
to the letter is characterized by unbelief, pride and rebellion against
God, whereas life according to the spirit is characterized by faith,
humility and obedience to God. It is perhaps therefore hardly sur-
prising that Luther declares that the ability to distinguish letter and
spirit is the hallmark of the true theologian![40]

Luther's early biblical exegesis is therefore essentially based upon
the *Quadriga*, with the three spiritual senses of scripture subordinated
to the literal–prophetic sense.[41] Luther, in fact, tends to play down
the anagogical, and shows an increasing interest in the tropological
sense of scripture.[42] It is at this point that an important difference

---

37 WA 4.475.1–4; 11–13. For the distinction between the 'back' and the 'face' of God, as
developed in the *theologia crucis*, see McGrath, *Luther's Theology of the Cross*, pp. 147–50.
38 WA 3.116.5–8.
39 For example, WA 4.134.20.
40 WA 55 I.4.25–7.
41 WA 3.46.28–9. Cf. Ebeling, 'Anfänge von Luthers Hermeneutik', pp. 60–1.
42 Ebeling, 'Anfänge von Luthers Hermeneutik', pp. 61–8. Ebeling suggests (p. 62) that Luther's
concept of faith is already sufficiently future-orientated to permit him to treat it merely as one
aspect of the *sensus propheticus*.

between Luther on the one hand, and Erasmus and Bucer on the other, must be noted. For Erasmus, the tropological sense of scripture is concerned with the moral demands which are made of the believer. Thus his discussion of the faith of Abraham ends with an exhortation to children to emulate the virtues of their parents.[43] Luther, however, adopts a quite different understanding of this sense of scripture: for him the tropological sense refers to the gracious work of Jesus Christ in the individual believer, so that the *bonum tropologicum* is to be defined as faith.[44] As Ebeling points out, Luther treats the concept as pertaining to God's *acta* rather than man's *facta*.[45] 'Via dei est, qua nos ambulare facit.'[46] Thus Luther interprets *iudicium Dei*, *iustitia Dei* and similar terms troplogically in terms of what God *does for* man, rather than in terms of what God *expects of* man.[47] At this point, Luther diverges from the medieval hermeneutical tradition, and it is far from clear why he should do so. The possible (but disputed) importance of the tropological sense of *iustitia Dei* to his theological breakthrough[48] gives added emphasis to the importance of establishing the origins of Luther's views on the tropological sense will be evident. The following suggestion may be of some use in this respect. It is evident that Luther regards the central message of scripture – both Old and New Testaments – to concern the *acta Dei*. Three particular arenas of this work of God are identified: the *acta Dei*

---

43 Erasmus, *Opera Omnia*, vol. 7, p. 789 F.

44 WA 3.532.23–6.

45 Ebeling, 'Anfänge von Luthers Hermeneutik', pp. 64–6.

46 WA 3.529.33. Cf. WA 3.156.2–3; 195.2–3; 530.21–2.

47 WA 3.465.33–5; 4.22.36 'id est quo nos sapientes, fortes, iusti et humiles vel iudicati sumus'.

48 J. S. Preus, *From Shadow to Promise: Old Testament Interpretation from Augustine to the Young Luther* (Cambridge, Mass., 1969), argued that the tropological sense hindered rather than assisted Luther's theological reflections. This improbable suggestion clearly rests upon a confusion of what Luther understands by *sensus propheticus*, among other points. See the convincing rebuttals by Gordon Rupp, *Journal of Theological Studies* 23 (1972), pp. 276–8; Scott Hendrix, *Ecclesia in via: Ecclesiological Developments in the Medieval Psalms Exegesis and the Dictata super Psalterium of Martin Luther* (Leiden, 1974). A more important criticism of the theory that Luther's breakthrough rests upon the *sensus tropologicus* concerns the apparent absence of any genuine breakthrough at this point – what is encountered is a terminological clarification within the framework of his *existing* thought: see McGrath, *Luther's Theology of the Cross*, pp. 113–28; 146. Recently, Helmar Junghans has suggested that Luther's theological breakthrough, including his discovery of the 'new' meaning of *iustitia Dei*. resulted from a new attitude to the Word of God, particularly a new manner of attending to the text of scripture: Junghans, *Der junge Luther und die Humanisten* (Göttingen, 1985), p. 287. While we remain unconvinced by Junghans' arguments on this specific point, it is clear that Luther's scholastic approach to the *interpretation* of scripture at this stage has indeed been supplemented by a new concern to *revere* scripture, perhaps deriving from Erfurt humanism in the manner Junghans suggests.

in Christ, in the church, and in the individual believer.[49] Luther's frequently repeated assertion that power lies with God in his Word, and not in us,[50] inevitably leads to an emphasis upon *acta Dei*, rather than *facta nostra*. This is evident in Luther's use of the allegorical sense of scripture to refer to God's *acta* in the church, and consistency would suggest that a similar approach should be encountered in relation to the tropological sense, which concerns *acta Dei in nobis* rather than *facta nostra*.

These points should be borne in mind, in considering the important thesis developed by Karl Bauer,[51] according to which the origins of Luther's reforming theology are to be explained upon the basis of the development of a new hermeneutic. This new hermeneutic, according to Bauer, was characterized by two leading features. First, an emphasis upon the Christological orientation of scripture; second, the tendency to treat the immediate practical concerns of the individual believer as the primary concern of the exegete. According to Bauer, this new hermeneutic was derived by Luther from Staupitz, and emerged in the period 1516–19.[52] The suggestion that Luther's hermeneutical insights were derived from Staupitz seems improbable in the light of recent research,[53] and is probably best regarded as an initially fruitful, but now untenable, suggestion. The associated suggestion that Luther's reforming theology is the direct consequence of the discovery of a new hermeneutic is considerably more exciting, and requires careful evaluation.

The first point to be considered is the dating of Luther's theological breakthrough. Although the debate is still unresolved,[54] it is clear that Luther's theology of justification was totally transformed by the year 1516. By this time, a 'new' understanding of the vital theologoumenon 'the righteousness of God (*iustitia Dei*)' had been established, and the priority of God over man in justification unequivocally stated.[55] This

---

49 WA 3.369.2–10; 541.38–542.2; 4.189.1–4.
50 For example, WA 4.216.40–1.
51 Karl Bauer, *Die Wittenberger Universitätstheologie und die Anfänge der Deutschen Reformation* (Tübingen, 1928), especially pp. 145–7.
52 Bauer, *Wittenberger Universitätstheologie*, pp. 21–2; 147. See further Ebeling, 'Anfänge von Luthers Hermeneutik', pp. 4–6.
53 See, e.g., David C. Steinmetz, *Luther and Staupitz: An Essay in the Intellectual Origins of the Protestant Reformation* (Durham, NC, 1980), pp. 35–67, especially pp. 65–7.
54 See McGrath, *Luther's Theology of the Cross*, pp. 141–7 for a discussion.
55 McGrath, *Luther's Theology of the Cross*, pp. 95–136.

is not necessarily to say that Luther's theological breakthrough is to be identified with his new theology of justification, although it is evident that it is its central feature.[56] Luther's theology of justification, as we noted earlier, was initially (1513) that of the *via moderna*, and was subjected to gradual modification over the period 1513–15 as new insights appeared. These new insights into man's justification *coram Deo* were essentially complete by early 1516, and almost certainly date from 1515.[57] Since Bauer has suggested that Luther's new hermeneutic dates from 1516–19, it would seem that his thesis concerning the hermeneutical basis of Luther's reforming theology has to be called into question, in that the origins of that theology appear to antedate his reforming hermeneutic.

The seriousness of this difficulty was considerably lessened by recognition of the fact that important hermeneutical developments are already evident in the *Dictata super Psalterium* itself.[58] Although Luther's new hermeneutic is indeed to be associated with the period 1516–19, important anticipations of its leading features may be found in the period 1513–15.[59] For this reason, the possibility that Luther's reforming theology owes its origins to new hermeneutical insights is still plausible.

It is evident that, although Luther continues to employ the *Quadriga* throughout the *Dictata* – and, indeed, would continue to regard it as a permissible hermeneutical tool for some years to come – an important modification to that four-fold scheme takes place within the *Dictata*. Although Luther *initially* follows the medieval tradition in general in insisting that the *literal* (that is, literal–prophetic, to use Lefèvre's terms) sense of scripture is fundamental, by the end of the *Dictata*, we find him insisting with equal vehemence that it is the *tropological* sense which is fundamental: 'sensus tropologicus ultimatus et principaliter intentus in scriptura'.[60] We have already noted how Luther eschews the

---

56 In my study of the development of Luther's reforming theology over the period 1513–19, noted above (n. 54), I pointed out how Luther's *theologia crucis* may be understood as the outcome of a theological programme based upon Luther's insights into the nature of *iustitia Dei*. The origins of this programme may be dated from 1515, and its conclusion in 1518–19.
57 McGrath, *Luther's Theology of the Cross*, pp. 128–33; McGrath, *Iustitia Dei: A History of the Christian Doctrine of Justification* (2 vols: Cambridge, 1986), vol. 2, pp. 3–10.
58 See, e.g., Ebeling, 'Anfänge von Luthers Hermeneutik', pp. 4–7.
59 For an excellent analysis, see Ebeling, 'Anfänge von Luthers Hermeneutik', pp. 8–12.
60 WA 3.335.21–2; 531.33–5.

traditional moral interpretation of the *sensus tropologicus*,[61] regarding it instead as a means of illuminating the work of God in Christ within man. As Ebeling has pointed out, it is the tropological sense which Luther comes to regard as embodying the existential dimension of the gospel,[62] representing the existential impact of Christ upon the believer. The significance of such concepts as *iustitia Dei* and *iudicium Dei* lies in the Christologically derived existential impact which they have upon the believer – and Luther's 1516–19 emphasis upon the immediate practical religious concerns of the individual believer is unquestionably foreshadowed here.

The strongly subjective dimension of Luther's exegesis, which is so intimately linked with the development of his theology of justification, is evident in the manner in which he transforms the *Quadriga* to the point at which it must be questioned whether he continues to use it at all.[63] The literal–prophetic and the tropological senses are increasingly viewed as one and the same thing, as the perceived signficance of Christ *pro nobis* comes to be identified as the supreme Christological insight of scripture. In view of Luther's idiosyncratic understanding of the *sensus tropologicus*, it would therefore seem that Luther's theological development over the crucial period 1513–15 took place *within*, but not necessarily *on account of*, the traditional medieval hermeneutical scheme. It is beyond dispute that Luther was able to employ the tropological sense of scripture as a vehicle for the development of his distinctive theology – but the evidence does not permit the conclusion that it was the occasion, still less the cause, of that development. The evidence suggests that Luther's hermeneutical and soteriological insights developed symbiotically, with each dimension to his thought reinforcing and stimulating the other, until eventually the old wineskins of the *Quadriga* proved incapable of containing the new wine which had fermented within them.

---

61 Cf. Holl, 'Luthers Bedeutung für den Fortschritt der Auslegungskunst', p. 546 '[Luther] betont diesen Sinn so stark, daß er ihn auch als den sensus primarius scripturae bezeichnen kann. Dazu kommt aber noch: was Luther unter diesem Titel vorträgt, sind nicht einzelne zufällig herausgegriffene sittliche Weisungen, wie man sie nach jeweiligem Bedünken an den Text anschließen mochte, sondern etwas Einheitliches, scharf Umrissenes, immer wieder von ihm Eingeschärftes. Es ist kurz gesagt das paulinische Evangelium, was Luther als dem tropologischen Sinn aus den Psalmen herausholt.'

62 Ebeling, 'Anfänge von Luthers Hermeneutik', pp. 66–8.

63 See, e.g., Ebeling, 'Anfänge von Luthers Hermeneutik', p. 68 '*Das Schema des vierfachen Schriftsinnes ist von innen her zubrochen. Zunächst auf seine Angelpunkte reduziert: den sensus literalis propheticus und den sensus tropologicus, hat er sich zuletzt als in sich identisch erweisen.*'

Just as Luther's soteriological insights initially failed to gain general acceptance within the Wittenberg theological faculty, so his hermeneutical insights failed in the same way, and perhaps to an even greater extent. The most important document relating to the hermeneutics of the Wittenberg university theology in the period 1516–19 is Karlstadt's theses of May 1518. For Karlstadt, the fundamental sense of scripture is the literal sense: authoritative theological argumentation must be based upon this sense.[64] In many respects, Karlstadt's dicta concerning the priority of the literal sense parallel those of his mentor, Thomas Aquinas,[65] reflecting in turn the medieval tradition as a whole. For Karlstadt, the meaning of a scriptural text (expressed in terms such as *verbi significatio* or *proprietas verborum*) can only be determined with reference to its literal sense.[66] But what is to be understood by the literal sense of scripture?

In an important study, Bubenheimer has drawn attention to the importance of the juristic tradition for Karlstadt's hermeneutics.[67] The model upon which Karlstadt appears to base his understanding of the literal sense of scripture is testamentary law. Thus the *circumstantiae scribentis* are not deemed relevant to the establishment of the literal sense. In marked contrast to Gerson and others, who insisted that the *sensus literalis* was determined by the intentions of the author, Karlstadt insists that the text *as written* is the primary object for investigation.[68] Karlstadt's frequent use of the term *sensus legibilis* is important in this context, as is his distinction between the 'intrinsic'

---

64 For example, *Apol. Concl.* fol. A. 2v 'Praemissae conclusiones verae sunt, si dicto doctoris testimonium sanctum secundum litteralem sententiam suffragaretur'; Valentin Ernst Löscher, *Vollständige Reformations-Acta und Documenta II: Auf das Jahr 1518* (Leipzig, 1723), pp. 80–1. Cf. his comments on Augustine's *de spiritu et litera*: '*vidi, legi* et relegi illum textum, *ad literam* autem legere hoc nequivi'; Ernst Kähler, *Karlstadt und Augustin: Der Kommentar des Andreas Bodenstein von Karlstadt zu Augustins Schrift De spiritu et litera* (Halle, 1952), 102.12–13.
65 For example, Thomas Aquinas, *Summa Theologiae*, Ia q.1 a.10 ad 1um 'Et ita etiam nulla confusio sequitur in sacra scriptura: cum omnes sensus fundentur super unum, scilicet literalem; ex quo solo potest trahi argumentum, non autem ex his quae secundum allegoriam dicuntur.'
66 *Apol. Concl.* fol. A 3r 'Sed eum, qui ad verbum seu verbi significationem accipitur, litteralem dicimus.'
67 Ulrich Bubenheimer, *Consonantia Theologiae et Iurisprudentiae: Andreas Bodenstein von Karlstadt als Theologe und Jurist zwischen Scholastik und Reformation* (Tübingen, 1977), pp. 126–37.
68 *Apol. Concl.* fol. A 2v 'Contra Gers[on] negamus, esse sensum litteralem, qui ex intentione, et circumstantiis scribentis colligitur'; Löscher, *Reformations-Acta*, p. 81. Cf. Gerson's principle, 'Est autem sensus literalis non solum grammaticalis, sed nec stricte logicalis; verum ille quem Spiritus sanctus principaliter intendebat, qui ex circumstantia literae, cum causis dicendi et modis exponendi, magis patet.' *Opera*, vol. 1, p. 11 D.

and 'extrinsic' exposition of scripture.[69] This radical narrowing of the concept of the 'literal sense of scripture' is of considerable importance in the development of the Reformation scripture principle, which increasingly came to be based upon the written letter of scripture. For present purposes, however, it is more important to note that Karlstadt – believing himself to be an authentic interpreter of Augustine – adopted an approach to the literal sense of scripture which was quite distinct from, and potentially diametrically opposed to, that of Luther in the same period. Although Karlstadt and Luther demonstrate significant convergence at points in their soteriology, this does not reflect common hermeneutical presuppositions, but if anything, a mutual respect for Augustine. The remarkable application of the tropological sense of scripture, so characteristic of Luther's formative period, is conspicuous by its absence, and – if anything – is the subject of implicit criticism within Karlstadt's 1518 hermeneutical theses. The Wittenberg university theology was not based upon a common hermeneutical programme: indeed, the ultimate unifying basis of that theology remains remarkably elusive.[70] The Wittenberg theology may indeed have been characterized by a return to the 'bible and Augustine' – but there appears to have been little agreement on the mode of interpretation of the first of these sources within the Wittenberg faculty in the crucial period 1516–18.

It is, nevertheless, significant that early Lutheran hermeneutics demonstrate significant continuity with those of the later medieval period. In particular, Luther's hermeneutics are clearly continuous with the scholastic *Quadriga*, the chief innovation (the use of Lefèvre's concept of the *sensus literalis propheticus*) being paralleled among other scholastic exegetes of the period, such as Wendelin Steinbach. Although the evidence suggests that hermeneutical developments may be of lesser significance in relation to Luther's theological development than was formerly thought to be the case, those developments initially took place within a hermeneutical (and also soteriological) framework well-established in certain theological circles by the year 1510. The framework within which the intellectual origins of the Wittenberg Reformation are to be sought was bequeathed to its chief propagators by the Middle Ages. The importance of this point becomes

---

69 Bubenheimer, *Consonantia Theologiae et Iurisprudentiae*, pp. 130–3.
70 Luther uses (or, more accurately, invents) the verb *wittenbergescere* to refer to this theology: WABr 12.16.6–9.

more apparent when the very different context of early Reformed hermeneutics is considered – to which we now proceed.

HERMENEUTICS AND THE ORIGINS
OF THE REFORMED CHURCH

Any account of early Reformed hermeneutics must be primarily concerned with the development of the exegetical methods and presuppositions of Huldrych Zwingli. In an earlier chapter, the considerable influence of humanist literary and textual techniques upon the development of the theology of the early Reformed church was noted. That same influence must now be considered in relation to the exegetical techniques employed in the interpretation of scripture.

Erasmus' initial preference for Origenistic allegorical exegesis, which gradually gave way (through the development of his philological techniques) to an increased emphasis upon the literal word of scripture, has already been described. The comparison of Zwingli and Erasmus in regard to their biblical hermeneutics has frequently been grossly confused through the tendency to assume that the latter's *Enchiridion* (1503) embodies his hermeneutical programme – whereas it is evident that, as his philological work developed, Erasmus' hermeneutics altered accordingly.[71] The man who edited the New Testament in 1516 was no longer the young humanist who wrote the *Enchiridion* in 1503. As is evident from a comparison between Erasmus' Matthew paraphrase of 14 January 1522, and Zwingli's important *Von clarheit und gewüsse oder unbetrogliche des wort gottes* of 6 September of the same year, the two men demonstrate a remarkable degree of convergence in their presuppositions, methods and doctrines. Although questions relating

---

71 See, e.g., Christine Christ, 'Das Schriftverständnis von Zwingli und Erasmus im Jahre 1522', *Zwingliana* 16 (1983), pp. 111–25; pp. 122–3 'In der Zwingliforschung wurde bis anhin ein Zwingli, den man vielfach von seinen Spätschriften her interpretierte, dem Verfasser des "Enchiridions" (1503) gegenübergestellt. Wurden spätere Erasmusschriften herangezogen, so wurden ihre "reformatorisch" klingenden Abschnitte mit Zitaten aus dem "Enchiridion" sofort abgeschwächt. Wohl ist es richtig, daß etwa Bibelzitate aus dem "Enchiridion" vom Programm der "humanistischen Bildungsform" (Schottenloher) her verstanden werden müssen, und wo das in der Erasmusforschung unterlassen wurde, ist das "Enchiridion" auch mißverstanden worden. Aber der Herausgeber der Neuen Testaments nach 1516 ist nicht mehr der junge Humanist von 1503. Erasus hatte inzwischen die Bibel lang genug studiert, um etwa den Unterschied zwischen einem platonisierenden Bildungsaufsteig und der christlichen Erlösung durch Gottes Gnade zu kennen.'

to the capacities of man (the freedom of the will, and the pedagogic aspect of the Reformation, discussed previously, being obvious examples) divide the two men, it is evident that in many other respects they are in agreement,[72] both in regard to the importance of scripture and the manner in which it is to be interpreted.

Zwingli makes extensive use of the distinction between the 'natural' and non-literal senses of scripture. In common with the medieval tradition, he insists that nothing should be believed which is established on the basis of a non-literal sense of scripture, unless it can first be demonstrated on the basis of the letter of scripture. The spiritual senses should be regarded as the embellishment of an exegetical argument, rather than its foundation.[73] Like Erasmus, Zwingli insists that the best possible exegeticals aids (such as a knowledge of the Hebrew and Greek languages, and of the various figures of speech employed in scripture) should be employed in an effort to establish the natural sense of scripture. The humanist influence is perhaps at its most evident in the emphasis which Zwingli lays upon the philological–historical method, which is given far greater weight that it would ever gain at Wittenberg. Furthermore, Zwingli draws extensively upon humanist rhetorical theory in his attempt to distinguish various tropes, such as alloiosis, catachresis and synecdoche, which were of potential theological significance.

The influence of humanism upon Zwingli is most evident in his early exegetical works, such as his marginal comments of 1516–17 to Erasmus' *Novum Instrumentum*.[74] At every point Zwingli depends upon Erasmus: his translation of the text, his textual criticism, his illustrations and his patristic references. Indeed, in terms of the *testimonia patrum* he employs, the strongly Origenistic bias of Erasmus is evident, particularly in his exposition of natural law, the nature of sin and eschatology. Finally, the anthropocentricity of Zwingli's exegesis is evident, here paralleling the younger Erasmus. Attention has also been drawn to the manner in which Zwingli uses humanist rhetorical techniques to deal with the inner meaning of a scriptural text,

---

72 Christ, 'Schriftverständnis von Zwingli und Erasmus', pp. 121–5.

73 For example, CR (Zwingli) 2.398.17–400.6; 6 I.404.2–9.

74 Walther Köhler, 'Die Randglossen Zwinglis zum Römerbrief in seiner Abschrift der paulinischen Briefe 1516/17', in *Forschungen zur Kirchengeschichte und zur christlichen Kunst: Johannes Ficker als Festgabe zum 70. Geburtstag dargebracht* (Leipzig, 1931), pp. 86–106. The dependence of Zwingli upon humanist philology in his translation of this letter has also been carefully documented: Adolf Meier, 'Zwinglis Übersetzung des Römerbriefs', *Evangelische Theologie* 19 (1959), pp. 40–52.

and particularly the extensive use of pagan classical authors in the course of his exegesis[75] – once more, indicating the considerable influence of humanism at this point. The Erasmian emphasis upon the tropological or moral sense of scripture is also evident in Zwingli's exegesis. Zwingli emphasizes the moral dimension of scripture, drawing attention to the contemporary moral relevance of Old Testament *exempla*. Zwingli's development of the Erasmian concept of the tropological sense of scripture (although Zwingli does not appear to use either this term, or the related term *sensus moralis*) clearly indicates his moralist concerns, and sets him apart from the young Luther in this crucial respect.

Despite the intense humanist preoccupation with the natural sense of scripture, noted above, Zwingli argues that Paul's use of the Old Testament legitimates the use of allegory in its interpretation (with 2 Corinthians 8.15 and Galatians 4.22–6 functioning as 'proof-texts'). Zwingli thus distinguishes between the literal sense of the Old Testament and its spiritual meaning. To read the Old Testament according to the letter is to adopt the carnal exegetical methods of the Jews, referring such accounts to an earthly Israel or Jerusalem; rather, it should be read in a spiritual manner, as prefiguring something which was accomplished and perfected in Christ.[76] Even here, the influence of humanism cannot be overlooked, particularly in view of the Origenist allegorizing characteristic of Erasmus' earlier works, such as the *Enchiridion*. In effect, Zwingli treats what Lefèvre termed the *sensus literalis historicus* as the natural sense, and the *sensus literalis propheticus* as the spiritual sense, although the parallel is not exact. Zwingli's understanding of the nature and relation of these senses is highly idiosyncratic, and requires careful analysis.

For Zwingli, concrete historical events recounted in the Old Testament possessed a deeper symbolical meaning. As an accommodation to human weakness, God prefigured what would eventually be accomplished and fulfilled in Christ in the form of external events or persons. Zwingli thus employs the term 'allegory' to refer to that mode of scriptural exegesis which is to be contrasted with a purely literal and carnal exegesis of the Old Testament.[77] In an important study, Edwin Künzli demonstrated that Zwingli's use of allegory could

75 Gerhard Krause, 'Zwinglis Auslegung der Propheten', *Zwingliana* 11 (1960), pp. 257–65.
76 CR 6 II.305.28–308.14; 13.213.8–12; 299.31–2; 374.24–7.
77 CR 6 II.305.28–308.14.

be rationalized with some success if a distinction was drawn between 'typology' and 'allegory'.[78] The 'typological' exegesis was primarily concerned with the Christological interpretation of individuals or events in the Old Testament as 'types' of Christ, and the 'allegorical' with passages where there was some uncertainty regarding the exegesis. In fact, however, Zwingli's use of both the concept and term of allegory is so broad and diffuse that it is difficult to analyse convincingly.[79] The chief difficulty is that, despite Zwingli's critique of those who imposed arbitrary interpretations upon obscure passages,[80] he appears to be forced to do precisely the same thing himself. On the basis of his own understanding of the natural sense, Zwingli is able to 'read back' his own theology into otherwise obscure passages, thus inevitably laying himself open to the accusation of indulging in *eisegesis* rather than *exegesis*.[81]

The influence of Erasmian humanism is perhaps even more marked upon the hermeneutics of Martin Bucer.[82] Earlier (pp. 52–3), we noted how Bucer took up and developed Erasmus' concept of the gospel as *lex Christi*, establishing as axiomatic the principle *nam et sacra doctrina proprie moralis est*. Bucer thus treats the tropological exegesis of scripture – the essentially timeless application of any biblical statement to practical piety on the grounds that it may be said to be *propter nos* – as fundamental.[83] The Old Testament histories must thus be regarded as having something significant to say to contemporary piety, rather than as purely historical narratives. Particularly in the emphasis upon *imitatio*, Bucer approximates closely to Erasmus. Thus Bucer follows Zwingli in asserting that scripture was written for our sake,[84] and not merely as an objective and disinterested account of God's dealings with mankind.

---

78 Edwin Künzli, 'Quellenproblem und mystischer Schriftsinn in Zwinglis Genesis- und Exoduskommentar', *Zwingliana* 9 (1949–54), pp. 185–207; 253–307, especially pp. 257–80. This analysis illustrates with some brilliance both the wide range of and the inherent contradiction within Zwingli's use of allegory.

79 See W. P. Stephens, *The Theology of Huldrych Zwingli* (Oxford, 1986), pp. 78–9.

80 For example, CR 6 II.305.6–27; 13.14.23–15.8; 361.27–35; 373.2–4.

81 Two particularly suspicious cases may be noted: CR 13.66.1–8; 347.7–10. There is also a certain fluidity in Zwingli's typology: Abraham is treated as a type of God at one point, and of the faithful people of God at another; Isaac represents Christ at one point, the faithful people of God at another, and God himself at a third.

82 The best study remains Johannes Müller, *Martin Bucers Hermeneutik* (Gütersloh, 1965).

83 Müller, *Martin Bucers Hermeneutik*, pp. 142–50, with important documentation.

84 Müller, *Martin Bucers Hermeneutik*, pp. 142–4; cf. CR (Zwingli) 1.421.12–423.9.

Bucer's emphasis upon *imitatio* allows him to interpret both the existential and moral statements of scripture pedagogically, with Christ being treated as the *unicus magister*, the prototype whom Christians are under obligation to follow.[85] In this respect, Bucer's scriptural exegesis can be regarded as both a continuation of the spirituality of the *devotio moderna* and a precursor of seventeenth century Pietism. It will also be evident that the apparent similarity between Bucer and the young Luther (in that both lay emphasis upon the tropological sense of scripture) is misleading: although both understand the tropological sense to refer to the existential dimension of scripture, Luther regards it as the work of Christ within man, whereas Bucer treats it as an example to be imitated by man, through the assistance of the Holy Spirit.

In one important respect, Bucer may be regarded as a more faithful interpreter than Zwingli of the later Erasmus. Despite Erasmus' increasing emphasis upon the literal sense of scripture, Zwingli had made extensive use of allegorization, particularly in relation to the interpretation of the Old Testament. Bucer rejects the use of allegory, in that it permits any meaning to be read into, or imposed upon, a passage, thus allowing its direct meaning to be overlooked or lost.[86] This is not, however, to say that Bucer abstains from the use of allegory altogether: Bucer appears to employ the device to a limited extent when the meaning is unequivocal.[87] It is not, however, treated as the primary sense of scripture – and here Bucer shows his affinities with the later Erasmus, rather than the author of the *Enchiridion*. Whereas the young Erasmus regarded allegory as the means of distinguishing letter and spirit, Bucer's theology of the Holy Spirit as the authentic interpreter of scripture, who allows the believer to read the text *ex intento auctoris*, allows him to dispense with this unreliable hermeneutical tool.

From this brief survey of early Reformed biblical hermeneutics, it will be evident that late medieval exegetical methods – such as the *Quadriga* – exercised little, if any, influence in this field. The hermeneutics of both Zwingli and Bucer may be regarded as Erasmian, and their theological programme as an attempt to return *ad fontes*, to interpret scripture in terms of its own parameters, rather than in

---

85 Müller, *Martin Bucers Hermeneutik*, pp. 145–7.
86 Müller, *Martin Bucers Hermeneutik*, pp. 100–14.
87 See the valuable discussion of Müller, *Martin Bucers Hermeneutik*, pp. 106–11.

terms of an imposed hermeneutical framework – scriptura sui ipsius interpres! The strongly moralist cast of early Reformed theology, linked with the Erasmian concept of *imitatio*, serves only to emphasize the differences between the early Reformed and Lutheran approaches to scripture. If the intellectual origins of the Reformation are to be explained in terms of the return to scripture as the source of Christian theology, the considerable divergence within the movement over the question of hermeneutics raises serious questions concerning the viability of this approach. The radical divergence within the Reformation as a whole, as well as within both the Lutheran and Reformed wings of that movement, over the exegesis of the sixth chapter of the Fourth Gospel, illustrates how wide the rift between the various Reformers could be when hermeneutical *cruces* (especially those apparently employing non-literal statements) could be. A further point is all too often overlooked: the *political* hermeneutics which served to propagate the Reformation in Switzerland and southern Germany during the third decade of the sixteenth century owed little, if anything, to the more theological hermeneutics which were being developed by Zwingli and others.

The importance of the 'First Zurich Disputation' of 29 January 1523 (pp. 43–4) in connection with the origins of the Reformed church has already been noted. The conclusions of this disputation are often regarded as a civic endorsement of Zwingli's reforming programme, establishing the *sola scriptura* principle as normative in matters of doctrine and preaching. In fact, however, it is clear that the city council introduced a subtle twist to the hermeneutical debate then raging within Zurich, by declaring that it was the city council itself (more strictly, the Lesser Council) which had the authority to determine what was in accordance with scripture, and what was not.[88] The outcome of the First Disputation was initially interpreted by the Lesser Council to mean that any teaching or practice might be permitted, subject to the provision that it be shown to have a formal basis in scripture. A similar decision was reached at Basle at the end of May 1523.[89] In both cases, the council's decision appears to have been conceived as an 'Interim' – a formula designed to gain time before a final decision

---

88 See Heiko A. Oberman, *Werden und Wertung der Reformation* (Tübingen, 1977), pp. 248–66. On the city council, see Norman Birnbaum, 'The Zwinglian Reformation in Zurich', *Past and Present* 15 (1959), pp. 27–47.
89 Oberman, *Werden und Wertung der Reformation*, pp. 250–1.

on the matters under consideration was reached. Thus Zwingli was informed that he might continue his preaching until he should be informed of a better theology (by the council).[90] In fact, the Lesser Council adopted a remarkably moderate approach to the question of formal agreement with scripture, refusing, for example, to allow the Zwinglian faction to paint the interiors of Zurich's churches in white. Contemporary sources suggest that only a minority of the Lesser Council were disposed favourably towards the evangelical faction,[91] with the result that the Zurich political scriptural hermeneutic tended to be surprisingly conservative. This situation changed significantly on 11 January 1524, when the Greater Council relieved the Lesser of its duty to interpret scripture, and assumed this office itself. What radical evangelicals such as Sprüngli had wished to see happen at Zurich, only to have it blocked by the Lesser Council, subsequently took place through the enhanced (if self-appropriated) spiritual authority of the Greater Council.

The point I want to emphasize will be obvious. The extent of the progress of the Reformation at Zurich, as elsewhere, was determined by political considerations, largely concerning the city council.[92] At Zurich, and subsequently elsewhere in Switzerland and southern Germany, the Reformation was propagated through public disputations based upon the *sola scriptura* principle. As this chapter has suggested, scripture requires interpretation – and the political dimension of the Zurich Reformation in particular (and the Swiss and southern German Reformation in general) was such that it was a *political* body which appropriated the authority to determine what was in accordance with scripture, and what was not. In other words, whatever the hermeneutics of the early theological proponents of the Reformation may have been, a secondary hermeneutic of political character was at least on occasion instrumental in the propagation of that movement.

90 CR (Zwingli) 1.471.2 '. . . so lang unnd vil, biß er eins besseren bericht werde'. As Oberman points out (p. 249), 'er' must be understood to refer to 'Zwingli' and not 'the Council' (*der Rat*, which takes the masculine pronoun in German).
91 According to Adam Sprüngli, only 14 out of the 48 members of the council favoured evangelicalism: see Oberman, *Werden und Wertung der Reformation*, pp. 258–9. Although Sprüngli's criteria for 'evangelicalism' were a little severe, his analysis appears to have been along the right lines.
92 The parallels with Geneva and Erfurt are instructive: Robert M. Kingdom, 'Was the Protestant Reformation a Revolution? The Case of Geneva', in *Transition and Revolution: Problems and Issues of European Renaissance and Reformation History*, ed. R. M. Kingdom (Minneapolis, 1974), pp. 53–107; Robert W. Scribner, 'Civic Unity and the Reformation in Erfurt', *Past and Present* 66 (1975), pp. 29–60.

This present chapter has examined the hermeneutics of the early Lutheran and Reformed churches, and found them to have little in common. The general Reformation principle of a return *ad fontes* was not accompanied by universal agreement, or anything even approaching this, over how scripture might be interpreted. While it is unquestionably true that many of the divergences within the early Reformation, particularly in relation to sacramental theology, arise from prior disagreement over hermeneutics, it is difficult to sustain the thesis that the distinctive foundational ideas of the Reformation themselves arose on account of a novel hermeneutic, even in the case of Luther himself. In fact, as the following chapter will show, there are excellent reasons for supposing that the *testimonium patrum* – the witness of the fathers – may have exercised a considerable restraining influence over both early Lutheran and Reformed hermeneutics, compensating to a significant extent for the absence of a general hermeneutical consensus. It is the role of the *testimonium patrum* in the theological method of the Reformers that will next be considered.

7

Sources and Methods:
The Patristic Testimony

The influence of the patristic heritage, and supremely the thought of Augustine of Hippo, upon the medieval period is beyond dispute.[1] Indeed, the theology of the medieval period may be regarded as thoroughly Augustinian to the extent that it was virtually a series of footnotes to Augustine: theological speculation was essentially regarded as an attempt to defend, develop and, where necessary, modify, the Augustinian legacy. Anselm of Canterbury virtually equated orthodoxy with the views of the 'catholic fathers, and especially Augustine'.[2] The standard text-book of medieval theology, still in use in the sixteenth century, was Peter Lombard's *Sentences* – a collection of patristic *dicta*, drawn largely from the writings of Augustine. The Lombard's book may be regarded as developing the procedure found in Prosper of Aquitaine's *Liber sententiarum ex operibus Augustini*, which is often pointed to as an early representative of 'medieval Augustinianism' – an attempt to bring together the main features of Augustine's theology, in order that they might be identified and developed.[3] The theological renaissance of the twelfth century, which may be regarded as laying the foundations for the theology of the medieval period as a whole, was largely based upon the writings of Augustine. In every major sphere of theological debate,

---

1 For example, David C. Steinmetz, *Misericordia Dei: The Thought of Johannes von Staupitz in its Late Medieval Setting* (Leiden, 1968), p. 33 'All medieval theologians, even the most Pelagian, were indebted to the great father of western theology for many of their ideas. All medieval theologians are, in some measure at least, Augustinian theologians. The question is not whether a theologian is indebted to Augustine but rather what is the degree and nature of his indebtedness.'

2 *Monologion*, prologue 'Quam ego saepe retractans nihil potui invenire me in ea dixisse, quod non catholicorum patrum et maxime beati Augustini scriptis cohaereat.'

3 See D. M. Cappuyns, 'Le premier représentant de l'Augustinisme médiévale', *RThAM* 1 (1929), pp. 309–37.

the point of departure appears to have been the views of Augustine.[4]

The chief difficulty facing the theologians of the twelfth and early thirteenth centuries was that Augustine's writings tended to be occasional, written in response to the challenges of his opponents, so that his theological distinctions and terminology were frequently shaped by the challenges of his opponents. Thus Augustine's concepts of 'operative' and 'cooperative' grace were formulated in response to the Pelagian distinction between a 'good will' and a 'good act', and proved to be incapable of bearing the strain placed upon them in a period which was characterized by increasing precision and systematization.[5] A similar difficulty was encountered in connection with Augustine's emphatic assertion that man could not merit justification: what precisely was meant by the term 'merit'? As theological systematization proceeded,[6] it became increasingly clear that the term 'merit' could bear a number of senses, necessitating a reformulation of Augustine's rejection of merit prior to justification, while retaining the theological insight which it expressed.[7] The twelfth and early thirteenth centuries may be regarded as consolidating the Augustinian heritage by retaining the *dogmatic content* of that heritage, while restating it employing distinctions, terms, concepts and methods unknown to Augustine himself. As the thirteenth century progressed, however, the process of reinterpreting Augustine appears to have become increasingly detached from its primary sources. There is every indication that Augustine's thought became obscured through the development of a tradition of Augustine interpretation. This process appears to have been catalysed by a number of factors.

First, Augustine tended to be studied atomistically, in the form of isolated quotations, or 'sentences', culled from his writings. In that the medieval reader of these sentences had no way of knowing their

---

4 This is particularly evident in relation to the doctrine of justification, one of the areas of theology to be most exhaustively discussed in the twelfth and early thirteenth centuries: see Alister E. McGrath, *Iustitia Dei: A History of the Christian Doctrine of Justification* (2 vols: Cambridge, 1986), vol. 1, *passim*. More generally, see M. D. Chenu, *La théologie au XIIe siècle* (Paris, 1957); J. de Ghellinck, *Le mouvement théologique de XIIe siècle* (Brussels, 2nd edn, 1969). On the twelfth century renaissance in general, see G. Paré, A. Brunet and P. Tremblay, *La renaissance du XIIe siècle* (Paris, 1933).

5 Witness Thomas Aquinas' difficulties with the concepts: McGrath, *Iustitia Dei*, vol. 1, pp. 103–8.

6 For a useful introduction, see H. Cloes, 'La systématisation théologique pendant la première moitié du XIIe siècle', *EThL* 34 (1958), pp. 277–329.

7 McGrath, *Iustitia Dei*, vol. 1, pp. 109–14.

immediate context, the possibility of seriously misinterpreting such isolated Augustinian gobbets was ever present.[8] The medieval Augustine interpretation tradition tended to treat such 'sentences' as proof texts for the particular position being defended, without any real attempt to engage directly with the complete primary sources. Such sources, it may naturally be added, were not generally available in the medieval period, through the physical impossibilty of transporting fragile manuscripts from one location to another. It is for this reason that the invention of printing and the production of the great Augustine editions of the early sixteenth century are so important – a point we shall return to presently.

Secondly, numerous works were in circulation during the medieval period purporting to be authentic works of Augustine.[9] The authenticity of some such works had been called into question in the pre-destinarian controversies of the ninth century, in which the views of Augustine were treated as authoritative by both sides – for example, the *Hypomnesticon*.[10] Other inauthentic works which were treated as authentic by medieval theologians included some which were thoroughly Pelagian, such as *De vita Christiana*,[11] thus confusing still further the already difficult task of interpreting Augustine's theology of grace. Perhaps the most influential work in establishing the medieval attitude to penance – a subject that would loom large in the Reformation debates – was the pseudo-Augustinian *De vera et falsa poenitentia*,[12] which propagated a view of penance which the Reformers would later dismiss as quasi-Pelagian. The widespread circulation of such tracts, however, created a serious problem for medieval theologians, in that it was not clear which of the various 'sentences' in circulation embodied the authentic views of Augustine.

The only means by which this difficulty could be overcome was by intensive source-critical work, such as that characteristic of the revival

---

8 See Alister E. McGrath, 'Reformation to Enlightenment', in *The History of Theology I: The Science of Theology*, ed. P. D. L. Avis (Basingstoke/Grand Rapids, Mich., 1986), pp. 000–00.
9 M. de Kroon, 'Pseudo-Augustin im Mittelalter: Entwurf eines Forschungberichts', *Augustiniana* 22 (1972), pp. 511–30.
10 Note the views of Hincmar of Reims and Florus of Lyons: McGrath, *Iustitia Dei*, vol. 1, pp. 131–2. For a detailed study, see J. E. Chisholm, *The Pseudo-Augustinian Hypomnesticon against the Pelagians* (Fribourg, 1967).
11 R. Evans, 'Pelagius, Fastidius and the Pseudo-Augustinian *De vita Christiana*', *Journal of Theological Studies* 13 (1962), pp. 72–98.
12 C. Fantini, 'Il trattato pseudo-agostiniana *De vera et falsa poenitentia*', *Ricerche di storia religiosa* 1 (1954–7), pp. 200-9.

of academic Augustinianism now recognized to be linked with the genesis of the *schola Augustiniana moderna* (see pp. 86–93). This may be illustrated by the recognition of the Pelagian character of the *Epistola ad Demetriadem* by both Thomas Bradwardine and Gregory of Rimini in the fourteenth century[13] (although this important conclusion did not gain general acceptance, both Johann Eck and Johannes Capreolus preferring to ascribe the work to Jerome.[14]) The source-critical work typical of this movement is evident in Gregory's *Commentary on the Sentences*, which appears to have been read as much as a source-book for reliable and authentic Augustine gobbets as for the views of Gregory himself.[15] A further feature of the academic Augustinianism of the fourteenth century, characteristic of the *schola Augustiniana moderna* and its immediate precursor at Oxford, is the emphasis upon the anti-Pelagian writings. In that Gregory of Rimini was widely recognized (for example, by an influential sixteenth century catholic theologian)[16] as *maximus et studiosissimus divi Augustini propugnator*, it is necessary to point out that this judgement was based upon Gregory's appeal to Augustine's doctrine of grace, as expounded in the anti-Pelagian writings. It is significant that an important aspect of Gregory's critique of Bradwardine centred upon the latter's non-Augustinian views on the significance of the Fall (pp. 91–2).

The rise of source-critical studies, within the Augustinian Order and elsewhere, in the fourteenth century inevitably led to a re-evaluation of the tradition-encrusted delineation of Augustine's theology, to the extent that it may be recognized as a rediscovery of the anti-Pelagian dimension to his thought. The rise of the ferociously anti-Pelagian soteriology of the *schola Augustiniana moderna* may be regarded as owing its origins, at least in considerable part, to the 'rediscovery' of the anti-Pelagian theology of Augustine. The priority of Augustine's views on the doctrine of grace over the *testimonia patrum* in general was justified on the basis of the considerable parallels – both biographical and theological – between Augustine and St Paul. Both, as Bradwardine pointed out, were unbelievers who owed their conversion to the remarkable agency of divine grace (to use the terms of twentieth

13 Heiko A. Oberman, *Werden und Wertung der Reformation* (Tübingen, 1977), p. 87.
14 As pointed out by Oberman, *Werden und Wertung der Reformation*, pp. 91–3.
15 Damasus Trapp, 'Augustinian Theology of the Fourteenth Century: Notes on Editions, Marginalia, Opinions and Book-Lore', *Augustiniana* 6 (1956), pp. 146–274, especially pp. 188–9.
16 Andreas de Vega, *Opusculum de iustificatione, gratia et meritis* (Venice, 1546), fol. 147. Note the accompanying reference to Bradwardine.

century popular religion, both were 'born again'), and who were thus well placed to speak of the sovereignty and precedence of divine grace over human actions.[17]

It is within this context of a continuing re-reception and re-evaluation of the theological, and especially the soteriological, legacy of Augustine in the late medieval period that the Reformation debates over its interpretation and the relative priority of its elements must be sought. The potential tension between its various elements, highlighted through the Hussite controversy and still unresolved on the eve of the Reformation, may be regarded as a significant contribution to the intellectual origins of the Reformation. It was the conviction on the part of the Wittenberg Reformers that the church of their day had lapsed into some form of Pelagianism – irrespective of whether this conviction was justified or not – which forced them to address the question of the relative priority and theological significance of the anti-Donatist and anti-Pelagian writings. Thus, at least in Luther's view, the Reformation did not arise as the result of any *direct* ecclesiological argument, but simply on the basis of the evangelical conviction that the church had defected from the gospel.[18] 'The Reformation, inwardly considered, was just the ultimate triumph of Augustine's doctrine of grace over Augustine's doctrine of the church.'[19] Such was the importance that the Wittenberg Reformers came to attach to Augustine's anti-Pelagian writings that a theology of justification consistent with those writings came to function as a criterion of the catholicity of the church. Although the Reformation is often regarded as essentially a debate over the theological status and interpretation of scripture, the truth of this statement has tended to obscure the fact that it was equally the continuation of a debate over the status, and supremely the interpretation, of Augustine, inherited from the late medieval period.

The particular form which the debate assumed in the first three decades of the sixteenth century was significantly influenced by the

17 Bradwardine, *De causa Dei* (London, 1618) lib. i, cap. 35; fol. 311 B–C.

18 Note Luther's famous remarks of 1535: 'Papa, ego voli tibi osculari pedes teque agnoscere summum pontificem, si adoraveris Christum meum et permiseris, quod per ipsius mortem et resurrectionem habeamus remissionem peccatorum et vitam aeternam, non per observationem tuarum traditionum. Si hoc cesseris, non adimam tibi coronam et potentiam tuam'; WA 40 I.357.18–22. For a careful study of Luther's attitude to the papacy and schism over the crucial period 1517–20, see Scott H. Hendrix, *Luther and the Papacy: Stages in a Reformation Conflict* (Philadelphia, 1981).

19 Benjamin B. Warfield, *Calvin and Augustine* (Philadelphia, 1956), p. 322.

substantial humanist editorial undertakings, which gave to the sixteenth century the magnificent (by contemporary standards) Amerbach edition of Augustine's works.[20] This 11-volume edition was complete by 1506,[21] and although it is not clear when the enterprise began, there are certainly excellent reasons for supposing that it was under way by 1490, and possibly even 1489. The initial print run of this work appears to have been restricted to 200 copies of each volume,[22] which lends some plausibility to the suggestion that a second edition of the *Opera omnia Augustini* was produced at Paris in 1515. This hypothesis has become influential in relation to the investigation of the Augustine-renaissance in the early sixteenth century: for example, wide circulation has been given to Kähler's suggestion that it was this edition of Augustine which Karlstadt purchased at the Leipzig book fair on 13 April 1517.[23] In fact, there was no 1515 edition of the Amerbach work: the suggestion that it was reprinted rests upon an error in an early Bodleian library catalogue.[24] The error arose in this way: one of the nine 1506 volumes of the Amerbach edition was misplaced, and its place on the Bodleian bookshelf taken by Badius' edition of the sermons of Augustine, published at Paris in 1515. The error was noticed in the early twentieth century, and the missing Amerbach volume substituted for the Badius volume. Catalogue entries prior to 1918 read thus: 'D. Aurelius Augustinus, episc. Hipponensis...Opera IX Tom. per Amerbachium, & c. Bas. 1506

20 See Joseph de Ghellinck, 'La première édition imprimée des *Opera omnia S. Augustini*', in *Miscellanea J. Gessler I* (Antwerp, 1948), pp. 530–47. The spelling 'Amorbach' is ccasionally encountered.

21 It is to be assumed that a typographical error underlies the statement of Oudinus to the effect that the edition was complete in 1586, and that '1506' is intended: 'Primus igitur Joannes Amerbachus huic collectioni vigilias suas, operamque haud vulgarem posuit, tanta diligentia, ut opus anno 1586 applausu omnium eruditorum Basileae completum fuerit.' C. Oudinus, *Commentarius de scriptoribus ecclesiae antiquis I* (Leipzig, 1722), p. 934. On the following page, Oudinus refers to the 1515 Paris edition of this work: see the reference at note 24 for comment.

22 This estimate is based on the statement by Conrad Pellikan to the effect that Amerbach produced 2,200 copies of the 11-volume work: 'Fuerunt tunc pariter impressi a Magistro Amorbachio Joanne duo millia exemplariorum et ducenta in undecim tomis.' *Das Chronikon des Konrad Pellikan*, ed. B. Riggenbach (Basle, 1877), p. 27. Cf. Oberman, *Werden und Wertung der Reformation*, p. 90 n. 37.

23 Ernst Kähler, *Karlstadt und Augustin: Der Kommentar des Andreas Bodenstein von Karlstadt zu Augustins Schrift De spiritu et littera* (Halle, 1952), p. 54 n.1. Cf. Gordon Rupp, *Patterns of Reformation* (London, 1969), p. 56. Kähler correctly pointed out that Karlstadt used the Amerbach edition of 1492 as a source for Augustine's letters.

24 This was pointed out by Luchesius Smits, *Saint Augustin dans l'oeuvre de Jean Calvin* (Assen, 1956), pp. 197–9.

& Par. 1515'. This gave the impression of *two* editions of the Amerbach work, one published at Basle in 1506, the other at Paris in 1515.

The significant decline in patristic studies in general, and the study of Augustine in particular, associated with the later Middle Ages, was thus reversed through the invention of printing and the development of the new humanist editorial techniques, which combined to make available reliable editions of important patristic texts. The importance of this development to the nascent reforming movements in Germany and Switzerland can hardly be overstated. The same movement, however, which gave the Reformers their editions of Augustine also came to pose the most significant challenge to his theological authority. The humanist appeal to the *testimonia patrum* was essentially an appeal to antiquity, an aspect of the general desire to return *ad fontes*. The fathers were to be preferred to the scholastics for three reasons. First, because of their superior Latin style; second, on account of their simplicity of theological expression; third, because of their chronological proximity to the period of the New Testament. In all these respects, the fathers were to be compared favourably with the scholastics, whose barbarous Latin, arcane theological terminology and temporal distance from the documents they purported to interpret were sufficient, in humanist eyes, to discredit them theologically. It will be noted that none of the three criteria employed by the humanists can be regarded as 'theological': the sole legitimate criteria, according to the humanists, were elegance and clarity of expression, and antiquity. At no point could 'theological orthodoxy' be acknowledged as a criterion in this respect.

It will therefore be evident that the humanist appeal to the *testimonia patrum* was essentially an appeal to the patristic corpus as a whole, and not to any particular theologian within it. An appeal, to give an obvious example, to Augustine as *inter theologos summus* was to be rejected out of hand, as involving the application of an impermissible *doctrinal* criterion. The humanist re-evaluation (or, perhaps we should say, *devaluation*) of the significance of Augustine is perhaps best seen from the editorial undertakings of Erasmus.

Initially, as was noted in an earlier chapter (p. 167), Erasmus demonstrated a marked preference for Origen among the fathers, apparently on account of his allegorical method of scriptural exegesis. However, as Erasmus' own editorial undertakings in relation to the Greek text of the New Testament proceeded, it is evident that he began to regard his fellow editor and philologist Jerome with the greatest of respect. In a significant letter to Leo X of 21 May 1515, Erasmus declared his intention to work towards the emergence of Jerome, 'the only Latin theologian worthy of the name', as *inter theologos summus*.[25] The first Jerome edition appeared from the Froben press at Basle in nine volumes in 1516,[26] prefaced by a biography of Jerome which included a point-by-point comparison of Jerome and Augustine, invariably to the latter's detriment.[27] The theological significance of this development was not overlooked at the time: in a letter of February 1518, Johann Eck noted with distaste the manner in which Erasmus had toppled Augustine from his place of primacy among the fathers.[28] In the series of editions of patristic writings which followed in the period 1520–9, Augustine was treated simply as a patristic writer on the same level as Arnobius Junior (a noted critic of Augustine's doctrine of grace, interestingly), rather than as pre-eminent among them.[29] Furthermore, both the second and third Jerome editions (1524 and 1533) retained the *vita Hieronymi* which was found objectionable by the increasing number of those disposed to find the basis of the *vera theologia* in the anti-Pelagian writings of Augustine.

As has been suggested, the Reformation may be regarded as a continuation, and to a certain extent an intensification, of the sporadic late medieval debate concerning the reception of the anti-Pelagian thought of Augustine. The influence of the *testimonia patrum*, and particularly the *vera theologia nostri Augustini*, upon the intellectual origins of the Reformation is more complex than is generally appreciated. The two sections which follow will consider the influence of the patristic witness upon the development of both the Lutheran and Reformed churches. First, the developments at Wittenberg in the second decade of the sixteenth century are considered.

25 *Opus Epistolarum*, ed. Allen, vol. 2, 86.220–2; 88.292; cf. 220.358–9.
26 *Omnium Operum divi Eusebii Hieronymi* (9 vols: Basel, 1516). In fact, only the first four volumes – the letters – may be regarded as demonstrating Erasmus' editoral methods: the remaining five drew upon earlier editions. Cf. Fritz Husner, 'Die Handschrift der Scholien des Erasmus von Rotterdam zu den Hieronymusbriefen', in *Festschrift für Gustav Binz* (Basel, 1935), pp. 132–46.
27 See Oberman, *Werden und Wertung der Reformation*, pp. 93–5.
28 Interestingly, it is Jerome who receives Reuchlin into heaven in Erasmus' 1522 *Apotheosis of Reuchlin*.
29 A number of editions of works of Augustine, in addition to those of Amerbach and Erasmus, also made their appearance in the early sixteenth century: see Smits, *Saint Augustin dans l'oeuvre de Jean Calvin*, pp. 199–201, for a list.

THE PATRISTIC TESTIMONY AND THE
ORIGINS OF THE LUTHERAN CHURCH

The influence of Augustine upon Luther at every stage of his theological development is undeniable.[30] Thus in his critique of the Aristotelian concept of the created habit, Luther makes a direct appeal to Augustine's doctrine of the union of the believer with God through the Holy Spirit.[31] Similarly, Luther's growing awareness of the impotence of the human *liberum arbitrium*, explicitly incorporated into his theology of justification by 1515–16,[32] appears to be based upon a close reading of Augustine's anti-Pelagian writings. Nevertheless, perhaps Luther's most important statement concerning his theological development – the autobiographical fragment of 1545[33] – indicates that Augustine is implicated in an essentially peripheral manner in relation to this development. According to Luther, his crucial reflections on the nature of 'the righteousness of God (*iustitia Dei*)' were essentially complete *before* he encountered a similar interpretation of the concept in Augustine's *De spiritu et litera*. It is, of course, possible that Luther may be defensively minimizing his debt to Augustine in order to strengthen his own claim to theological originality or independence. Luther first begins to cite *De spiritu et litera* in late 1515, by which time his theological breakthrough has almost certainly taken place.[34] It is also clear that the concept of *iustitia Dei* which Luther 'discovered' is quite distinct from that of Augustine.[35] While Luther and Augustine

30 For example, see A. Hamel, *Der junge Luther und Augustin* (2 vols: Gütersloh, 1934–5), vol. 1, pp. 5–25; Bernhard Lohse, 'Die Bedeutung Augustins für den jungen Luther', *Kerygma und Dogma* 11 (1965), pp. 116–35; Leif Grane, 'Augustins "Expositio quarundam propositionum ex epistola ad Romanos" in Luthers Römerbriefvorlesung', *ZThK* 69 (1972), pp. 304–30; Grane, 'Divus Paulus et S. Augustinus, interpres eius fidelissimus: Über Luthers Verhältnis zu Augustin', in *Festschrift für Ernst Fuchs*, ed. G. Ebeling, E. Jüngel and G. Schunack (Tübingen, 1973), pp. 133–46. According to Friedensburg, a large collection of patristic texts was available at Wittenberg from 1513: W. Friedensburg, *Geschichte der Universität Wittenberg* (Halle, 1917), p. 154.
31 WA 9.44.1–4.
32 For example, WA 56.385.15–22 (note the explicit reference to Augustine). See further Alister E. McGrath, *Luther's Theology of the Cross: Martin Luther's Theological Breakthrough* (Oxford, 1985), pp. 128–32.
33 WA 54.185.12–186.21. English translation in McGrath, *Luther's Theology of the Cross*, pp. 95–8.
34 McGrath, *Luther's Theology of the Cross*, pp. 132–3. Cf. C. Boyer, 'Luther et le "De spiritu et litera" de Saint Augustin', *Doctor Communis* 21 (1968), pp. 167–87; Leif Grane, *Modus loquendi theologicus: Luthers Kampf um die Erneuerung der Theologie (1515–1518)* (Leiden, 1975), pp. 65–6. Cf. WA 56.36.11; 172.5.
35 This has been pointed out elsewhere: McGrath, *Iustitia Dei*, vol. 2, pp. 7–9. Earlier studies tended to suggest that Luther's concept was essentially identical with that of Augustine.

concur in the view that *iustitia Dei* is a righteousness *given by*, rather than *belonging to*, God, Luther develops two major aspects of this righteousness which have no parallel in Augustine. First, this righteousness is revealed in the cross of Christ; second, this righteousness contradicts human expectations and preconceptions of the form it should take.[36] A detailed comparison of Luther and Augustine in relation to their doctrines of justification indicates a common anti-Pelagian theology of grace, along with points of significance at which Luther and Augustine diverge radically,[37] making it impossible to argue that Luther merely reproduced Augustine's soteriology, or altered its emphasis slightly. Although Luther may – in common with many late medieval theologians – retain an Augustinian soteriological *framework*, the novel elements of his reforming theology appear to originate elsewhere.

A very different conclusion may be drawn in the case of Andreas Bodenstein von Karlstadt. Using the anti-Pelagian *corpus* as a criterion, Luther recognized by 1516 that the highly influential treatise *de vera et falsa poenitentia* was pseudo-Augustinian. This conclusion had not been drawn by the editors of the editions of the *Opera Augustini* which Luther had used earlier. The 1489 Strasbourg edition of the *Opuscula Augustini*, used by Luther in 1509, included the work as authentic,[38] as did the authoritative Amerbach edition.[39] In a disputation of 25 September 1516, alluded to earlier (pp. 61–2), Luther outraged Karlstadt through his suggestion that the treatise was not Augustinian.[40] In that Luther had also suggested that Augustine did not countenance the view that man could fulfil the commandments of God through his own abilities,[41] the scene was clearly set for a significant confrontation within the Wittenberg theological faculty over Augustine's doctrine of grace. Karlstadt's purchase of an edition of Augustine on 13 January 1517 appears to have convinced him that Luther was right (at least, on these points of interpretation), with the result that on

---

36 For Augustine, there was an essential continuity between *iustitia Dei* and *iustitia humana*: see McGrath, *Iustitia Dei*, vol. 1, pp. 35–6; P. A. Schubert, *Augustins Lex-Aeterna-Lehre nach Inhalt und Quellen* (Münster, 1924).
37 McGrath, *Iustitia Dei*, vol. 2, pp. 17–18. The concept of *iustitia Christi aliena* is of particular importance in this respect.
38 WA 9.4 no. 13.
39 Luther appears to have been using the eighth volume of this edition in 1516: WABr 1.70.12.
40 Luther's gleeful recollection of this event is contained in a letter of the following month: WABr 1.65.24–5 'Est enim...nihil ab Augustini eruditione et sensu remotius.'
41 For Luther's comments, see WABr 1.65.29–66.1.

26 April of the same year he publicly defended 151 theses drawn from the works of Augustine (particularly *de spiritu et litera*), before delivering a pioneering lecture course on this same anti-Pelagian work during the academic year 1517–18.

It is clear from the text of this lecture course that Karlstadt's theology of grace is thoroughly Augustinian, exhibiting none of the radical points of departure so characteristic of Luther by this stage. Thus Karlstadt interprets *iustitia Dei* in throroughly Augustinian terms,[42] develops a dialectic between law and *grace*, rather than law and *gospel* (as with Luther), and emphasizes the priority of *grace* rather than *faith*.[43] Luther's views on the radical dichotomy between divine and human righteousness is conspicuously absent, as is the Christological (more accurately, staurological) concentration, so characteristic of Luther's theological deliberations at this point.

From this point onwards, the Wittenberg theological faculty appears to have moved towards adopting a reforming theology based upon 'the bible and Augustine',[44] embodying the essence of Augustine's anti-Pelagian theology. The publication of Staupitz' *Libellus de exsecutione aeternae praedestinationis*, developing a radical doctrine of double predestination similar to that of the *schola Augustiniana moderna*,[45] on 6 February 1517 unquestionably served to strengthen the hand of those at Wittenberg who wished to treat Augustine as *summus theologus*: it also served to call into question the Augustinian provenance of the medieval theological axiom *si non es praedestinatus, fac ut praedestineris*,[46] thus facilitating the task of defending their radical interpretation of Augustine's theology of grace to those, such as Eck, who preferred to read their Augustine through the mirror of tradition.

This programme of reform through a return to the primary theological sources clearly captured the imagination of Philip Melanchthon, who joined the Wittenberg faculty as professor of Greek in 1518.[47]

---

42 Kähler, *Karlstadt und Augustin*, 69.27–31 'Non est sensus, quod illa iusticia dei sit per legem testificatam qua deus in se iustus est, sed illa, qua iustificat impium, qua induit hominem, qua instaurat imaginem dei in homine; de hac iusticia, qua deus suos electos iustos et pios efficit, tractamus.' Cf. 55.32–56.2.
43 McGrath, *Iustitia Dei*, vol. 2, pp. 21–3 for a full discussion. The suggestion of Ronald J. Sider, *Andreas Bodenstein von Karlstadt: The Development of his Thought 1517–1525* (Leiden, 1974), pp. 67–8; 122–5; 258–9, that Karlstadt's doctrine of justification is *forensic* at this point, is to be rejected as resting upon confusion concerning what 'forensic' actually means.
44 WABr 1.99.8–13.
45 See Steinmetz, *Misericordia Dei*, pp. 75–92, for an analysis of the work.
46 See Oberman, *Werden und Wertung der Reformation*, pp. 98–102.
47 The oration of 1519 is particularly informative: CR (Melanchthon) 11.32.

For Melanchthon, there was no conflict between the principle of the supreme authority of scripture and that of the positive theological evaluation of the witness of the early church. The fathers were to be valued primarily as early exponents of scripture.[48] Of particular interest is Melanchthon's justification for the emphasis placed by the Wittenberg Reformers upon the views of Augustine. According to Melanchthon, the period of the early church in the first four centuries was characterized by a gradual defection from the *primum et verum*, the 'authentic' gospel.[49] This process was particularly associated with Origen, whose allegorizing method proved seriously misleading to his readers, distracting them from the true (literal) meaning of the scriptural text.[50] According to Melanchthon, the situation was redressed through the influence of Augustine, who Melanchthon treats as embodying the primitive gospel, with its Origenistic corruptions eliminated.[51] The identification of Augustine as the criterion of theological orthodoxy led Melanchthon to argue that he served as a model for all subsequent reformations of the church. In this respect, the Wittenberg Reformation was simply the application to the sixteenth century situation of the principles of the 'Augustinian Reformation' of the early fifth century.

Although the influence of Augustine upon the personal theological development of the young Luther may have been less than decisive, the evidence suggests that his influence over the Wittenberg Reformation as a whole was pivotal. Karlstadt's conversion to the evangelical cause in 1517 effectively established the dominance of Augustine over the corporate reforming theology associated with the Wittenberg theological faculty, so that the *vera theologia* was essentially scripture as interpreted in the anti-Pelagian writings of Augustine. This point should be borne in mind when attempting to evaluate the possible influence of the *schola Augustiniana moderna* over this movement: in that

---

48 The function of the *testimonia patrum* within the context of Melanchthon's reforming theology has been carefully studied by Peter Fraenkel, *Testimonia Patrum: The Function of the Patristic Argument in the Theology of Philip Melanchthon* (Geneva, 1961). The relation of the substance of Melanchthon's theology to the patristic testimony has been analysed by E. P. Meijering, *Melanchthon and Patristic Thought: The Doctrines of Christ and Grace, The Trinity and the Creation* (Leiden, 1983).
49 Fraenkel, *Testimonia Patrum*, pp. 70–86, for a careful and well-documented study.
50 Fraenkel, *Testimonia Patrum*, pp. 86–93. Note how Melanchthon treats Origen as a precursor of Pelagius.
51 Fraenkel, *Testimonia Patrum*, pp. 93–6. Cf. CR (Melanchthon) 2.884 'So man nun fragt, warum sondert ihr euch denn von der vorigen rechten Kirchen. Ich halte eben das, welches Ambrosius und Augustinus gelehret haben.'

both movements appealed to scripture and the anti-Pelagian *corpus*, a certain degree of theological convergence would be expected, and cannot be assumed necessarily to reflect the direct textual influence of the *schola Augustiniana moderna* over the Wittenberg Reformation.

THE PATRISTIC TESTIMONY AND THE
ORIGINS OF THE REFORMED CHURCH

Froben is reported to have given Zwingli a copy of one of the volumes of the Amerbach Augustine edition of 1506.[52] Although the library which Zwingli took with him from Glarus to Einsiedeln in 1516 included annotated copies of Augustine, including the 1515 edition of *De civitate Dei*, he does not appear to have used them extensively. At this point, Zwingli appears to follow Erasmus in his predilection for Jerome. Writing to Beatus Rhenanus in June 1520, Zwingli omits any direct reference to Augustine in his references to patristic writers.[53] It is, in fact, extremely difficult to establish the extent and nature of Zwingli's use of Augustine prior to moving to Zurich in 1519.[54] Thus, for example, the most important marginal glosses to Zwingli's Augustine editions are to be found in the Amerbach edition – yet it is not clear precisely when Zwingli came into possession of this edition, let alone whether the marginal comments were entered at Einsiedeln or Zurich. In practice, most of these marginal comments must be recognized as dating from the Zurich period, if they can be dated at all, and chiefly to concern sacramental theology. There is also a conspicuous absence of any reference to Augustine in the celebrated letter to Myconius of 24 July 1520, which is often regarded as marking Zwingli's break with humanism.[55] This absence suggests that Zwingli did not regard his break with humanism as resulting from any direct influence of Augustine. The evidence which some (particularly Köhler) have suggested indicates a prolonged engagement with the thought of Augustine since 1516 is both circumstantial and

---

52 Alfred Schindler, *Zwingli und die Kirchenväter* (Zurich, 1984), p. 26. Schindler suggests, on the basis of CR (Zwingli) 7.440.9–11, that it may have been the first volume in this series.
53 CR 7.324.23–5.
54 As pointed out by J. M. Usteri, 'Initia Zwinglii', *Theologische Studien und Kritiken* 58 (1885), pp. 607–72; 59 (1886), pp. 95–159; p. 98; Schindler, *Zwingli und die Kirchenväter*, p. 31.
55 Schindler, *Zwingli und die Kirchenväter*, pp. 28–31.

ambiguous,[56] and is insufficient to permit any conclusions of substance to be drawn. Rather, Zwingli appears to have used the patristic testimony initially in a characteristically humanist fashion, and to have been drawn to Augustine in the Zurich period as much for his sacramental views as for his theology of grace – an area of theology which, the reader is reminded, never possessed the same importance for Zwingli as it did for Luther or Karlstadt.

This initial lack of interest in Augustine's theology of grace gave way to increasing concern with the anti-Pelagian corpus in the 1530s and 1540s. Thus Calvin clearly understood the Reformation to be a restoration or recapitulation of the theology of Augustine, occasionally suggesting that everything he himself had written might be regarded as a paraphrase of Augustine's writings.[57] In this, he is clearly in agreement with the Wittenberg *vera theologia* – but it is not clear that this point alone explains Calvin's high estimate of Augustine. The suggestion that Calvin's conversion is itself due to Augustine,[58] thus explaining the high regard entertained for the latter by the former, is ingenious, but lacks documentation. While the possibility that the origins of Calvin's distinctive ideas may lie with a close reading of Augustine is not to be totally rejected out of hand, the fact that Calvin belongs to the second generation of Reformers must serve as a reminder that we are dealing increasingly with the *mediated* influence of the patristic testimony, through the medium of the Reformation itself. Whereas the late medieval period based its theology upon a tradition-encapsulated Augustine, the later Reformation increasingly developed its own tradition concerning the great African theologian.

The patristic testimony must therefore be regarded as having an ultimately indeterminable, but probably slight, influence upon the intellectual origins of the Reformed church. It is probably true to say that the fathers influenced Zwingli to much the same extent as they influenced Erasmus – as exegetical, moral and spiritual, but not primarily *doctrinal* guides. There is no substantial evidence to indicate that the intellectual origins of the Reformed evangelical faction are

---

56 See the careful study of Schindler, *Zwingli und die Kirchenväter*, pp. 34–41.

57 *Institutio* (1559) III.xxii.8. Cf. CR (Calvin) 8.266 'Augustinus...totus noster est'. For a careful study of Calvin's views on the status of Augustine, see Smits, *Saint Augustin dans l'oeuvre de Jean Calvin*, pp. 265–70, with valuable documentation. More generally, see the useful analysis of A. N. S. Lane, 'Calvin's Use of the Fathers and Medievals', *Calvin Theological Journal* 16 (1981), pp. 149–205.

58 Smits, *Saint Augustin dans l'oeuvre de Jean Calvin*, pp. 17–24; 261.

to be explained even partly upon the basis of a direct rediscovery of Augustine's anti-Pelagian writings, whereas there are excellent reasons for suggesting that such a 'rediscovery' underlay the origins of the Wittenberg theology of 1517–19, particularly as developed by Karlstadt. However, it must be observed that the early Reformed church in the period 1515–20 displayed nothing that even approached the Wittenberg preoccupation with the doctrine of grace at the same time and which lay behind their wrestling with the anti-Pelagian Augustinian corpus. The sharply different theological concerns of the early Lutheran and Reformed evangelical movements goes some way towards accounting for their different evaluation and reception of Augustine's anti-Pelagian writings. The Reformation may indeed have been a 'rediscovery' of Augustine – but the Augustines whom the Wittenberg and Zurich theologians rediscovered were rather different.

The manner in which the Reformers exploited the *testimonia patrum* illustrates one of the many difficulties attending any attempt to establish the precise relationship between the Renaissance and the Reformation. In many respects, the reforming educational programme developed by the Wittenberg theological faculty parallels that favoured by the humanists – the return to the study of original sources (such as the bible and the fathers), the study of the three sacred languages (Hebrew, Greek and Latin), and the elimination from the curriculum of works of 'scholastic' theology.[59] This indicates the necessity to distinguish the *substance* of the theological method of the early Reformation from its *underlying motivation*. It is not enough merely to consider *what* theological sources and methods the Reformers adopted: the reasons *why* they adopted them must be established, if those aspects of the Reformation which serve to distinguish it from the Renaissance are to be identified. In the case of the Wittenberg Reformation, the study of the bible (including the associated necessary philological and textual techniques) was undertaken in an attempt to recapture the Word of God, in order that the church might be reformed upon its basis, both as an institution in itself and in relation to its doctrine. The study of the fathers was regarded as a valuable ancillary tool towards this end, and as justifying the emphasis upon Augustine within the patristic

59 Thus Grossmann, *Humanism in Wittenberg 1485–1517* (Nieuwkoop, 1975), treats the Wittenberg reforms as the logical outcome of the development of the *studia humanitatis* under Christoph Scheurl.

corpus on the basis of an explicitly acknowledged *doctrinal* criterion.[60]

Although this distinction may be maintained with relative ease with regard to the Wittenberg Reformation, it encounters serious difficulties in the case of Zwingli and the early Zurich Reformation. Zwingli does not appear to have studied the bible, biblical languages or the fathers with the same underlying presuppositions as those which governed contemporary developments at Wittenberg. The early Reformed church shows considerably greater affinity with the Renaissance than its Wittenberg counterpart, both in terms of the substance of its theological method, and its underlying motivation. Although this situation would be altered, initially through Bullinger's reworking of Zwingli's theology,[61] and subsequently through the rise of Geneva as the political and theological centre of the Reformed church,[62] the fact remains that the *origins* of the Reformed church are considerably more closely linked with the Renaissance than are their Lutheran equivalents.

---

60 This point is developed elsewhere: McGrath, *Luther's Theology of the Cross*, pp. 48–53.
61 Gottfried W. Locher, 'Praedicatio verbi Dei est verbum Dei: Heinrich Bullinger zwischen Zwingli und Luther; Ein Beitrag zu seiner Theologie', *Zwingliana* 10 (1954), pp. 47–57.
62 Gottfried W. Locher, 'Von Bern nach Genf: Die Ursachen der Spannung zwischen zwinglischer und calvinistischer Reformation', in *Wegen et Gestalten in het Gereformeerd Protestantisme*, ed. W. Balke, C. Graafland and H. Harkema (Amsterdam, 1976), pp. 75–87.

8

Sources and Methods: Towards the Universalization of Method

Earlier chapters have drawn attention to the considerable affinity and continuity between early Reformed theology and humanism. This present chapter will consider a further aspect of the relation between Reformed theology and humanism – the trend towards the universalization of method within Reformed theology in the final four decades of the sixteenth century. In one sense, this development lies outside the scope of the present study, in that it dates from a period which cannot be considered to have any direct bearing upon the question of the intellectual *origins* of the Reformation. However, the renewed influence of Renaissance humanism upon later Reformed theology is of relevance to the present study, in that it indicates how Reformed theologians, in their quest to develop a coherent theological method in the face of increasing Lutheran and catholic polemics, adopted the methodological insights of the late Italian Renaissance. Just as their predecessors within the Reformed church had adopted the literary, philological and exegetical methods of the Renaissance in establishing the characteristic features of Reformed theology, so they took the crucial step of adopting the methodological insights developed at Padua in the fifteenth century.

It has already been noted that Aristotelianism stubbornly persisted throughout the Italian Renaissance, to the intense irritation of those who prefer to regard the Renaissance as essentially a Platonist reaction against scholastic Aristotelianism.[1] The most significant Aristotelian school was associated with Padua,[2] and it was at this university that the new methodological insights which were to exercise such influence

1 P. O. Kristeller, *La tradizione aristotelica nel Rinascimento* (Padua, 1972).
2 Bruno Nardi, *Saggi sull'Aristotelismo padovana dal secolo XIV al XVI* (Florence, 1958); P. O. Kristeller, *Aristotelismo e sincretismo nel pensiero di Pietro Pomponazzi* (Padua, 1983).

over later Reformed theology were developed. In a seminal essay Randall demonstrated the development at Padua of a methodology based upon the concepts of 'resolution' and 'composition' (later to be known as *analytica* and *synthetica*), applicable to various intellectual disciplines, in the late fourteenth and fifteenth centuries, culminating in the work of Giacomo Zabarella (1532–89).[3] The impact of these insights upon the 'new science' of the late sixteenth and early seventeenth centuries is considerable, as is evident from Galileo Galilei's use of the *metodo risolutivo* and *metodo compositivo*.[4] For Zabarella, Aristotelian syllogistic logic and method were essentially identical, so that method came to be identified with the procedure of a single specific discipline (in this case, Aristotelian syllogistic logic).

It has long been suspected that Theodore Beza adopted these Paduan methodological insights. It is known that Beza was particularly interested in the works of Pomponazzi,[5] and recent work on Beza's theological method has indicated the influence of his Aristotelian presuppositions, particularly in relation to his doctrine of God.[6] Similar findings have been established in the case of Girolamo Zanchi, the Italian Aristotelian turned Reformed divine.[7] It is possible that the influence of Vermigli may be also significant in this connection, as he is known to have had associations with the Aristotelian school at Padua. This decisive methodological shift involves a shift from the soteriological (and hence Christocentric) analytic and inductive methodology employed by the earlier Reformed theologians, such as Calvin, to a logical (and hence theocentric) synthetic and deductive methodology. The results of this shift are perhaps most evident in

---

3 John Herman Randall, 'The Development of Scientific Method in the School of Padua', in *Renaissance Essays*, ed. P. O. Kristeller and P. P. Wiener (New York, 1968), pp. 217–51.

4 John Herman Randall, *The Career of Philosophy* (2 vols: New York, 1962–70), vol. 1, pp. 339–60.

5 Note his request to Grataroli, dated 11 August 1563, for a copy of Pomponazzi's *De naturalium effectuum causis*, published by Grataroli at Basle in 1556: *Correspondance de Théodore de Bèze*, ed. Meylan, Dufour and Tripet (11 vols: Geneva, 1960–83), vol. 4, no. 282; pp. 182–3. This entry is interpreted by the editors as substantiation of Beza's scholastic tendencies: *Correspondance*, vol. 4, p. 9; 183 n.5. Cf. P. Bietenholz, *Der italienische Humanismus und die Blütezeit des Buchdrucks in Basel* (Basle, 1959), pp. 131–2.

6 Walter Kickel, *Vernunft und Offenbarung bei Theodor Beza: Zum Problem des Verhältnisses von Theologie, Philosophie und Staat* (Neukirchen, 1967), p. 167 'Die Folge des aristotelischen Einflusses ist die Verdrangung Christi und des Wortes aus ihrer zentralen Stellung in der Theologie und der Ersatz der Christozentrik durch ein rationales finalkausales System.'

7 Otto Gründler, *Die Gotteslehre Giralmo Zanchis und ihre Bedeutung für seine Lehre von der Prädestination* (Neukirchen, 1965).

the later Reformed discussion of predestination. Whereas Calvin defers discussion of predestination until a relatively late point in the *Institutio*, and then treats the doctrine with some caution, as an aspect of his soteriology, Beza effectively makes the divine decrees of predestination the logical starting point for a deductive theology. For Beza and Zanchi, predestination is an aspect of the doctrine of God, the logical starting point for theological speculation on the basis of Aristotelian syllogistic logic.[8] Thus for Beza – and, indeed, for Reformed Orthodoxy in general – it is predestination which is the central theological principle.[9] This development, it should be emphasized, is essentially the result of the appropriation and theological application of the methodological insights of the late Renaissance Paduan school.

That these developments were essentially due to methodological presuppositions is indicated by the reaction to them within the Reformed church. Thus Arminius argued that theology was a practical science, which necessitated an analytical, rather than a synthetical, method:

> It has long been a maxim with those philosophers who are the masters of method and order, that the theoretical sciences ought to be delivered in a synthetical manner (*ordine compositivo*), but the practical in an analytical order (*vero resolutivo*), on which account, and because theology is a practical science, it follows that it must be treated according to the analytical method (*methodo resolutiva*).[10]

For Arminius, to treat theology as a theoretical science – which is the procedure of Beza, following Zabarella – is quite improper. More

---

8 See Alister E. McGrath, 'Reformation to Enlightenment', in *The History of Theology I: The Science of Theology*, ed. P. D. L. Avis (Basingstoke/Grand Rapids, Mich., 1986), pp. 154–60. Kickel designates Beza's doctrine of predestination as a rationalization of the more restrained statements of Calvin: *Vernunft und Offenbarung bei Theodor Beza*, pp. 159; 167.

9 Kickel, *Vernunft und Offenbarung bei Theodor Beza*, pp. 167–9. Cf. the celebrated study of Alexander Schweizer, *Die protestantischen Centraldogen in ihrer Entwicklung innerhalb der reformierten Kirche* (2 vols: Zurich, 1854–6), in which predestination is unequivocally identified as the *Centraldogma* of the Reformed church.

The useful study of John Platt, *Reformed Thought and Scholasticism: The Arguments for the Existence of God in Dutch Theology* (Leiden, 1982), is a particularly valuable guide to the developments within Reformed theology in this period.

10 Arminius, *Private Disputation II*; in *Works* (3 vols: London, 1825–75), vol. 2, p. 319.

significant, however, was the reaction of the Salmurian Academy against the Bezan doctrine of predestination.

Under the influence of Beza, Aristotelian syllogistic logic became an essential component of the curriculum of the Genevan Academy.[11] Beza's refusal to allow Peter Ramus a teaching position at the academy was based upon his hostility towards Ramus' anti-Aristotelian programme, evident in his logic. Although the Genevan Aristotelian pattern was adopted by many Reformed academies throughout Europe, Ramus' logic was taught at the Protestant academy of Saumur – and on the basis of this logic, which declined to deduce the particular from the general, the later Salmurian academicians, such as Amyraut, challenged the foundations of the Orthodox doctrine of predestination.[12] Underlying both these challenges to this doctrine, as developed by Beza, was a critique of the methodological presuppositions, inherited from the Paduan school, on the basis of which it was perceived to be based.

It is beyond the scope of the present study to consider the methodological developments within late sixteenth century Reformed theology in any detail. Nevertheless, we wish to draw attention to an aspect of that development which is too easily overlooked – the continuing influence of late Renaissance humanism upon the Reformed understanding of theological sources and methods. The first phase of the Reformation saw questions of method being confined to textual, literary, philological, exegetical and hermeneutical matters (in all of which the influence of the Renaissance is conspicuous), but it did not witness sustained discussion of the nature of 'method' itself. This is evident from the internal organization of the successive editions of Calvin's *Institutio*, in which no single methodological principle governs its shape and form. In marked contrast, Beza's systematic works are dominated by methodological considerations: the very manner in which Beza's theological exposition takes place is governed by Zabarella's concept of method. Although the rhetorical brilliance of Calvin's *Institutio* ensured its permanent place in the history of Reformed

---

11 See, e.g., Robert M. Kingdom, *Geneva and the Consolidation of the French Protestant Movement* (Geneva, 1967), pp. 18; 120.

12 Jürgen Moltmann, 'Prädestination und Heilsgeschichte bei Moyse Amyraut', *ZKG* 65 (1954), pp. 270–303; François Laplanche, *Orthodoxie et prédication: l'oeuvre d'Amyraut et la querelle de la grâce universelle* (Paris, 1965); Brian G. Armstrong, *Calvinism and the Amyraut Controversy: Protestant Scholasticism and Humanism in Seventeenth Century France* (Madison, 1969).

theology, it is Beza who is to be credited with the systematization of that theology in a methodologically consistent manner. It is therefore perhaps paradoxical that the renaissance of scholasticism within Reformed theology is almost certainly ultimately due to the influence of late Renaissance humanism – but such an observation should serve to remind us that 'humanism' is a phenomenon more complex than is often appreciated. The influence of humanism upon Reformed theology during the sixteenth century is both consistent and considerable: both the origins and subsequent development of Reformed theology reflect the influence of the late Renaissance to an extent unparalleled within Lutheranism, which declined to adopt Aristotelianism until the seventeenth century.[13]

Although the influence of late medieval scholastic theology upon the development of Reformed theology initially appears to have been minimal, the influence of humanism upon that theology appears to have led to the rise of precisely such a scholasticism within a movement initially so opposed to it. It is for this reason that this present brief chapter has been included in this account, where it might seem seriously out of place – it serves to indicate the complexity of the manner in which intellectual movements interacted at the time, and to set the relation of Reformed theology to humanism in a broader context than is usually encountered.

The present study is particularly concerned with the relation between the two great movements in late medieval and Renaissance intellectual history: scholasticism and humanism. Although these movements are often presented as assuming a mutually antagonistic stance at the dawn of the sixteenth century, it must be appreciated that this generalization masks a dangerously simplistic understanding of both movements. The occasional positive mutual interaction of humanism and scholasticism, so evident at the university of Padua during the Renaissance, and subsequently in Reformed Orthodoxy, indicates the dangers of approaching the period with rigid preconceived stereotypes of either of these intellectual movements. The origins and subsequent development of Reformed theology throughout the sixteenth

---

13 See Emil Weber, *Die philosophische Scholastik des deutschen Protestantismus im Zeitalter der Orthodoxie* (Leipzig, 1907); Weber, *Der Einfluß der protestantischen Schulphilosophie auf die orthodox-lutherische Dogmatik* (Leipzig, 1908); M. Wundt, *Die deutsche Schulphilosophie des 17. Jahrhunderts* (Tübingen, 1939); Richard Schröder, *Johann Gerhards lutherische Christologie und die aristotelische Metaphysik* (Tübingen, 1983).

century were shaped by the humanist movement – but the form of that humanism varied from one period, one location and one individual to another. The anti-Aristotelian, anti-scholastic polemic of Zwingli and his circle gave way to a more positive appreciation of the virtues of both Aristotle and scholasticism – and *both* these attitudes may be properly designated as 'humanist'. This changing understanding of the nature of Renaissance humanism is charged with significance for the interpretation of the intellectual origins and subsequent development of the Reformation. The full complexity of the contours of the trialogue between humanism, scholasticism and the Reformation is only now beginning to emerge from the mists of history, and promises to stimulate still further the study of this already intriguing ripple in the millpond of intellectual history.

Conclusion

Was the Reformation inevitable? This final chapter will present a brief simplified overview of some of the conclusions of the present study. In view of the intricacy of much of the earlier discussion, this concluding chapter aims to assess the broad significance of this investigation to our understanding of the intellectual origins and nature of the European Reformation. Whereas much of the earlier part of this work was concerned with points of fine detail, it may prove helpful now to apply some very broad brush strokes to our canvas, in order that the finer ones may be better appreciated. By far the greater part of the analysis contained in this work cannot, however, be summarized succinctly, so this concluding chapter cannot be regarded as containing its results *in nuce*.

The first focus of attention is the complexity and heterogeneity of the origins of the ideas underlying the Reformation. Any attempt to adopt a reductionist approach to this remarkable historical phenomenon – whether by ignoring its theological dimension altogether or by imposing a preconceived interpretative framework upon obviously recalcitrant material – can only result in a misapprehension of its nature and significance. The movement so loosely designated 'The Reformation' arose from a complex heterogeneous matrix of social and ideological factors, the latter associated with individual personalities, intellectual movements, schools of thought and universities in such a manner as to defy the crass generalizations which are the substance of all too many interpretations of the phenomenon. The quest for the intellectual origins of the Reformation thus concerns not the identification of a single factor, nor even a group of factors, which may be said to have *caused* the movement, but rather concerns the unfolding of a complex matrix of creatively interacting intellectual currents, whose precise mode of interaction was determined as much by local as by cosmopolitan, by social as by academic, factors. Intellectual currents which interacted creatively in one locality did not do so elsewhere.

The heterogeneity of the theological concerns underlying the Reformation may be illustrated with reference to the religious questions underlying the movement. It may well be the case that many popular approaches to the origins of the Reformation identify the doctrine of 'justification by faith' as its central religious issue. While this judgement may be sustained in the case of the initial phase of the *Wittenberg* Reformation, it is clearly quite incorrect in the case of the southern German and Swiss Reformation. The theologians of this movement – such as Zwingli and Bucer – initially demonstrated a near-total disinterest in the doctrine, and subsequently appear to have misunderstood it, regarding it as detrimental to the development of piety. The independence of the origins of the Swiss Reformation from its Wittenberg counterpart is of considerable significance in this context, lending weight to the suggestion that the concerns of the two movements were different. The Reformed church, from its first phase onwards, demonstrated a concern (whether it may be designated as 'humanist' or not) to reform the morals and practices of the church on the basis of scripture, without in any way linking this development of the principle *sola scriptura* with that of justification *sola fide*. The suggestion that the principle of justification *sola fide* was the universal cause of the Reformation is quite unjustified. It was but one of a number of elements in a complex movement.

The heterogeneity of the Reformation may be further illustrated from the relation of its elements to scholasticism and humanism. In the case of both, serious difficulties of definition must be noted. The identification of 'scholasticism' with a degenerate Ockhamism, or 'humanism' with the personal preoccupations and predispositions of Erasmus of Rotterdam, has enormously hindered the proper evaluation of their relation to the Reformation. As was emphasized earlier, a careful study of the nature of both these movements is an essential prerequisite of modern Reformation historiography. It is for this reason that the recent clarification of the characteristics of both the *via moderna* and the *schola Augustiniana moderna*, and the pioneering studies of Kristeller on the nature of Renaissance humanism, are of such seminal importance to contemporary Reformation scholarship. The invalidation of many of the older studies of the relationship of the Reformation in general, or individual elements or personalities within it, to scholasticism and humanism is ultimately a consequence of our growing understanding of these latter movements.

In the light of these developments, it is clear that the Wittenberg Reformation was characterized by a direct engagement with scholasticism. Although both Luther and Karlstadt were unquestionably aided in this matter by the newly developed humanist textual and philological techniques, it seems that Luther employed the hermeneutics of the late medieval period in his biblical exegesis, during the course of which he gradually broke free from the soteriological framework of the *via moderna*. In other words, Luther's theological breakthrough must be regarded as a development within, rather than a radical break with, the framework of late medieval thought. Although it is fashionable to speak of 'Luther's Copernican Revolution', which substituted a theocentricity for the medieval anthropocentricity, the suggestion of such a radical discontinuity (implicit in the use of the term 'revolution') cannot be sustained. The 'theocentricity' in question was characteristic of the *schola Augustiniana moderna* in the later medieval period, with which Luther may have been familiar, and with which he certainly exhibits at least some degree of continuity. Far from breaking with the medieval theological tradition, Luther may be regarded merely as adopting a somewhat different position within its compass. The 'desk-bound' character of Luther's theology during the period 1513–19 has often been noted, reflecting the fact that at this point it was an academic, rather than a popular, reforming theology, directed against academic opponents.

The scholastic character of the early Wittenberg Reformation serves to highlight the divergence from the Reformed church at this point. The strongly Erasmian character of Zwingli's theology in the period 1515–20 illustrates the humanist character of the early Reformed theology. The direct engagement with scholasticism, so prominent a feature of the Wittenberg Reformation, is conspicuous by its absence. Where Luther criticized the scholastics in order to refute them, Zwingli criticized them in order to by-pass them altogether, in characteristic Erasmian style. The vitality of the early Reformed theology – which contrasts with the somewhat dull and stolid Wittenberg theology of the same period, 1515–20 – reflects the humanist conviction that religion concerns life in all its fullness, rather than theological formulations. Thus the very different environments in which the Wittenberg and Zurich reforming theologies emerged must be emphasized: the former was initially an academic, the latter a social and ecclesiastical, reforming movement. Although the impact of the new philological, textual and exegetical techniques was unquestionably felt at Wittenberg, the appropriation and exploitation of these techniques is particularly to be associated with the early period of the Reformed church. Whereas these techniques were employed to a limited extent at Wittenberg to develop a reformed academic Augustinianism, at Zurich they were exploited to forge a theology by which both city and church might be reformed.

The present study has been particularly concerned with the question of the intellectual origins of the Reformation. The intricacy of the discussion of this question in earlier sections of this work may inhibit identification of the broad features of the late medieval intellectual landscape against which these developments took place. It may therefore be helpful if three main developments are identified, in order to set the points of detail in a broader context.

First, the inherent doctrinal diversity of the late medieval period must be noted. The later Middle Ages, particularly the fifteenth century, was characterized by a theological pluralism arising from factors such as the rise of the different methodologies associated with the various theological schools. There was thus a spectrum of theological opinions within the late medieval church, raising the question of the relation of these 'opinions' to catholic dogma.

Second, the late medieval period witnessed a two-fold crisis of authority. The growing confusion, particularly evident during the fifteenth century, concerning what was merely 'theological opinion' and what was actually 'catholic dogma' inevitably led to the former being confused with the latter. The necessity of toleration in respect of divergent theological opinions was vigorously defended during the period as an essential aspect of constructive academic theological debate, and such 'opinions' were often recognized as possessing a purely heuristic, and hence provisional, validity. Nevertheless, in a period which witnessed an unprecedented proliferation of such 'opinions', authoritative pronouncements concerning the relation of 'opinions' to 'dogma' were conspicuously absent. The teaching authority of the *magisterium* had been seriously weakened through the obvious difficulties raised for such a concept of authority by the Great Schism, with the result that, in the absence of any magisterial guidance, theological opinions became confused with catholic dogma. As we noted, there are excellent reasons for suggesting that Martin Luther's views concerning the alleged 'Pelagianism' of the medieval church may well arise from his confusing the theological opinions of the *via moderna* with the official teaching of the church.

Accompanying this erosion of the teaching authority of the church was an apparent disinclination (whether through unwillingness or inability) on the part of the *magisterium* to take decisive forcible action to suppress opinions of which it disapproved. This development has its roots in the fifteenth century, but is most evident in the third decade of the sixteenth century. Thus the German diocesan and provincial synods, traditionally the enforcers of religious orthodoxy, do not appear to have been convened during the crucial years 1522–3, when the forcible suppression of the ideas of the Reformers was a real possibility.

The third consideration concerns the perceived nature of theology in the later medieval period. There was a general tendency (with certain exceptions within the Franciscan Order) to regard theology as essentially the exposition of scripture. This understanding of the nature of theology inevitably entailed a crisis in the wake of the rise of the new philological, literary and exegetical techniques of the Renaissance, in that 'scripture' could no longer be equated with 'the Vulgate text, as traditionally received'. The possibility that the content of Christian theology might be significantly altered through the impact of the new learning could not be excluded. To many catholics, 'sacred philology' seemed to undermine certain traditional catholic teachings, particularly in relation to Mariology and the theology of penance – teachings which the Reformers were more than happy to dispense with, while retaining the idea of theology as the exposition of scripture.

For reasons such as these it may be stated that a crisis developed within the world of religious ideas in the late fifteenth century, reaching a climax in the first two decades of the sixteenth. These developments need not necessarily have led to a Reformation, as we now understand the term: it is, however, difficult to see how the crisis could have been resolved without a major clarification of the nature and limits of the Christian faith, along with the development of means by which orthodoxy might be enforced where necessary – and the church of the early sixteenth century gives every indication of simply not having been in a position to do either.

A final summary concerns the continuity and discontinuity between the late medieval period and the Reformation. In terms of theological sources and methods, it is evident that the Wittenberg Reformers demonstrate a remarkable degree of continuity with the late medieval period: indeed, one might go so far as to suggest that, in the period 1513–17, no significant discontinuities in matters of theological method between the Wittenberg Reformers and the late medieval period may be discerned. Although doctrinal divergence from the later medieval period is evident in Luther's thought from 1514 onwards, this does not initially arise through any radically new insights into theological sources or methods – for example, through the discovery of a new hermeneutic. In marked contrast, however, the early Reformed theology demonstrates little affinity with later scholasticism, but a corresponding greater continuity with both Erasmian and non-Erasmian humanism in the period 1515–20. In that humanism is perhaps the most important intellectual movement of the first two decades of the sixteenth century, it must be regarded as an essential constituent of late medieval thought. The intricacies of the earlier discussion of the continuity and discontinuity between the medieval period and the Reformation defy succinct summarization, but suffice it to say that both wings of the Reformation initially demonstrate, although in different manners, a considerable degree of continuity with the thought of the late medieval period, which gradually gave way to an increasing discontinuity as development took place. Both movements may thus be said to develop initially *within* the context of late medieval thought, rather than marking an immediate and radical break with it.

Was the Reformation an inevitability? This survey of the intellectual currents on the eve of the Reformation indicates that some form of upheaval within contemporary catholicism was highly probable. The factors which have been documented in the present study suggest that a significant degree of doctrinal instability had developed within catholicism by the end of the first decade of the sixteenth century, with little immediate prospect of its resolution. The development of such instability would have important consequences for the self-understanding of the church at this point. This, however, need point to no more that a shift in attitudes within contemporary catholicism, rather than the development of schism within it. The Reformation, considered as an historical phenomenon, cannot be explained on the basis of the religious ideas underlying it alone. The rise of nationalism, the growing political power of both the south German and Swiss cities and the German princes, the rise in lay piety and theological awareness – all these coincided with this crisis within the world of religious ideas, turning an essentially intellectual movement into a political upheaval. It was this combination of social, political and religious parameters which must be regarded as underlying the specific historical form which the Reformation took. The quest for the intellectual origins of the European Reformation is an essential aspect of the study of that movement – but it cannot claim to define the specific historical form which that movement adopted. There was unquestionably an irreducible religious and intellectual element to the Reformation, which contributed significantly to its shaping – but it was not the only such element. The historian of ideas must become a social historian if he is to come to terms with the full complexity of this fascinating movement in the flux of human history – just as the social historian must also become an historian of ideas.

The quest for the intellectual origins of the Reformation will, on account of its inherent complexity, continue to exercise a fascination over the historian of ideas for some considerable time to come. Indeed, it is quite possible that future research will demonstrate still more clearly how complex and heterogeneous the Reformation was as an intellectual phenomenon. Just as the simplifications of yesteryear, although congenial to the purposes of historians, have been called into question by the intensive research of the past quarter of a century, it must be recognized that even the tentative conclusions of today may be invalidated through future intensification of the quest for the intellectual origins of the Reformation. Nevertheless, it is hoped that the present study will at least indicate the current state of knowledge on the question, and perhaps stimulate others to undertake further work in what is perhaps one of the most intriguing areas of academic research.

Select Bibliography

M. J. B. Allen, 'Marsilio Ficino on Plato, the Neoplatonists and the Christian Doctrine of the Trinity', *Renaissance Quarterly* 37 (1984), pp. 555–84.

H. Ankwick-Kleehoven, *Der Wiener Humanist Johannes Cuspinian, Gelehrter und Diplomat zur Zeit Kaiser Maximilians* (Graz, 1959).

R. Bäumer, 'Die Reformkonzilien des 15. Jahrhunderts in der neueren Forschung', *Annuarium Historiae Conciliorum* 1 (1969), pp. 153–64.

—— 'Die Zahl der allgemeinen Konzilien in der Sicht von Theologen des 15. und 16. Jahrhunderts', *Annuarium Historiae Conciliorum* 1 (1969), pp. 288–313.

K. Bannach, *Die Lehre von der doppelten Macht Gottes bei Wilhelm von Ockham: Problemgeschichtliche Voraussetzungen und Bedeutung* (Wiesbaden, 1975).

H. Baron, *The Crisis of the Early Italian Renaissance: Civic Humanism and Republican Liberty in an Age of Classicism and Tyranny* (Princeton, NJ, revised edn, 1966).

—— 'Leonardi Bruno: "Professional Rhetorician" or "Civic Humanist"?', *Past and Present* 36 (1967), pp. 21–37.

G. Bauch, 'Die Anfänge des Studiums der griechischen Sprache und Literatur in Nord-Deutschland', *Gesellschaft für deutsche Erziehungs- und Schulgeschichte* 6 (1896), pp. 47–98.

—— *Die Rezeption des Humanismus in Wien* (Breslau, 1903).

—— 'Die Einführung des Hebräischen in Wittenberg mit Berücksichtigung der Vorgeschichte des Studiums der Sprache in Deutschland', *Monatschrift für Geschichte und Wissenschaft des Judentums* 48 (1904), pp. 22–32; 77–86; 145–60; 214–23; 283–99; 328–40; 461–90.

K. Bauer, *Die Wittenberger Universitätstheologie und die Anfänge der Deutschen Reformation* (Tübingen, 1928).

O. Bayer, *Promissio: Geschichte der reformatorischen Wende in Luthers Theologie* (Göttingen, 1971).

J. H. Bentley, 'Erasmus' *Annotationes in Novum Testamentum* and the Textual Criticism of the Gospels', *ARG* 67 (1976), pp. 33–53.

P. Bietenholz, *Der italienische Humanismus und die Blütezeit des Buchdrucks in Basel* (Basle, 1959).

N. Birnbaum, 'The Zwinglian Reformation in Zurich', *Past and Present* 15 (1959), pp. 27–47.

J. Bohatec, *Budé und Calvin: Studien zur Gedankenwelt des französischen Früh-humanismus* (Graz, 1950).

J. Boisset, *Sagesse et saintété dans la pensée de Jean Calvin* (Paris, 1959).

C. Bonorand, *Vadians Weg vom Humanismus zur Reformation und seine Vorträge über die Apostelgeschichte* (Vadian-Studien 7: St Gallen, 1962).

—— 'Die Bedeutung der Universität Wien für Humanismus und Reformation, insbesondere in der Ostschweiz', *Zwingliana* 12 (1964–8), pp. 162–80.

—— *Aus Vadians Freundes- und Schülerkreis in Wien* (Vadian-Studien 8: St Gallen, 1965).

—— *Vadian und die Ereignisse in Italien im ersten Drittel des 16. Jahrhunderts* (Vadian-Studien 13: St Gallen, 1985).

E. Borchert, *Der Einfluß des Nominalismus der Spätscholastik nach dem Traktat de communicatione idiomatum des Nikolaus Oresme* (Münster, 1940).

W. J. Bouwsma, 'The Two Faces of Humanism: Stoicism and Augustinianism in Renaissance Thought', in *Itinerarium Italicum: The Profile of the Italian Renaissance in the Mirror of its European Transformations*, ed. H. A. Oberman with T. A. Brady (Leiden, 1975), pp. 3–60.

C. Boyer, 'Luther et le "De spiritu et litera" de Saint Augustin', *Doctor Communis* 21 (1968), pp. 167–87.

L. E. Boyle, 'Innocent III and Vernacular Versions of Scripture', in *The Bible in the Medieval World*, ed. K. Walsh and D. Wood (Studies in Church History: Subsidia 4: Oxford, 1985), pp. 131–55.

V. Branca, 'Ermolao Barbaro and Late Quattrocento Venetian Humanism', in *Renaissance Studies*, ed. J. R. Hale (Totowa, NJ, 1973), pp. 218–43.

Q. Breen, *John Calvin: A Study in French Humanism* (Hamden, 2nd edn, 1968).

U. Bubenheimer, *Consonantia Theologiae et Iurisprudentiae: Andreas Bodenstein von Karlstadt als Theologe und Jurist zwischen Scholastik und Reformation* (Tübingen, 1977).

E. Buechler, *Die Anfänge des Buchdrucks in der Schweiz* (Berne, 2nd edn, 1951).

H. O. Burger, *Renaissance, Reformation, Humanismus* (Bad Homburg, 1969).

J. Cadier, 'Le prétendu stoïcisme de Calvin', *Etudes théologiques et religieuses* 41 (1966), pp. 217–26.

—— 'Le conversion de Calvin', *Bulletin de la societé de l'histoire du protestantisme français* 116 (1970), pp. 142–51.

S. I. Camporeale, *Lorenzo Valla: umanesimo e teologia* (Florence, 1972).

D. Cantimori, 'Sulla storia del concetto di Rinascimento', *Annali della scuola normale superiore di Pisa: lettere, storia e filosophia*, 2nd series, 1 (1932), pp. 229–68.

G. Cervani, 'Il Rinascimento italiano nella interpretazione di Hans Baron', *Nuova rivista storica* 39 (1955), pp. 492–503.

J. Chomorat, 'Les *Annotations* de Valla, celles de Erasme et la grammaire', in *Histoire de l'exégèse au XVIᵉ siècle*, ed. O. Fatio and P. Fraenkel (Geneva, 1978), pp. 202–28.

C. Christ, 'Das Schriftverständnis von Zwingli und Erasmus im Jahre 1522', *Zwingliana* 16 (1983), pp. 111–25.

K. W. Clark, 'Observations on the Erasmian Notes in Codex 2', *Texte und Untersuchungen* 73 (1959), pp. 755–6.

W. J. Courtenay, 'Covenant and Causality in Pierre d'Ailly', *Speculum* 46 (1971), pp. 94–119.

—— 'The King and the Leaden Coin: The Economic Background to Sine Qua Non Causality', *Traditio* 28 (1972), pp. 185–209.

—— 'Nominalism and Late Medieval Thought: A Bibliographical Essay', *Theological Studies* 33 (1972), pp. 716–34.

—— 'John of Mirecourt and Gregory of Rimini on whether God can undo the Past', *RThAM* 39 (1972), pp. 224–56; 40 (1973), pp. 147–74.

—— 'Nominalism and Late Medieval Religion', in *The Pursuit of Holiness in Late Medieval and Renaissance Religion*, ed. C. Trinkaus and H. A. Oberman (Leiden, 1974), pp. 26–59.

—— *Adam Wodeham: An Introduction to his Life and Writings* (Leiden, 1977).

—— 'Late Medieval Nominalism Revisited: 1972–1982', *Journal of the History of Ideas* 44 (1983), pp. 159–64.

J. Courvoisier, *De la Réforme au Protestantisme: essai d'ecclesiologie réformé* (Paris, 1977).

M. Del Pra, 'Linguaggio e conoscenza assertiva nel pensiero di Roberto Holkot', *Rivista critica di storia della filosofia* 11 (1956), pp. 15–40.

—— 'La teoria del "significato totale" delle propositione nel pensiero di Gregorio da Rimini', *Rivista critica di storia della filosofia* 11 (1956), pp. 287–311.

W. Dettloff, *Die Lehre von der Acceptatio Divina bei Johannes Duns Scotus mit besonderer Berücksichtigung der Rechtfertigungslehre* (Werl, 1954).

—— *Die Entwicklung der Akzeptations- und Verdienstlehre von Duns Skotus bis Luther* (Münster, 1963).

J. P. Donnelly, *Calvinism and Scholasticism in Vermigli's Doctrine of Man and Grace* (Leiden, 1976).

G. Ebeling, 'Die Anfänge von Luthers Hermeneutik', in *Lutherstudien I* (Tübingen, 1971), pp. 1–68.

W. Eckermann, *Wort und Wirklichkeit: Das Sprachverständnis in der Theologie Gregors von Rimini und seine Weiterwirkung in der Augustinerschule* (Würzburg, 1978).

E. Egli, 'Zur Einführung des Schriftprinzips in der Schweiz', *Zwingliana* 1 (1903), pp. 332–9.

F. Ehrle, *Der Sentenzenkommentar Peters von Candia des Pisaner Papstes Alexanders V: Ein Beitrag zur Scheidung der Schulen in der Scholastik des vierzehnten Jahrhunderts und zur Geschichte des Wegestreits* (Münster, 1925).

E. L. Eisenstein, *The Printing Press as an Agent of Change* (2 vols: Cambridge, 1979).

O. Engels, 'Zur Konstanzer Konzilsproblematik in der nachkonziliaren Historiographie des 15. Jahrhunderts', in *Von Konstanz nach Trient: Beiträge zur Kirchengeschichte von den Reformkonzilien bis zum Tridentinum*, ed. R. Bäumer (Paderborn, 1972), pp. 233–59.

H. Entner, 'Der Begriff "Humanismus" als Problem der deutschen Literatur-geschichtsschreibung', *Klio* 40 (1962), pp. 260–70.

—— 'Probleme der Forschung zum deutschen Frühhumanismus 1400–1500', *Wissenschaftliche Zeitschrift der Ernst-Moritz-Arndt-Universität Greifswald* 15 (1966), pp. 587–90.

J. Etienne, *Spiritualisme érasmien et théologiens louvainistes: un changement de problématique au début du XVIᵉ siècle* (Louvain/Gembloux, 1956).

G. R. Evans, *The Language and Logic of the Bible: The Earlier Middle Ages* (Cambridge, 1984).

—— *The Language and Logic of the Bible: The Road to Reformation* (Cambridge, 1985).

O. Fatio, *Méthode et théologie: Lambert Daneau et les débuts de la scolastique réformée* (Geneva, 1976).

H. Feld, *Martin Luthers und Wendelin Steinbachs Vorlesungen über den Hebräer-brief: Eine Studie zur Geschichte der neutestamentlichen Exegese und Theologie* (Wiesbaden, 1971).

—— *Die Anfänge der modernen biblischen Hermeneutik in der spätmittelalterlichen Theologie* (Wiesbaden, 1977).

W. K. Ferguson, *The Renaissance in Historical Thought: Five Centuries of Inter-pretation* (Boston, 1948).

P. Fraenkel, *Testimonia Patrum: The Function of the Patristic Argument in the Theology of Philip Melanchthon* (Geneva, 1961).

W. Friedensburg, *Urkundenbuch der Universität Wittenberg I: (1502–1611)* (Magdeburg, 1926).

A. L. Gabriel, '"Via Antiqua" und "Via Moderna" and the Migration of Paris Students and Masters to the German Universities in the Fifteenth Century', in *Antiqui und Moderni: Traditionsbewußtsein und Fortschrittbewußtsein im späten Mittelalter*, ed. A. Zimmermann (Berlin/New York, 1974), pp. 439–83.

F. Gaeta, *Lorenzo Valla: filologia e storia nell'umanesimo* (Naples, 1955).

G. Gál, 'Adam of Wodeham's Question on the "complexe significabile" as the Immediate Object of Scientific Knowledge', *FcS* 37 (1977), pp. 66–102.

A. Ganoczy, *Le jeune Calvin: genèse et évolution de sa vocation réformatrice* (Wiesbaden, 1966).

E. Garin, 'Le traduzioni umanistiche di Aristotele nel secolo XV', *Atti e memorie dell'Accademia fiorentini di scienze morali 'La Columbaria'* 16 (1951), pp. 55–104.

D. Geanokoplos, 'The Discourse of Demetrius Chalcondyles on the Inaugu-ration of Greek Studies at the University of Padua in 1463', *Studies in the Renaissance* 21 (1974), pp. 119–44.

J. de Ghellinck, 'La première édition imprimée des *Opera omnia S. Augustini*', in *Miscellanea J. Gessler I* (Antwerp, 1948), pp. 530–47.

B. Girardin, *Rhétorique et théologique: Calvin, le commentaire de l'epître aux Romains* (Paris, 1979).

A. Godin, *L'homélaire de Jean Vitrier: spiritualité franciscaine en Flandre au XVIᵉ siècle* (Geneva, 1971).

— 'Fonction d'Origène dans la pratique exégètique d'Erasme: les annotations sur l'epître aux Romains', in *Histoire de l'exégèse au XVIᵉ siècle*, ed. O. Fatio and P. Fraenkel (Geneva, 1978), pp. 17–44.

E. Gössmann, *Antiqui und Moderni im Mittelalter: Eine geschichtliche Standortsbestimmung* (Munich/Paderborn, 1974).

J. F. G. Goeters, 'Zwinglis Werdegang als Erasmianer', in *Reformation und Humanismus: Robert Stupperich zum 65. Geburtstag*, ed. M. Greschat und J. F. G. Goeters (Witten, 1969), pp. 255–71.

M. Grabmann, 'Johannes Capreolus O. P., der "Princeps Thomistarum", und seine Stellung in der Geschichte der Thomistenschule', in *Mittelalterliches Geistesleben III*, ed. L. Ott (Munich, 1956), pp. 370–410.

L. Grane, *Contra Gabrielem: Luthers Auseinandersetzung mit Gabriel Biel in der Disputatio contra scholasticam theologiam 1517* (Gyldendal, 1962).

— 'Gregor von Rimini und Luthers Leipziger Disputation', *Studia Theologica* 22 (1968), pp. 29–49.

— 'Augustins "Expositio quarundam propositionum ex epistola ad Romanos" in Luthers Römerbriefvorlesung', *ZThK* 69 (1972), pp. 304–30.

— 'Divus Paulus et S. Augustinus, interpres eius fidelissimus: Über Luthers Verhältnis zu Augustin', in *Festschrift für Ernst Fuchs*, ed. G. Ebeling, E. Jüngel and G. Schunack (Tübingen, 1973), pp. 133–46.

— *Modus loquendi theologicus: Luthers Kampf um die Erneuerung der Theologie (1515–1518)* (Leiden, 1975).

S. S. Gravalle, 'Lorenzo Valla's Comparison of Latin and Greek and the Humanist Background', *BHR* 44 (1982), pp. 269–89.

H. H. Gray, 'Renaissance Humanism: The Pursuit of Eloquence', in *Renaissance Essays*, ed. P. O. Kristeller and P. P. Wiener (New York, 1968), pp. 199–216.

M. Greschat, 'Die Anfänge der reformatorischen Theologie Martin Bucers', in *Reformation und Humanismus: Robert Stupperich zum 65. Geburtstag*, ed. M. Greschat and J. F. G. Goeters (Witten, 1969), pp. 124–40.

— 'Martin Bucers Bücherverzeichnis', *Archiv für Kulturgeschichte* 57 (1975), pp. 162–85.

— 'Der Ansatz der Theologie Martin Bucers', *Theologische Literaturzeitung* 103 (1978), 81–96.

H. von Greyerz, 'Studien der Kulturgeschichte der Stadt Bern am Ende des Mittelalters', *Archiv des Historischen Vereins des Kantons Bern* 35 (1940), pp. 175–491.

E. Grislis, 'Calvin's Use of Cicero in the Institutes I:1–5 – A Case Study in Theological Method', *ARG* 62 (1971), pp. 5–37.

M. Grossmann, *Humanism in Wittenberg 1485–1517* (Nieuwkoop, 1975).

O. Gründler, *Die Gotteslehre Giralmo Zanchis und ihre Bedeutung für seine Lehre von der Prädestination* (Neukirchen, 1965).

H. Haf[f]ter, 'Vadian und die Universität Wien', *Wiener Geschichtsblätter* 20 (1965), pp. 385–90.

B. Hägglund, 'Martin Luther über die Sprache', *Neue Zeitschrift für systematische*

Theologie und Religionsphilosophie 26 (1984), pp. 1–12.

A. Hamel, *Der junge Luther und Augustin* (2 vols: Gütersloh, 1934–5).

B. Hamm, *Promissio, Pactum, Ordinatio: Freiheit und Selbstbindung Gottes in der scholastischen Gnadenlehre* (Tübingen, 1977).

H. Hargreaves, 'The Wycliffite Versions [of the Bible]', in *Cambridge History of the Bible* (3 vols: Cambridge, 1963–70), vol. 2, pp. 387–415.

—— 'Popularising Biblical Scholarship: The Role of the Wycliffite *Glossed Gospels*', in *The Bible and Medieval Culture*, ed. W. Lourdaux and D. Verhelst (Louvain, 1979), pp. 171–89.

D. Harmening, 'Faust und die Renaissance-Magie: Zum ältesten Faust-Zeugnis (Johannes Trithemius an Johannes Viridung, 1507)', *Archiv für Kulturgeschichte* 55 (1973), pp. 56–79.

H. Heller, 'The Evangelicalism of Lefèvre d'Etaples: 1525', *Studies in the Renaissance* 19 (1972), pp. 42–77.

H. Hermelink, *Die theologische Fakultät in Tübingen vor der Reformation 1477–1534* (Tübingen, 1906).

G. Hobbs, 'Martin Bucer on Psalm 22: A Study in the Application of Rabbinical Exegesis by a Christian Hebraist', in *Histoire de l'exégèse au XVIe siècle*, ed. O. Fatio and P. Fraenkel (Geneva, 1978), pp. 144–63.

—— 'Monitio amica: Pellican à Capito sur le danger des lectures rabbiniques', in *Horizons européens de la Réforme en Alsace*, ed. M. de Kroon and M. Lienhard (Strasbourg, 1980), pp. 81–93.

E. Hochstetter, 'Nominalismus?', *FcS* 9 (1949), pp. 370–403.

F. Hoffmann, 'Der Satz als Zeichen der theologischen Aussage bei Holcot, Crathorn und Gregor von Rimini', in *Der Begriff der Repräsentatio im Mittelalter* (Berlin, 1971), pp. 296–313.

H. H. Holfelder, *Solus Christus: Die Ausbildung von Bugenhagens Rechtfertigungslehre in der Paulusauslegung (1524/25) und ihre Bedeutung* (Tübingen, 1981).

K. Holl, 'Luthers Bedeutung für den Fortschritt der Auslegungskunst', in *Gesammelte Aufsätze zur Kirchengeschichte* (3 vols: Tübingen, 7th edn, 1948), vol. 1, pp. 544–82.

M. Hurley, '*Scriptura Sola*: Wyclif and His Critics', *Traditio* 16 (1960), pp. 275–352.

J. IJsewijn, 'The Coming of Humanism to the Low Countries', in *Itinerarium Italicum: The Profile of the Italian Renaissance in the Mirror of its European Transformations*, ed. H. A. Oberman with T. A. Brady (Leiden, 1975), pp. 193–304.

H. Jedin, 'Ein Turmerlebnis des jungen Contarinis', in *Kirche des Glaubens – Kirche der Geschichte: Ausgewählte Aufsätze und Vorträge I* (Freiburg, 1966), pp. 167–90.

H. Junghans, 'Der Einfluß des Humanismus auf Luthers Entwicklung bis 1518', *Luther-Jahrbuch* 37 (1970), pp. 37–101.

—— *Der junge Luther und die Humanisten* (Göttingen, 1985).

E. Kähler, *Karlstadt und Augustin: Der Kommentar des Andreas Bodenstein von Karlstadt zu Augustins Schrift De Spiritu et Litera* (Halle, 1952).

W. Kickel, *Vernunft und Offenbarung bei Theodor Beza: Zum Problem des Verhältnisses von Theologie, Philosophie und Staat* (Neukirchen, 1967).

R. M. Kingdom, 'Was the Protestant Reformation a Revolution? The Case of Geneva', in *Transition and Revolution: Problems and Issues of European Renaissance and Reformation History*, ed. R. M. Kingdom (Minneapolis, 1974), pp. 53–107.

G. Kisch, *Humanismus und Jurisprudenz: Der Kampf zwischen mos italicus und mos gallicus an der Universität Basel* (Basle, 1955).

— 'Forschungen zur Geschichte des Humanismus in Basel', *Archiv für Kulturgeschichte* 40 (1958), pp. 194–221.

J. M. Kittelson, *Wolfgang Capito: From Humanist to Reformer* (Leiden, 1975).

R. Klibansky, *The Continuity of the Platonic Tradition during the Middle Ages* (Munich, 1981).

K. Koch, *Studium Pietatis: Martin Bucer als Ethiker* (Neukirchen, 1962).

W. Köhler, *Huldrych Zwinglis Bibliothek* (Zurich, 1921).

— 'Die Randglossen Zwinglis zum Römerbrief in seiner Abschrift der paulinischen Briefe 1516/17', in *Forschungen zur Kirchengeschichte und zur christlichen Kunst: Johannes Ficker als Festgabe zum 70. Geburtstag dargebracht* (Leipzig, 1931), pp. 86–106.

R. Kolb, *Nikolaus von Amsdorf: Popular Polemics in the Preservation of Luther's Legacy* (Nieuwkoop, 1978).

P. O. Kristeller, 'Renaissance Aristotelianism', *Greek, Roman and Byzantine Studies* 6 (1965), pp. 157–74.

— 'The European Diffusion of Italian Humanism', in *Renaissance Thought II: Humanism and the Arts* (New York, 1965), pp. 69–88.

— *La tradizione aristotelica nel Rinascimento* (Padua, 1972).

— *Renaissance Thought and Its Sources* (New York, 1979).

— *Aristotelismo e sincretismo nel pensiero di Pietro Pomponazzi* (Padua, 1983).

M. de Kroon, 'Pseudo-Augustin im Mittelalter: Entwurf eines Forschungberichts', *Augustiniana* 22 (1972), pp. 511–30.

F. Kropatschek, *Das Schriftprinzip der lutherischen Kirche I: Die Vorgeschichte: Das Erbe des Mittelalters* (Leipzig, 1904).

F. Krüger, *Bucer und Erasmus: Eine Untersuchung zum Einfluß des Erasmus auf die Theologie Martin Bucers* (Wiesbaden, 1975).

E. Künzli, 'Quellenproblem und mystischer Schriftsinn in Zwinglis Genesis- und Exoduskommentar', *Zwingliana* 9 (1949–54), pp. 185–207; 253–307.

D. Kurze, 'Der niedere Klerus in der sozialen Welt des späten Mittelalters', in *Beiträge zur Wirtschafts- und Sozialgeschichte des Mittelalters*, ed. K. Schultz (Cologne/Vienna, 1976), pp. 273–305.

A. N. S. Lane, 'Calvin's Use of the Fathers and Medievals', *Calvin Theological Journal* 16 (1981), pp. 149–205.

G. Leff, *Bradwardine and the Pelagians: A Study of His 'De Causa Dei' and Its Opponents* (Cambridge, 1957).

— *William of Ockham: The Metamorphosis of Scholastic Discourse* (Manchester, 1977).

H. Leube, *Kalvinismus und Luthertum im Zeitalter der Orthodoxie I: Der Kampf um die Herrschaft im protestantischen Deutschland* (Leipzig, 1928).

G. W. Locher, 'Praedicatio verbi Dei est verbum Dei: Heinrich Bullinger zwischen Zwingli und Luther; Ein Beitrag zu seiner Theologie', *Zwingliana* 10 (1954), pp. 47–57.

— 'Zwingli und Erasmus', *Zwingliana* 13 (1969), pp. 37–61.

— 'Von Bern nach Genf: Die Ursachen der Spannung zwischen zwinglischer und calvinistischer Reformation', in *Wegen en Gestalten in het Gereformeerd Protestantisme*, ed. W. Balke, C. Graafland and H. Harkema (Amsterdam, 1976), pp. 75–87.

G. M. Logan, 'Substance and Form in Renaissance Humanism', *Journal of Medieval and Renaissance Studies* 7 (1977), pp. 1–34.

F. Luchsinger, *Der Baslerbuchdruck als Vermittler italienischer Geistes* (Basle, 1953)

A. E. McGrath, '"Augustinianism"? A Critical Assessment of the so-called "Medieval Augustinian Tradition" on Justification', *Augustiniana* 31 (1981), pp. 247–67.

— 'Humanist Elements in the Early Reformed Doctrine of Justification', *ARG* 73 (1982), pp. 5–20.

— 'Forerunners of the Reformation? A Critical Examination of the Evidence for Precursors of the Reformation Doctrines of Justification', *HThR* 75 (1982), pp. 219–42.

— '*Homo assumptus?* A Study in the Christology of the *Via Moderna*, with Particular Reference to William of Ockham', *EThL* 60 (1985), pp. 283–97.

— *Luther's Theology of the Cross: Martin Luther's Theological Breakthrough* (Oxford, 1985).

— *Iustitia Dei: A History of the Christian Doctrine of Justification* (2 vols: Cambridge, 1986).

— 'John Calvin and Late Medieval Thought: A Study in Late Medieval Influences upon Calvin's Theological Development', *ARG* 77 (1986), pp. 58–78.

F. Machilek, 'Die Frömmigkeit und die Krise des 14. und 15. Jahrhunderts', *Medievalia Bohemica* 3 (1970), pp. 209–27.

H. J. McSorley, *Luther – Right or Wrong? An Ecumenical-Theological Study of Luther's Major Work, The Bondage of the Will* (Minneapolis, 1969).

K. Maeder, *Die via media in der schweizerischen Reformation: Studien zum Problem der Kontinuität im Zeitalter der Glaubenspaltung* (Zurich, 1970).

W. Maurer, 'Melanchthons Loci Communes von 1521 als wissenschaftliche Programmschrift: Ein Beitrag zur Hermeneutik der Reformationszeit', *Luther-Jahrbuch* 27 (1960), pp. 1–50.

B. Moeller, 'Die deutschen Humanisten und die Anfänge der Reformation', *ZKG* 70 (1959), pp. 46–61.

— 'Frömmigkeit in Deutschland um 1500', *ARG* 56 (1965), pp. 5–31.

— 'Probleme der Reformationsgeschichtsforschung', *ZKG* 76 (1965), pp. 246–57.

— 'Zwinglis Disputationen: Studien zu den Anfängen der Kirchenbildung und des Synodalwesens im Protestantismus', *Zeitschrift der Savigny-Stiftung für Rechtsgeschichte,* Kanonische Abteilung, 56 (1970), pp. 275–324; 60 (1974), pp. 213–364.

— 'Die Ursprünge der reformierten Kirche', *Theologische Literaturzeitung* 100 (1975), 642–53.

— 'Luther und die Städte', in *Aus der Lutherforschung: Drei Vorträge* (Opladen, 1983), pp. 9–26.

E. Monnerjahn, *Giovanni Pico della Mirandola: Ein Beitrag zur philosophischen Theologie des Humanismus* (Wiesbaden, 1960).

A. V. Müller, *Luthers theologische Quellen: Seine Verteidigung gegen Denifle und Grisar* (Giessen, 1912).

J. Müller, *Martin Bucers Hermeneutik* (Gütersloh, 1965).

W. Näf, *Vadian und seine Stadt St Gallen* (2 vols: St Gallen, 1944–57).

— 'Schweizerische Humanismus: Zu Glareans "Helvetiae Descriptio"', *Schweizerische Beiträge zur allgemeinen Geschichte* 5 (1947), pp. 186–98.

C. G. Nauert, 'The Clash of Humanists and Scholastics: An Approach to Pre-Reformation Controversies', *Sixteenth Century Journal* 4 (1973), pp. 1–18.

W. H. Neuser, *Die reformatorische Wende bei Zwingli* (Neukirchen, 1977).

R. Newald, *Probleme und Gestalte des deutschen Humanismus* (Berlin, 1963).

T. Nipperdey, 'Die Reformation als Problem der marxistischen Geschichtswissenschaft', in *Reformation, Revolution, Utopie: Studien zum 16. Jahrhundert* (Göttingen, 1975), pp. 9–34.

H. A. Oberman, *Archbishop Thomas Bradwardine; A Fourteenth Century Augustinian: A Study of His Theology in Its Historical Context* (Utrecht, 1957).

— '*Facientibus quod in se est Deus non denegat gratiam*: Robert Holcot O.P. and the Beginnings of Luther's Theology', *HThR* 55 (1962), pp. 317–42.

— *The Harvest of Medieval Theology: Gabriel Biel and Late Medieval Nominalism* (Cambridge, Mass., 1963).

— 'Headwaters of the Reformation: *Initia Lutheri – Initia Reformationis*', in *Luther and the Dawn of the Modern Era*, ed. H. A. Oberman (Leiden, 1974), pp. 40–88.

— 'Tuus sum, salvum me fac: Augustinréveil zwischen Renaissance und Reformation', in *Scientia Augustiniana: Studien über Augustinus, den Augustinismus und den Augustinerorden*, ed. C. P. Mayer and W. Eckermann (Würzburg, 1975), pp. 349–94.

— 'Reformation: Epoche oder Episode?', *ARG* 68 (1977), pp. 56–111.

— *Werden und Wertung der Reformation: Vom Wegestreit zum Glaubenskampf* (Tübingen, 1977).

— 'Fourteenth Century Religious Thought: A Premature Profile', *Speculum* 53 (1978), pp. 80–93.

— *Forerunners of the Reformation: The Shape of Late Medieval Thought Illustrated by Key Documents* (Philadelphia, 1981).

A. K. Offenberg, 'Untersuchungen zum hebräischen Buchdruck in Neapel um 1490', in *Buch und Text im 15. Jahrhundert*, ed. L. Hellinga and H. Härtel (Hamburg, 1978), pp. 129–41.

S. E. Ozment, *The Reformation in the Cities: The Appeal of Protestantism to Sixteenth-Century Germany and Switzerland* (New Haven, Conn., 1975).

R. Paqué, *Das Pariser Nominalistenstatut: Zur Entstehung des Realitätsbegriffs der neuzeitlichen Naturwissenschaft (Occam, Buridan und Petrus Hispanicus, Nikolaus von Autrecourt und Gregor von Rimini)* (Berlin, 1970).

J. B. Payne, 'Towards the Hermeneutics of Erasmus', in *Scrinium Erasmianum II*, ed. J. Coppens (Leiden, 1970), pp. 13–49.

R. Peter, 'Rhétorique et prédication selon Calvin', *Revue d'histoire et de philosophie religieuses* 55 (1975), pp. 249–72.

A. Poppi, 'Il problema della filosofia morale nella scuola padovana del Rinascimento: Platonismo e Aristotelismo nella definizione del metodo dell'ethica', in *Platon et Aristote à la Renaissance* (XVIe Colloque Internationale de Tours: Paris, 1976), p. 105–46.

R. R. Post, *The Modern Devotion: Confrontation with Reformation and Humanism* (Leiden, 1968).

S. Prete, 'Leistungen der Humanisten auf dem Gebiete der lateinischen Philologie', *Philologus* 109 (1965), pp. 259–69.

G. Radetti, 'Le origini dell'umanesimo civile fiorentino nel 1400', *Giornale critico della filosophia italiana*, 3rd series, 12 (1959), pp. 98–112.

S. Raeder, *Das Hebräische bei Luther untersucht bis zum Ende der ersten Psalmenvorlesung* (Tübingen, 1961).

— *Die Benutzung des masoretischen Textes bei Luther in der Zeit zwischen der ersten und zweiten Psalmenvorlesung* (Tübingen, 1967).

— *Grammatica Theologica: Studien zu Luthers Operationes in Psalmos* (Tübingen, 1977).

J. H. Randall, 'The Development of Scientific Method in the School of Padua', in *Renaissance Essays*, ed. P. O. Kristeller and P. P. Wiener (New York, 1968), pp. 217–51.

R. Raubenheimer, 'Martin Bucer und seine humanistischen Speyerer Freunde', *Blätter für pfälzische Kirchengeschichte und religiöse Volkskunde* 32 (1965), pp. 1–52.

A. Renaudet, *Préréforme et humanisme à Paris pendant les premières guerres d'Italie (1494–1517)* (Paris, 2nd edn, 1953).

K. Reuter, *Das Grundverständnis der Theologie Calvins* (Neukirchen, 1963).

— *Vom Scholaren bis zum jungen Reformator: Studien zum Werdegang Johannes Calvins* (Neukirchen, 1981).

M. van Rhijn, 'Wessel Gansfort te Heidelberg en de strijd tussen de "via antiqua" en de "via moderna"', in *Studiën over Wessel Gansfort en zijn tijd* (Utrecht, 1933), pp. 23–37.

E. F. Rice, 'The Humanist Idea of Christian Antiquity: Lefèvre d'Etaples and His Circle', *Studies in the Renaissance* 9 (1962), pp. 126–60.

A. Rich, *Die Anfänge der Theologie Huldrych Zwinglis* (Zurich, 1949).

G. Ritter, *Studien zur Spätscholatik I: Marsilius von Inghen und die okkamistische Schule in Deutschland* (Heidelberg, 1921).

— *Studien zur Spätscholastik II: Via antiqua und via moderna auf den deutschen*

Universitäten des XV. Jahrhunderts (Heidelberg, 1922).

— 'Die geschichtliche Bedeutung des deutschen Humanismus', *Historische Zeitschrift* 127 (1922–3), pp. 393–453.

D. Robey, 'P. P. Vergerio the Elder: Republicanism and Civic Values in the Work of an Early Humanist', *Past and Present* 58 (1973), pp. 3–37.

J. Rogge, *Zwingli und Erasmus: Die Friedensgedanken des jungen Zwinglis* (Stuttgart, 1962).

H. P. Rüger, 'Karlstadt als Hebraist an der Universität Wittenberg', *ARG* 75 (1984), pp. 297–309.

P. Saenger, 'Silent Reading: Its Impact on Late Medieval Script', *Viator: Medieval and Renaissance Studies* 13 (1982), pp. 367–414.

V. Schenker-Frei, *Biblioteca Vadiana: Die Bibliothek des Humanisten Joachim von Watt nach dem Katalog des Josua Kessler von 1553* (Vadian-Studien 9: St Gallen, 1973).

H. Schepers, 'Holkot contra dicta Crathorn', *Philosophisches Jahrbuch* 77 (1970), pp. 320–54; 79 (1972), pp. 106–36.

J. Schilling, 'Determinatio secunda almae facultatis theologiae Parisiensis super Apologiam Philippi Melanchthonis pro Luthero scriptam', in *Lutheriana: Zum 500. Geburtstag Martin Luther* (Archiv zur Weimarer Ausgabe 5: Vienna, 1984), pp. 351–75.

H. Schüssler, *Der Primät der Heiligen Schrift als theologisches und kanonistisches Problem im Spätmittelalter* (Wiesbaden, 1977).

M. Schulze, '"Via Gregorii" in Forschung und Quellen', in *Gregor von Rimini: Werk und Wirkung bis zur Reformation*, ed. H. A. Oberman (Berlin/New York, 1981), pp. 1–126.

J. E. Seigel, '"Civic Humanism" or Ciceronian Rhetoric? The Culture of Petrarch and Bruni', *Past and Present* 34 (1966), pp. 3–48.

R. J. Sider, *Andreas Bodenstein von Karlstadt: The Development of His Thought 1517–1525* (Leiden, 1974).

M. Sieber, 'Glarean in Basel, 1514–1517 und 1522–1529', *Jahrbuch des Historischen Vereins des Kantons Glarus* 60 (1963), pp. 53–75.

B. Smalley, *The Study of the Bible in the Middle Ages* (Oxford, 3rd edn, 1983).

L. W. Spitz, *The Religious Renaissance of the German Humanists* (Cambridge, Mass., 1963).

— 'The Course of German Humanism', in *Itinerarium Italicum: The Profile of the Italian Renaissance in the Mirror of its European Transformations*, ed. H. A. Oberman with T. A. Brady (Leiden, 1975), pp. 371–436.

L. Smits, *Saint Augustin dans l'oeuvre de Jean Calvin I: étude de critique littéraire* (Assen, 1956).

P. Sprenger, *Das Rätsel um die Bekehrung Calvins* (Neukirchen, 1960).

J. von Stackelberg, 'Renaissance: "Wiedergeburt" oder "Wiederwunsch"? Zur Kritik an J. Triers Aufsatz über die Vorgeschichte des Renaissance-Begriffs', *BHR* 22 (1960), pp. 406–20.

E. Stakemeier, *Der Kampf um Augustin: Augustinus und die Augustiner auf dem Tridentinum* (Paderborn, 1937).

C. Stange, 'Über Luthers Beziehungen zur Theologie seines Ordens', *Neue kirchliche Zeitschrift* 11 (1900), pp. 574–85.

—— 'Luther über Gregor von Rimini', *Neue kirchliche Zeitschrift* 13 (1902), pp. 721–7.

R. Stauffer, 'Lefèvre d'Etaples, artisan ou spectateur de la Réforme?', *Bulletin de la societé de l'histoire du protestantisme français* 113 (1967), pp. 405–23.

—— 'Einfluß und Kritik des Humanismus in Zwinglis "Commentarius de vera et falsa religione"', *Zwingliana* 16 (1983), pp. 97–110.

J. M. Stayer, 'Zwingli before Zürich: Humanist Reformer and Papal Partisan', *ARG* 72 (1981), pp. 55–68.

D. C. Steinmetz, *Misericordia Dei: The Theology of Johannes von Staupitz in its Late Medieval Setting* (Leiden, 1968).

—— *Luther and Staupitz: An Essay in the Intellectual Origins of the Protestant Reformation* (Durham, NC, 1980).

J. N. Stephens, 'Heresy in Medieval and Renaissance Florence', *Past and Present* 54 (1972), pp. 25–60.

W. P. Stephens, *The Theology of Huldrych Zwingli* (Oxford, 1986).

R. Stupperich, *Das Herforder Fraterhaus und die Devotia Moderna: Studien zur Frömmigkeitsgeschichte Westfalens an der Wende zur Neuzeit* (Münster, 1975).

—— 'Das Enchiridion Militis Christiani des Erasmus von Rotterdam nach seiner Entstehung, seinem Sinn und Charakter', *ARG* 69 (1978), pp. 5–23.

G. H. Tavard, *Holy Writ or Holy Church: The Crisis of the Protestant Reformation* (London, 1959).

B. Tierney, 'Ockham, the Conciliar Theory, and the Canonists', *Journal of the History of Ideas* 15 (1954), pp. 40–70.

—— 'Pope and Council: Some New Decretist Texts', *Medieval Studies* 19 (1957), pp. 197–218.

—— '"Tria quippe distinguit iudicia . . ." A Note on Innocent III's Decretal *Per venerabilem*', *Speculum* 37 (1962), pp. 48–59.

G. Toffanin, *Storia letteraria d'Italia: Il Cinquecento* (Milan, 6th edn, 1960).

—— *Storia dell'umanesimo II: l'umanesimo italiano* (Bologna, 1964).

T. F. Torrance, 'La philosophie et la théologie de Jean Mair ou Major (1469–1550)', *Archives de philosophie* 32 (1969), pp. 531–47; 33 (1970), pp. 261–94.

—— 'Intuitive and Abstractive Knowledge from Duns Scotus to John Calvin', in *De doctrina Ioannis Duns Scoti: Acta tertii Congressus Scotistici Internationalis* (Rome, 1972), pp. 291–305.

D. Trapp, 'Augustinian Theology of the Fourteenth Century: Notes on Editions, Marginalia, Opinions and Book-lore', *Augustiniana* 6 (1956), pp. 146–274.

J. Trier, 'Zur Vorgeschichte des Renaissance-Begriff', *Archiv für Kulturgeschichte* 33 (1955), pp. 45–63.

—— 'Wiederwuchs', *Archiv für Kulturgeschichte* 43 (1961), pp. 177–87.

C. Trinkaus, *In Our Image and Likeness: Humanity and Divinity in Italian Humanist Thought* (2 vols: Chicago, 1970).

— 'A Humanist's Image of Humanism: The Inaugural Orations of Bartolommeo della Fonte', *Studies in the Renaissance* 7 (1960), pp. 90–147.

K. Trodinger, *Stadt und Kirche im spätmittelalterlichen Würzburg* (Stuttgart, 1978).

H. Trümpy, 'Glarner Studenten im Zeitalter des Humanismus', *Beiträge zur Geschichte des Landes Glarus: Festgabe des Historischen Vereins des Kantons Glarus* (Glarus, 1952), pp. 273–84.

K. H. Ullmann, *Reformatoren vor der Reformation vornehmlich in Deutschland und den Niederlanden* (2 vols: Hamburg, 1841–2).

W. Urban, 'Die "via moderna" an der Universität Erfurt am Vorabend der Reformation', in *Gregor von Rimini: Werk und Wirkung bis zur Reformation*, ed. H. A. Oberman (Berlin/New York, 1981), pp. 311–30.

P. Vignaux, *Justification et prédestination au XIVᵉ siècle: Duns Scot, Pierre d'Auriole, Guillaume d'Occam, Grégoire de Rimini* (Paris, 1934).

R. G. Villoslada, *La Universidad de Paris durante los estudios de Francisco de Vitoria O.P. (1507–1522)* (Rome, 1938).

P. de Vooght, *Les sources de la doctrine chrétienne d'après les théologiens du XIVᵉ siècle et du début du XVᵉ* (Paris, 1954).

D. Weinstein, 'In Whose Image and Likeness? Interpretations of Renaissance Humanism', *Journal of the History of Ideas* 33 (1972), pp. 165–76.

F. Wendel, *Calvin: The Origins and Development of His Religious Thought* (London, 1974).

— *Calvin et l'humanisme* (Paris, 1976).

V. Wendland, 'Die Wissenschaftlehre Gregors von Rimini in der Diskussion', in *Gregor von Rimini: Werk und Wirkung bis zur Reformation*, ed. H. A. Oberman (Berlin/New York, 1981), pp. 241–300.

K. Werner, *Die Scholastik des späteren Mittelalters III: Der Augustinismus in der Scholastik des späteren Mittelalters* (Vienna, 1883).

E. Wolf, *Staupitz und Luther: Ein Beitrag zur Theologie des Johannes von Staupitz und deren Bedeutung für Luthers theologischen Werdegang* (Leipzig, 1927).

K.-H. Wyss, *Leo Jud: Seine Entwicklung zum Reformator 1519–1523* (Berne/Frankfurt, 1976).

L. Zanta, *La renaissance du stoïcisme au XVIᵉ siècle* (Geneva, 1975).

C. Zürcher, *Konrad Pellikans Wirken in Zürich 1526–1556* (Zurich, 1975).

A. Zumkeller, *Dionysius de Montina: Ein neuentdeckter Augustinertheologe des Spätmittelalters* (Wurzburg, 1948).

— 'Hugolin von Orvieto über Urstand und Erbsünde', *Augustiniana* 3 (1953), pp. 35–62; 165–93; 4 (1954), pp. 25–46.

— 'Hugolin von Orvieto über Prädestination, Rechtfertigung und Verdienst', *Augustiniana* 4 (1954), pp. 109–56; 5 (1955), pp. 5–51.

— 'Die Augustinertheologen Simon Fidati von Cascia und Hugolin von Orvieto und Martin Luthers Kritik an Aristoteles', *ARG* 54 (1963), pp. 13–37.

— 'Die Augustinerschule des Mittelalters: Vertreter und philosophisch-theologische Lehre (Übersicht nach dem heutigen Stand der Forschung)', *Analecta Augustiniana* 27 (1964), pp. 167–262.

— 'Der Wiener Theologieprofessor Johannes von Retz und seine Lehre von Urstand, Erbsünde, Gnade und Verdienst', *Augustiniana* 22 (1972), pp. 118–84; 540–82.

— 'Johannes Klenkok O.S.A. im Kampf gegen den "Pelagianismus" seiner Zeit: Seine Lehre über Gnade, Rechtfertigung und Verdienst', *Recherches Augustiniennes* 13 (1978), pp. 231–333.

— 'Die Lehre des Erfurter Augustinertheologen Johannes von Dorsten über Gnade, Rechtfertigung und Verdienst', *Theologie und Philosophie* 53 (1978), pp. 27–64; 127–219.

— 'Der Augustinertheologe Johannes Hiltalingen von Basel über Erbsünde, Gnade und Verdienst', *Analecta Augustiniana* 43 (1980), pp. 57–162.

— 'Erbsünde, Gnade und Rechtfertigung im Verständnis der Erfurter Augustinertheologen des Spätmittelalters', *ZKG* 92 (1981), pp. 39–59.

— 'Der Augustiner Angelus Dobelinus, erster Theologieprofessor der Erfurter Universität, über Gnade, Rechtfertigung und Verdienst', *Analecta Augustiniana* 44 (1981), pp. 69–147.

Index